GREAT DINNERS from LIFE

GREAT DINNERS from LIFE

by
Eleanor
Graves

Photographs by
John Dominis
Milton Greene
Henry Groskinsky
Mark Kauffman
Fred Lyon

TIME-LIFE BOOKS, ALEXANDRIA, VIRGINIA

Other Publications:

THE GOOD COOK

THE SEAFARERS

THE ENCYCLOPEDIA OF COLLECTIBLES

THE GREAT CITIES

WORLD WAR II

HOME REPAIR AND IMPROVEMENT

THE WORLD'S WILD PLACES

THE TIME-LIFE LIBRARY OF BOATING

HUMAN BEHAVIOR

THE ART OF SEWING

THE OLD WEST

THE EMERGENCE OF MAN

THE AMERICAN WILDERNESS

THE TIME-LIFE ENCYCLOPEDIA OF GARDENING

LIFE LIBRARY OF PHOTOGRAPHY

THIS FABULOUS CENTURY

FOODS OF THE WORLD

TIME-LIFE LIBRARY OF AMERICA

TIME-LIFE LIBRARY OF ART

GREAT AGES OF MAN

LIFE SCIENCE LIBRARY

THE LIFE HISTORY OF THE UNITED STATES

TIME READING PROGRAM

LIFE NATURE LIBRARY

LIFE WORLD LIBRARY

FAMILY LIBRARY:

HOW THINGS WORK IN YOUR HOME

THE TIME-LIFE BOOK OF THE FAMILY CAR

THE TIME-LIFE FAMILY LEGAL GUIDE

THE TIME-LIFE BOOK OF FAMILY FINANCE

Fourth printing. Revised 1979.
Published simultaneously in Canada.
Library of Congress catalogue card number 74-78949.

An Invitation to Good Dining

This is a book for people who like to have friends in to dinner. It is also a book for people who, every once in a while, are willing to put a little extra effort into cooking those dinners—*provided* that they know the results are going to be worth it. You won't use this book every day. But every time you have company you can rely on it to provide you with a menu that is right for the time of year, the number of guests and the mood you're in. It will tell you what to serve from appetizer to coffee, what to shop for, how long the preparation will take, when the tricky moments may occur and how to cope with them. A detailed timetable will guide you every step of the way. It will even remind you when to open the wine and when to change your clothes. As far as possible the menus are planned so that you do not have to spend the hour before you serve dinner in the kitchen. Most of the preparation is done before your guests arrive.

It may provide some comfort to know that all these dinners have been cooked in an average kitchen by an average housewife. They have all been put together under standard battle conditions—the normal number of small children and pets, the standard kitchen equipment and a total lack of household help. From the last I must except my gallant husband, who is always on hand when it comes to such manly chores as opening clams and getting lobsters into the pot.

Some of the dishes in this book will probably be new to you. One doesn't often run into *imam bayildi* or *ghivetch*. Be assured that though they sound outrageous they do not taste it. When dishes *are* particularly highly seasoned or laced with garlic you are forewarned not to invite the most conservative eaters you know. Except for the occasional exotic dish, the ingredients used in this book are standard and in most places will be easily available. In the few cases where a somewhat obscure ingredient is called for, an alternative is suggested. The same is true of equipment. The dinners do not assume more than the basic kitchen equipment discussed in the chapter on utensils at the back of this book. However, many of the tempting wares shown there would make your cooking easier and more fun. The cost of these dinners is, I think, reasonable. They are not budget parties, but they are not going to mean economizing until the *next* time somebody comes to dinner. If a particularly costly ingredient is asked for, an alternative is usually suggested.

This book is divided into seasons and takes into account the food that becomes available only at certain times of the year, and the weather—and therefore appetites. But these divisions should not be viewed too strictly. I would use fall and winter menus freely from September to April. The spring menus reflect the arrival of fruits and vegetables that have been missing all winter long in many parts of the country. And summer offers dinners guaranteed to wilt neither the guests nor the hostess.

I hope that as you make these dinners from start to finish, and get to know the recipes, some will become family favorites that you will use in other contexts. Many are quick and easy, far from elaborate productions. I rarely go through a summer fortnight without making lemon soup, for instance, and *seviche* is a first course I serve to friends all the time.

In these recipes, portions are large, but I rarely find myself with leftovers. I hope it is not immodest to assume that the reason for this is that the product is marvelously good to eat.

—*Eleanor Graves*

Contents

When the lid is lifted from a steaming
pot of cassoulet or carbonades,
everyone at the table breathes
deeply. Appetites are sturdy, and it
is the time of year for grand occasions
with abundant platters of
paella and holiday feasts with
baronial roasts so stately that they awe
every voracious eye.

winter

Crown Roast of Pork

To some people, having a Christmas dinner that doesn't vary by so much as a crumb from year to year is as essential as hanging the stockings. But for those who are turkey-stuffed and plum pudding-sated, this crown of pork dinner will be a savory change. And it is a splendid meal for any other gala midwinter occasion.

Pork, often in the form of suckling pig, was traditionally eaten in Europe at wintertime festivities. But modern appetites, particularly in America, find whole pigs, no matter how small, a bit overwhelming. A crown roast is both magnificent and manageable. It is made up of pork ribs, turned and tied to resemble a crown. Each portion is actually a rib chop, and the roast can be constructed of any number of chops to serve a moderate-size family or an avalanche of guests. It is easy to carve and the center can be heaped with any kind of stuffing. Properly cooked, the bones become delicately charred, the skin glistens and crackles and the crown takes on a golden glow.

It's too bad that manners prevent you from warning your guests to eat lightly the day before they come to this dinner. Every item in the menu —from soup to chestnuts—is so delicious that anyone who can't do justice to it is going to be furious with himself. As the hostess, the way to guard against anyone passing up dessert is to serve moderate-size portions and to be rather cool about offering second helpings.

For an all-out feast, which this is, it is relatively easy to prepare. The only drawback is its cost. Many of the ingredients would be extravagances at anything less than the dinner of the year—oysters, wild rice, the crown roast which butchers may charge extra for shaping, and imported chestnuts. But your guests will be served as handsomely as they're ever likely to be. In the interest of economy you can make certain changes: use brown rice and eliminate the champagne. Skip the bisque entirely but don't try to economize halfway by skimping on the oysters.

The holidays are the worst possible time of year to have to spend hours in the kitchen. It is the same time that you are helping with the costumes for the school pageant, worrying about your wardrobe for other people's parties and, up to the last minute, Christmas shopping. But this menu is flexible enough so you can either elect to do the whole thing the day of the dinner (working at it pretty steadily) or prepare some items in advance. You will, however, need to do some shopping ahead—the chestnuts are a special kind called *marrons glacés* (candied chestnuts), and may mean a trip to a gourmet store. The butcher should be forewarned that he has to make the crown. As to the cooking—you can make the bisque and dessert the day ahead and refrigerate them. But, if you do it all on the day of the party, make the cake the first thing in the morning and store it in the refrigerator. Start the bisque. Chill the champagne. In the afternoon organize the vegetables. As for the roast, the butcher has done the work—all you have to do is allow the right amount of cooking time.

MENU FOR EIGHT

OYSTER BISQUE

CROWN OF PORK WITH WILD RICE
Spiced fruits
Peas à la française
Baked squash Parmesan
Light red wine

CHESTNUT ROLL

Champagne

RECIPES

OYSTER BISQUE

Oysters have a glamorous past with such overtones of Diamond Jim Brady and Lillian Russell that they are a most suitable beginning to an elegant dinner. They are served here in soup—bisque simply means a thick cream soup. Either fresh or frozen oysters will do, and the size of the oyster is of no importance. If you buy fresh ones, have them shucked at the fish store—don't try it yourself.

1½ pints oysters	2 teaspoons salt
2 eight-ounce bottles clam juice	½ teaspoon whole peppercorns
1½ cups dry white wine	⅓ cup butter
2 stalks celery, sliced	⅓ cup flour
2 medium onions, sliced	2 eggs
2 carrots, sliced	3 cups light cream
3 slices lemon	¼ cup dry sherry
2 teaspoons dried parsley	Dash of cayenne pepper
1 bay leaf	2 tablespoons finely
1 pinch thyme	chopped fresh parsley
¼ teaspoon nutmeg	

Chop the oysters in a blender or by hand, saving all the oyster liquor. Put the oysters and liquor into a saucepan. Add clam juice, wine, celery, onions, carrots, lemon slices, herbs, nutmeg, salt and peppercorns. Bring to a boil, reduce heat, and simmer gently uncovered for 45 minutes. Strain through a fine sieve or cheesecloth. Measure this stock and, if necessary, add enough water to make five cups. Then melt butter in a large saucepan. Add flour and stir until smooth. Gradually stir in the oyster stock and cook, stirring constantly, until the mixture thickens. With a fork, beat the eggs with one-half cup of the cream. Stir about one cup of the hot bisque into the egg-cream mixture. Then gradually stir this mixture back into the bisque. Add the remaining cream and heat thoroughly but do not boil. Before serving, stir in the sherry and a dash of cayenne. Serve sprinkled with parsley.

CROWN OF PORK

A crown roast is one of the most splendid of all cuts of meat. Most often constructed of lamb, it is less expensive and every bit as good when made of pork. Allow two chops per person, with a few extra for really hearty eaters. Many butchers will sell the crowns only in multiples of seven since there are seven chops in each retail rib portion. Select meat that is firm and lean. Pork must be white or grayish when cooked, not tinged with pink. Pork does not generally need basting, but when roasting the crown, spoon cider and pan juices over the bones occasionally so that they get attractively brown.

Crown of pork, 18-21 ribs
1 cup apple cider
Wild rice (recipe below)

Preheat oven to 325°. Place the crown, bones sticking up, in a shallow roasting pan—no rack is needed. Insert a meat thermometer into the center of a meaty part of one of the chops, making sure it does not rest on bone. Roast the pork until the thermometer reaches 185° or for about three hours, basting the crown from time to time with apple cider and the pan juices. To serve, remove from the oven, fill the center of the crown with cooked wild rice, piling the rice high. If there is any rice left over, serve it separately.

WILD RICE

Wild rice, a native American delicacy, is not rice at all but the seed of a tall aquatic grass. It is literally wild—efforts to farm it have been failures. It is harvested from canoes, mostly by Indians in Minnesota. Considering all this, it's hardly surprising that it costs a fortune!

1½ cups wild rice
6 cups water
1½ teaspoons salt

Rinse the rice thoroughly. Combine rice, boiling water and salt in a saucepan. Boil, without stirring, until rice is tender, about 40 minutes. Drain well. Makes about five cups of rice.

PEAS À LA FRANÇAISE

1 tablespoon sugar	3 ten-ounce packages
¼ teaspoon chervil	frozen small peas
¼ teaspoon thyme	½ pound tiny white onions
1½ teaspoons salt	(about 24)
Freshly ground black pepper	¼ cup butter
2 cups shredded lettuce	¼ cup boiling water

Remove peas from freezer to thaw about an hour ahead of cooking time. Don't care what the package directions say: thaw them. With this quantity, they will be easier to handle. Peel the onions. If the onions are not the tiniest ones, remove one or two layers to reduce them to cocktail-onion size. Cook them in boiling salted water for five minutes; drain. Melt the butter in a large heavy saucepan. Add onions, the one-quarter cup boiling water, sugar, herbs, salt and pepper. Add the peas and toss to blend them with the seasonings. Add the lettuce and stir it in gently. Cover the pan and cook over medium heat just until the peas are tender, about five minutes.

BAKED SQUASH PARMESAN

4 acorn squash	Parmesan cheese
8 tablespoons butter	Salt
8 teaspoons grated	Freshly ground black pepper

Preheat oven to 325°. Scrub squash and cut them in half lengthwise. Scrape out the seeds and all the strings. Put squash, open side up, in a shallow baking pan. Sprinkle each half with salt and pepper. Put one tablespoon of butter and one teaspoon of cheese in each half. Be generous with both—the more you put in, the better the squash will taste. Bake for one hour or until tender.

CHESTNUT ROLL

This is one of the most impressive desserts you will ever turn out—to eat and to admire—so don't leave it off the menu just because it sounds hard. It really isn't. It takes an hour or so to put together but it is close to being foolproof. And it should cinch your reputation.

¾ cup sifted cake flour	1 teaspoon vanilla extract
1 teaspoon baking powder	Confectioners' sugar
¼ teaspoon salt	Chestnut butter cream
4 eggs	(recipe below)
¾ cup sugar	Shaved bitter chocolate

Preheat oven to 400°. Line the bottom of a jelly roll pan (15x10x1 inches) with wax paper or foil trimmed to fit. Don't use the plastic wrap that sticks to itself—it will melt. Butter the paper. Sift flour, baking powder and salt together. Beat the eggs until light and foamy. Continue beating, adding sugar slowly, until very thick and at least doubled in bulk. This will take about 10 minutes with an electric hand mixer. Sprinkle the sifted dry ingredients over the batter and fold them in gently. Fold in the vanilla. Bake for 12 to 15 minutes or until the cake is delicately browned and the top springs back when touched lightly. Loosen the cake around the edges with a knife and turn it out on a cloth sprinkled evenly with confectioners' sugar. Working quickly while the cake is still warm, carefully remove the paper. Cut off the crisp edges of the cake with a sharp knife. Starting at the long side—and be sure it *is* the long side, it is instinctive to want to start the other way—gently roll up the cake right along with the towel. The towel keeps the cake from sticking to itself. Place the roll, towel and all, on a cake rack to cool. When cool unroll the cake and remove the towel. Spread the top with one half of the chestnut butter cream. Reroll the cake, place it on a serving platter and frost the outside of the roll with the rest of the cream. Decorate the top with chocolate.

CHESTNUT BUTTER CREAM

2 six-ounce cans of *marrons glacés*	⅓ cup light corn syrup
	3 egg yolks
or 2 small jars of *marrons* in vanilla syrup, drained	½ pound sweet butter, softened
½ cup sugar	¼ cup dark rum

Finely chop *marrons*—which is what the can will read because all candied chestnuts are imported from France. Cut butter into small pieces. Put egg yolks into a mixing bowl. Set them all aside. Combine sugar and corn syrup in a small saucepan. Cook over medium heat, stirring constantly, until the mixture comes to a full bubbling boil. Remove from heat. Beat the egg yolks until foamy and lemon-colored. Add the hot syrup gradually, continuing to beat until the mixture is cool. Beat in the butter, a little at a time. Stir in the rum and chestnuts.

Cioppino: Seafood Stew

Every country in the world with more than a mile of seacoast can boast some kind of stew or soup made with the local catch. The U.S. has two that are well-known specialties—New England clam chowder and seafood gumbo from the Gulf. The equal of these, but less familiar, is a San Francisco specialty called cioppino (and pronounced *chuh-peen-o*). The invention, probably of Italians who fished the Pacific some 100 years ago, has many overtones, and some major chords too, that are struck in Italian cooking.

There is nothing in cioppino that restricts it to the Pacific coast. In fact, a cook a thousand miles from the nearest shore can still put together a respectable version. The choice of seafood is determined by what is available. Crab, of course, on the West Coast; lobster on the East Coast and frozen lobster tails in between, and whatever else the fish store or the frozen food counter has on hand. What makes cioppino distinctive is the pungent Mediterranean-style mixture of tomatoes, basil and oregano with plenty of red wine and garlic—a base which makes the finished dish very strong and heady stuff indeed.

Plan to have this dinner sometime when you are feeling bored with things in general. Shopping for the unusual ingredients is a kind of challenge and the cooking is free-wheeling.

This dinner makes some special demands on your china closet: you will need three sets of salad- or dessert-size dishes: one for the tarts, one for the salad and another for dessert. You should serve the cioppino in large individual bowls or soup dishes—it is much too liquid and runny to serve on flat dinner plates.

Leeks are the mildest member of the onion family, but have a distinctively earthy taste. If your grocer does not regularly carry them, ask him to order them for you. If he can't, use scallions instead. Substitutions in the cioppino matter less. If you can't get sea bass you can use almost any mildly flavored white fish as the base. Haddock or halibut would be fine. As for the shellfish, use what is most readily available and therefore the freshest and best tasting. If need be, you can use frozen lobster tails in-

MENU FOR EIGHT

LEEK AND SAUSAGE TARTS

CIOPPINO
Garlic bread
Red wine
Watercress and endive salad

GRAPES JUANITA

stead of fresh lobsters. And there is no reason why you can't use frozen fish. Of course, without having the lobsters, mussels and clams in their shells, the finished product will not look so pretty.

All of this dinner should be prepared on the day it is going to be eaten, but it does not take too long. The one thing you can do the day ahead is to make the tart shells.

On the morning of the dinner make the filling for the tarts and refrigerate it. Make the grape dessert and refrigerate that too. Wash and wrap the watercress and endive and store them in the refrigerator. Mix your favorite vinaigrette dressing and set it aside. Prepare the garlic bread and wrap it in foil. The cioppino takes about an hour to cook so put it on just as the guests arrive. You will have to duck into the kitchen occasionally to add the fish, batch by batch. Thirty minutes before dinner fill the tarts and heat them up. When you sit down to the first course, heat the garlic bread in a hot oven. As you clear the table, loosen the foil wrapping to let the bread brown a bit.

RECIPES

LEEK AND SAUSAGE TARTS

The only trick to preparing leeks is getting them thoroughly clean. Cut off all the green leaves first. Remove the outside white layer and slice off the bottom of the stem. Then slit open the top of the white stem and, under running water, bend back the layers, rinsing until the leek is free of sand. If you do not want to bother with making tart shells, buy baked patty shells or use frozen ones.

TART SHELLS

2 1/4 cups sifted flour	shortening
3/4 teaspoon salt	1/3 cup ice water
3/4 cup plus 2 tablespoons	

Mix the flour and the salt in a medium-size bowl. Using a pastry blender or two knives, cut the shortening into the flour until its resembles coarse meal. Sprinkle water over the mixture and toss quickly with a fork until mixture holds together. Turn dough out onto a lightly floured surface and form into a ball. Divide dough into two parts. Working with one part at a time for ease, roll out thinly. Use muffin or cupcake pans to shape the tart shells. Invert the pans, and with a piece of string, measure one of the cups—up one side, across the bottom and down the other side. Cut the string and use it as a guide to the size of the pastry cutter. Use a saucer, or the top of a can that is the same size across as the length of string. Fit pastry rounds over the bottom of the muffin pans, pinching the pastry into pleats to make it fit tightly. Prick well with a

fork. Bake in a 425° oven for 12 to 15 minutes, until golden. Cool, slide shells off pans.

8 medium-size leeks or 24 scallions	horseradish
1 1/4 cups chicken broth	1/2 teaspoon salt
2 tablespoons butter	Freshly ground black pepper
2 tablespoons flour	4 link breakfast sausages, cooked and drained
1/2 cup heavy cream	8 baked tart or patty shells
1 teaspoon prepared	

Trim and wash the leeks. Cut them into quarter-inch slices and rinse them well again. Drain thoroughly. Bring chicken broth to a boil, add the leek slices, cover and cook for 10 minutes, or until the leeks are tender. Drain the liquid into a measuring cup. There should be at least one cup. If less, add chicken broth to bring it up to one cup. Preheat oven to 325°. Melt butter in a saucepan, add flour and stir until smooth. Add broth and cream and cook, stirring constantly, until thickened and smooth. Add horseradish, salt and pepper and mix well. Stir in the leeks. Put the tart shells on a cookie sheet. Spoon the leek mixture into the tart shells. Cut the sausages into half-inch slices and arrange them on top. Bake the tarts for 10 minutes or until hot and bubbly. If the filling has been refrigerated, bake the tarts for 20 to 25 minutes.

CIOPPINO

The only work involved in putting this dish together will be the chopping—of which there is considerable. It can all be done ahead of time, if you prefer to do it early, and the ingredients stored separately in tightly covered containers in the refrigerator.

Serve the cioppino from the giant pot it was cooked in. If you want, you may put a round of garlic bread at the bottom of each soup plate to act as a blotter. After the cioppino course offer your guests finger bowls or warm moist napkins to clean their fingers.

Serve the salad as a separate course. The cioppino is really much too messy to have anything else going on at the same time.

1½ pounds boned sea bass, cut in 2-inch slices	½ cup olive oil
3 1½-pound lobsters, cut up	1 2-pound 3-ounce can Italian tomatoes with basil
1 pound shrimp, shelled and cleaned	1 6-ounce can tomato paste
12 hardshell clams	2 cups red wine
24 mussels	1 lemon, thinly sliced
2 cups chopped onion	1 cup chopped parsley
½ cup chopped green pepper	1 teaspoon basil
	1 teaspoon oregano
6 cloves garlic, minced	1 teaspoon salt
	Freshly ground black pepper

Combine the onion, green pepper and garlic with the olive oil in a large pot or kettle. Cook over low heat for 10 minutes, stirring occasionally. Add the tomatoes, tomato paste, wine, lemon, one-half cup of the parsley and all the other seasonings. Bring to a boil, reduce heat, cover and simmer for 20 minutes. Add the bass, lobsters and shrimp and simmer, covered, for 20 minutes. Scrub the clams and mussels with a stiff brush under cold running water. Remove the "beard" that may be attached to the mussels. Add the clams and mussels to the pot and simmer, covered, for 10 minutes more or until the clams

and mussels open and the fish is done. Serve the cioppino sprinkled with the remaining chopped parsley.

GARLIC BREAD

Many people who don't have strong convictions about other kinds of cooking are adamant about how to make garlic bread. Some insist on pressing the garlic, others on mincing it; some melt butter and brush it on, others soften it and smooth it on. There is even argument over whether you cut the bread halfway through or all the way. If you are open-minded, try this way. It is neat, simple and gives maximum garlicity.

2 large loaves Italian bread	2 cloves garlic, crushed
1 cup butter	

Preheat oven to 400°. Slice bread one inch thick. Add the crushed garlic cloves to the butter and melt over low heat. Tear off a sheet of foil two inches longer than first loaf of bread. Dip one side of each bread slice into butter and set it on foil, put the slices together until the loaf is reassembled. Repeat with second loaf. Pour any extra butter over loaves. Fold foil over the top of the bread; fold up ends to make a tight seal. Bake for 15 minutes. Open the foil and bake for five minutes more to brown and crisp the loaves.

GRAPES JUANITA

This dessert requires about 10 minutes to make. Use green seedless grapes and remove all of the stem.

2 pounds seedless grapes	½ cup light brown sugar
1 cup sour cream	Grated orange rind

Combine the grapes and sour cream. Sprinkle the brown sugar on top. Chill for at least two hours. Garnish with the grated rind.

A German Pot Roast

How you cook this dish is of relatively minor importance. It's how you soak it that counts. Sauerbraten, or German-style pot roast, takes on its distinguishing sweet-sour flavor from sitting in a pungent marinade. How long it sits, and in what, varies considerably. In the days when marinating was as much for tenderizing as for taste, the beef was soaked for a week. Today all but the most entrenched traditionalists settle for four days. In northern Germany the beef is soaked in buttermilk. In Bavaria, it's beer. The recipe shown here, which is most like the Rhineland marinade, combines white wine, vinegar, carrots and onions. The result is a culinary conundrum—a dish both smooth and sharp.

What it takes to bring off this dinner is foresight. There is nothing tricky about cooking good sauerbraten. But there is also no shortcut. Four days of soaking the meat is a must.

This is an easy dinner to put together. All of it—except the potatoes—can be done well ahead. It is robust, but your guests are almost guaranteed good appetites after smelling the sauerbraten as it cooks during the cocktail hour. It has a delicious, but strong, aroma, so if you don't want your guests to smell it as they come in the door be sure to turn on the fan or open the window when you first put it on to cook.

The first thing to start thinking about when you decide to make the sauerbraten is your refrigerator: you must make room for a large bowl for the next four days. The contents of the bowl are highly aromatic and even though you wrap it securely, don't plan to put any delicately flavored foods next to it in the refrigerator. You will have to turn the meat daily while it marinates.

On the morning of the dinner make the cherry tart.

MENU FOR SIX

SMOKED SALMON WITH HORSERADISH CREAM

SAUERBRATEN
Potato pancakes
Mustard-glazed carrots
Beer

CHERRY TART

Take the sauerbraten out of the refrigerator when you put the tart in. Do the salmon appetizer in the morning too. It will take you almost five hours to prepare the sauerbraten—three quarters of an hour for the final preparation and four hours of cooking time. An hour before your guests are due, butter the bread for the appetizer and set it aside, well wrapped. Whip the cream for the tart and refrigerate it. Cook the carrots and their sauce, to be reheated at the last moment.

Peel the potatoes and keep them in cold water, if you are going to make the potato pancakes from scratch. Even if you use a mix, the pancakes must be cooked just before serving, so allow yourself half an hour, although you do not have to be in constant attendance. You may find it more convenient to serve the salmon appetizers in the living room along with drinks rather than at the table. If so, cook the pancakes while guests are nibbling at these. If you decide to serve the first course at the table, make the pancakes before you sit down and keep them warm in a low oven.

RECIPES

SMOKED SALMON WITH HORSERADISH CREAM
Smoked salmon comes in several varieties. East Coast salmon, cured in a sugar-salt brine, then smoked, is called Nova Scotia smoked salmon. It is quite mild in flavor and more expensive than lox. Lox is West Coast salmon, which is saltier to begin with and is cured in a saltier brine than the Nova Scotia. Use Nova Scotia style in this recipe, but it will not hurt to use lox if it's all you can get or all you feel you can afford.

3/4 pound thinly sliced smoked salmon	1 teaspoon fresh lemon juice
1 1/2 teaspoons unflavored gelatin	1/4 teaspoon sugar
6 tablespoons cold water	6 thin slices pumpernickel, buttered
1/2 cup heavy cream	Lemon wedges
2 tablespoons prepared horseradish, drained	Watercress sprigs
	Freshly ground black pepper

Sprinkle gelatin over the cold water in a small saucepan. Place the pan over low heat and stir until the gelatin is completely dissolved. Let cool slightly, then chill 10 minutes. Whip the cream until stiff. Stir in the horseradish, lemon juice, sugar and gelatin mixture. Continue to beat until cream mixture is quite thick. Chill for a few minutes. Place a generous spoonful of the cream mixture down the center of each salmon piece. Gently fold the two sides over so they overlap just slightly. Place each cream-filled salmon roll seam-side down on a baking sheet lined with

wax paper; cover with plastic wrap and chill. Serve with triangles of buttered pumpernickel, garnish with lemon wedges and watercress. At the table pass a pepper mill.

SAUERBRATEN
Top or bottom round is equally good for this dish, although top round has a neater shape and is therefore a little easier to carve. Whichever you choose, have the butcher tie it well. Otherwise after four days of soaking and four hours of cooking it will begin to lose its shape.

5 pound pot roast of beef (bottom or top round)	sliced
	4 shallots, peeled
Marinade	8 peppercorns
2 cups white vinegar	6 whole cloves
2 cups dry white wine	3 bay leaves, halved
2 cups water	2 teaspoons salt
2 large onions, sliced	1 teaspoon mustard seed
6 carrots, scraped and	Few sprigs parsley

Place the meat in a four-quart bowl or pot. This is an unusual marinade because it is cooked. Put all the ingredients for it in a large saucepan; bring to a boil, lower heat and simmer for five minutes. Cool, then pour the marinade over the meat, cover the bowl well and refrigerate for four days. Turn the meat once a day, to be sure the entire piece gets well marinated. Remove the meat from the marinade and pat it as dry as possible with paper towels. Strain the marinade, pressing all the liquid from the vegetables. Reserve the juice, discard the vegetables.

5 tablespoons flour	1 bay leaf
1 teaspoon salt	2 tablespoons butter
1/4 cup cooking oil	2 tablespoons sugar
1 large onion, sliced	1/3 cup gingersnap crumbs
6 whole cloves	

Mix two tablespoons of the flour with the salt, and coat all sides of the meat with it. Heat the oil in a large casserole or Dutch oven. Add the meat and brown it well on all sides, over medium heat, which will take about 20 minutes. Remove meat and pour off all fat from the pot. Return meat to the pot and add the onion slices, cloves, bay leaf and three cups of the marinade. Cover and simmer until meat is almost tender, about three hours. Remove meat and strain the marinade. Return the meat and strained marinade to pot. In a small skillet, melt the butter, stir in the sugar and the remaining three tablespoons of flour, and cook, stirring, over low heat until a rich brown color. Stir this sugar-flour mixture into the marinade. Cover and continue cooking until meat is very tender, about one hour more. To serve, remove meat to a heated platter. Stir gingersnap crumbs into gravy and, using a whisk, cook and stir two or three minutes until gravy is smooth and thickened. Taste the gravy, add more salt and pepper if necessary. Slice the meat, not too thin, arrange overlapping slices on a hot platter, and coat with some of the gravy. Pass the remaining gravy in a sauceboat. If you prefer you may carve the beef at the table and serve gravy with each portion. Serve the sauerbraten with potato pancakes. They are the appropriate accompaniment and are worth the last-minute effort. Use a standard recipe or a mix.

MUSTARD-GLAZED CARROTS

2 pounds carrots	mustard
1 teaspoon salt	1/4 cup brown sugar
3 tablespoons butter	1/4 cup chopped parsley
3 tablespoons prepared	

Scrape the carrots and cut them in half lengthwise, then into two-inch sections. Cook in boiling water, with the salt added, covered, until just tender, about 20 minutes. Drain. In a small saucepan cook the butter, mustard and brown sugar until syrupy, about three minutes. Pour over carrots and simmer for five minutes. Sprinkle with the parsley just before serving.

CHERRY TART

This is a typical German fruit tart—made without a top crust and from a sweet buttery dough that is very much like a cookie. The dough is easy to make, does not get soggy, and is pressed into shape rather than rolled out. Make it in a flan ring or, as the American version is called, a slip-bottom pan. By setting the pan on top of a jar—after the tart is cooked of course—the sides will slip off with a little help from a sharp, small knife. Then, by using a spatula, the bottom can easily be slipped off as the tart is transferred to a serving dish.

Spread the whipped cream thinly and evenly over the top or decorate the tart with dabs of cream just before serving.

2 one-pound cans red sour pitted cherries (packed in water)	1 egg, lightly beaten
	1 tablespoon water
	2 teaspoons grated lemon rind
1 cup sugar	
2 tablespoons kirsch	4 teaspoons cornstarch
2 cups flour	1/4 teaspoon almond extract
1/8 teaspoon salt	1/2 cup of heavy cream, whipped
2/3 cup butter	

Drain the cherries and reserve the liquid. Sprinkle them with two-thirds cup of the sugar and the kirsch. Let them stand for an hour, stirring occasionally. Meanwhile, make the tart dough. Sift the flour with the remaining one-third cup sugar and salt into a mixing bowl. Cut in the butter with a pastry blender or two knives until it resembles fine meal. Make a well in the center of the dry ingredients, add the egg, water and lemon rind. Work flour and liquid together, using a fork or your fingers, until the dough will stick together and form a ball. Turn it out onto a lightly floured board. Using the heel of your hand, knead the dough three or four times. Reshape the dough into a ball, wrap in wax paper and chill for a half hour. When chilled, pat the pastry into a round nine-inch pan, pressing the dough evenly over bottom and up the sides of the pan with your fingers. Crimp dough to make an edge. Refrigerate the tart shell while you prepare the filling. Preheat the oven to 350°. Drain the sugared cherries well and reserve the liquid. Add enough liquid from the can, if needed, to make one cup. Measure cornstarch into a saucepan; stir in the cherry liquid. Bring to a boil, stirring, and simmer two to three minutes until it is clear and thickened. Add it to drained cherries, with the almond extract, and mix gently. Pour the fruit into the chilled tart shell. Bake for 50 minutes, until crust is golden and filling is bubbly. Serve warm, or cold, with whipped cream.

Welsh Rabbit

England, which gets little enough credit for its cooking, has one tasty tradition that is almost entirely overlooked. This is the custom of winding up dinner with a savory—a small portion of a highly flavored dish containing anything from meat to eggs to cheese. The best known is Welsh rabbit, a smooth mixture of Cheddar cheese and beer. The dish is ancient and a couple of centuries ago some cooks began calling it "rarebit," apparently because this sounded more refined. The name is actually a culinary joke. When a hunter's bag was poor, a Welsh housewife cooked cheese instead of rabbit. It is served on this menu after a gala main course of pheasant, a tangy and unexpected touch.

The very names on this menu —pheasant, Welsh rabbit, port —conjure up elegant Edwardian eating. This is a dinner to linger over, deserving of your best china and four of your most discriminating guests.

This dinner gets its style by combining simple ingredients in unusual ways. The soup mixes two familiar stocks for an exotic result. The sauce for the pheasants is basically two prosaic ingredients, apples and cream, lifted into something special by a little Calvados. Welsh rabbit, although familiar as a midnight supper, is a change from the usual cheese tray. Make the most of the many kinds of fruits available in the fall by tucking a few unusual items like persimmons and pomegranates among the apples and pears.

The key question concerns the pheasant: Are you going to buy it or shoot it? If you plan to do the former, decide on the menu early as the birds may have to be ordered in advance. If your husband is a hunter, presumably you will have the bird in hand before you invite dinner guests. If your pheasants are to be store-bought, they may arrive frozen, or, far worse, in full plumage. Be sure to specify that you want the birds plucked. Pheasants are not cheap. You can substitute a pair of small roasting chickens and get a fine dinner, but the rich gamey flavor will be lacking.

Select the cheese for the rabbit carefully; since Cheddars vary enormously from bland to sharp, sample before you buy. Sharp cheese is best for this dish, but be sure the one you pick suits your taste.

A call ahead of time to the liquor store is wise—be sure they have, or can get, Calvados. If they fail you

MENU FOR SIX

CLAM CONSOMMÉ

PHEASANT NORMAND
Wild rice
Gingered carrots
Red wine

WELSH RABBIT

Port
Fresh fruit and nuts

completely, you can use applejack.

Since you are probably going to make this a dressy party you will want to do everything that you can ahead of time, which consists of making the soup stocks and combining them. Early on the afternoon of the dinner make your fruit centerpiece, or at least put the fruit in the serving bowl. Include nuts —walnuts, pecans, Brazil nuts —and be sure you can find the nutcracker. Grate the cheese for the rabbit and cover it. Prepare the gingered carrots, then cover and refrigerate them. Set the table. An hour or so before the guests are due—sooner if you need more than a half hour to change—brown the pheasants and apples and prepare the Calvados sauce. Combine these ingredients in a casserole and set it aside. Open the wine. Whip the cream for the soup, cover and store it in the refrigerator. At this point get dressed yourself, remembering that you will have a little last-minute cooking to do. Be sure that you have an all-enveloping apron you can get in and out of easily. When the guests arrive, start the pheasant casserole. Enjoy your guests for 45 minutes, then return to the kitchen and start the wild rice and put the consommé on a low heat. Add the cream to the pheasant. Reheat the carrots. After you have finished the soup course, thicken the pheasant sauce and put the cheese into a double boiler to melt while you eat. When you clear the table of the main course, finish off the rabbit with the ingredients you've assembled earlier. During this brief lull your husband can make quite a thing of pouring the port —this is your big chance to trot out the decanter you got as a wedding present and haven't used yet. Give everyone clean plates after the rabbit, then pass the fruit.

RECIPES

CLAM CONSOMMÉ

The soup will taste best with homemade stock, but it is entirely possible to use canned chicken broth. You can even use bottled clam juice but if you do, taste the combination as you make it, since brands vary in flavor. For homemade soup the proportion is two parts of clam to one of chicken, so use that as a guide.

24 chowder clams	2 eggshells
1 quart water	Salt
½ teaspoon thyme	Black pepper
½ teaspoon marjoram	½ cup heavy cream
3 cups chicken broth	Chicken broth (recipe
2 egg whites, beaten	below)

Scrub clams and put them in a large pot with the water and herbs. Bring to a boil, reduce heat, cover and simmer

for 10 minutes or until all the clams open. Remove from heat. Drain the clams thoroughly and measure the stock. There should be about six cups; if you have less, add water. Combine this with the chicken broth in a large saucepan and bring to a boil. Stir in egg whites and then put the empty eggshells in. The whites and shells clarify the soup. Boil gently for five minutes. Let settle for 10 minutes. Strain the broth through a fine sieve. Season to taste. Whip cream and top each serving with a spoonful.

CHICKEN BROTH

1½ pounds chicken necks and backs	1 onion, coarsely chopped
	1 teaspoon salt
6 cups water	

Put all the ingredients in a large-size saucepan. Bring to a boil, reduce heat and simmer without a cover for two hours or until reduced to half the original quantity. Then strain the broth.

PHEASANT NORMAND
This is the way it is done in Normandy, where Calvados comes from.

2 pheasants, cleaned	¼ cup fresh lemon juice
¼ cup butter	2 teaspoons salt
2 cups coarsely chopped, peeled tart apples	½ teaspoon black pepper
	1 tablespoon cornstarch
½ cup Calvados	1 tablespoon cold water
2 cups heavy cream	

The pheasants should weigh two and a half to three pounds each. Preheat oven to 375°. Tuck pheasant wings under the body and tie legs together. Sauté the birds in the quarter cup of butter in a heavy frying pan until they are lightly browned on all sides. When pheasants are browned, remove and keep them warm. Sauté apple pieces briefly in butter that remains in the skillet. Scoop them out and spread them over the bottom of a good-sized casserole. Place the pheasants on top. Pour off fat from the skillet in which pheasants and apples have been browned. Add Calvados and swirl it around over high heat for a minute or two, scraping the bottom of pan to deglaze it. Pour over the birds. Cover the casserole and bake for 45 minutes. Add the cream, lemon juice, salt and pepper and bake uncovered for another 30 minutes or until the pheasants are tender when pricked with a fork. Juices should be clear not pink, and drumsticks should move easily. Pheasants never get terribly tender so don't expect them to be like chicken. Put the pheasants on the serving platter and keep them warm. Combine cornstarch with the water and stir the paste into liquid in the casserole. Cook on top of stove over moderate heat, stirring constantly for a minute or two until the sauce thickens to a gravylike consistency. Pour sauce over the pheasants. Serve with wild rice. Use one and a half cups rice boiled gently for 40 minutes in six cups of water. If you use chicken instead of pheasants, the cooking time will be about the same.

GINGERED CARROTS
Puréeing vegetables isn't strictly for babies and invalids. The French do it all the time.

2 pounds carrots	melted
2 cups water	1 teaspoon ground ginger
1¼ teaspoons salt	Freshly ground black pepper
6 tablespoons butter,	

Peel and slice the carrots and put them in a heavy saucepan with the water and three-quarters teaspoon of salt. Bring them to a boil over medium-high heat, then cover, reduce the heat and cook them for 20 to 25 minutes, until they are soft. Remove from the heat, drain off the water, and purée the carrots in a food mill or an electric

blender until completely smooth and lump-free. Place the purée in a saucepan. Add butter, ginger, the remaining one-half teaspoon of salt and a grinding of pepper. Reheat over a low flame until carrots are piping hot.

WELSH RABBIT
The trick to serving this dish as a savory is not to keep your guests waiting too long after the main course. Remember to start melting it when you begin to eat the pheasant, giving it a quick turn with a wire whisk if you are in the kitchen on another errand. Have the other ingredients ready, and mix the beer and egg yolks together beforehand. With these preparations it won't take more than five to ten minutes to finish the rabbit.

You can serve the cheese on toast or rusks that have been warmed in the oven. If your rabbit is slightly grainy, it is a good sign. The wheel-type cheeses are less smooth but have more bite than the processed cheddars.

6 cups grated Cheddar cheese (about 1½ pounds)	1 tablespoon Dijon mustard
	2 teaspoons Worcestershire
	1 teaspoon salt
2 tablespoons butter	3 drops Tabasco
4 egg yolks	6 slices hot toast
½ cup beer	

Melt the butter in the top of a double boiler or chafing dish over simmering water. Stir in the cheese and cook over low heat until it is completely melted. Stir until smooth. Stir the egg yolks into the beer with a fork. Add this mixture to the cheese very slowly—a spoonful or so at a time, stirring with a whisk as it cooks in. Add mustard, Worcestershire, salt and Tabasco. Continue cooking and stirring until the mixture is thickened. Taste, and add more seasoning if desired. Serve on hot toast.

"Claret is for boys," said Dr. Johnson, "and port is for men," so be prepared for the men to be more appreciative of this rich wine than the ladies. It is a sweet, heavy wine. The richest is the ruby type, the lightest is tawny. Whichever you select, serve it with the rabbit and with the fruits and nuts.

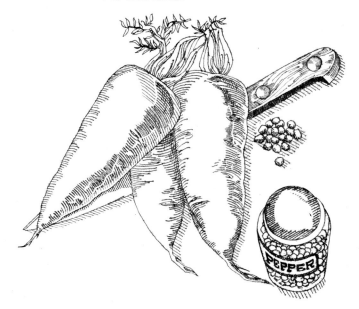

Cassoulet: A French Bean Dish

This is the world's most sumptuous version of baked beans. Like New England beans, cassoulet is a regional dish, native to southwestern France but enjoyed all over the country. It is rich with five kinds of meat, stocks, sauces and herbs. The particulars vary from Toulouse to Carcassonne, and from cook to cook. Common denominators are white beans, pork sausage and plenty of garlic.

The creation of a cassoulet is not something to be undertaken casually. Anatole France fondly recalled that his favorite version tasted as if it had been cooking for 20 years. It is a lot of work but feeds a lot of people. There isn't a better dish for a crowd, so the menu that accompanies it is planned for a party.

This menu lends itself well to a buffet dinner. The appetizer can be passed in the living room during cocktails. The cassoulet encourages people to dig down for the varied morsels beneath the surface. Dessert is light and easy to manage.

There is a lot of cooking in this dinner and you have to be able to keep many balls in the air. If you can cope with only one thing at a time, this menu will take up more hours of your day than it should.

The redeeming feature of this kind of meal is that it can all be done ahead. Either the cheesecake or the cassoulet *must* be done the day before, and in fact it is preferable if both of them are cooked ahead.

Be sure ahead of time that you are going to be able to get an assortment of fresh vegetables for the appetizer.

MENU FOR TWELVE

RAW VEGETABLES
with anchovy mayonnaise
and curry mayonnaise

CASSOULET
Green salad
with oil-and-lemon dressing
Hot French bread
Light red wine

CHEESECAKE

If you are going to do the cheesecake and cassoulet early, start by roasting the meats for the cassoulet. While they are in the oven prepare the beans and the sauce. When the roasts are done, assemble the cheesecake and put it in the oven. As the cake is baking, and then later as it is cooling, assemble the cassoulet and refrigerate it. Put the cheesecake in the refrigerator, too, when it has cooled.

Get extra ice if you need it. In the morning make the mayonnaise dips and refrigerate them. At your convenience wash and cut the vegetables and set the buffet table. Before your guests arrive, heat the cassoulet, arrange the vegetables on platters, open the wine. Assemble the salad. Just before dinner, toss the salad and pop the bread into the oven.

RECIPES

RAW VEGETABLES WITH MAYONNAISES
This is a light hors d'oeuvre that will not kill anyone's appetite for the cassoulet to come. It is supremely attractive and, if you like to think in terms of balanced menus, it supplies the vegetables that you won't get in the cassoulet.

To bring something new to this appetizer, don't use the perennial carrot sticks and celery. All nibbling cooks know that most vegetables are delicious raw, so use as much of this list as you want—your platter will look and taste best if you use them all.

1 fennel	1 bunch broccoli
2 red or green peppers	1 head Belgian endive
1/2 pound mushrooms	1 pint cherry tomatoes
1 head cauliflower	1/2 pound green beans

Wash the vegetables. All of them should be served in attractive, bite-size pieces, so cut the fennel and peppers into strips; slice the mushrooms; break the cauliflower and broccoli into flowerets; separate the endive into leaves; keep tomatoes and beans whole. Cover and chill until serving time. Then arrange them on two platters.

Make these dips with homemade mayonnaise if you have the time. It is creamier than any you can buy.

ANCHOVY MAYONNAISE

1 1/2 cups mayonnaise	2 teaspoons capers
1 two-ounce can flat anchovy fillets	1 tablespoon chopped fresh chives
1/4 cup chopped fresh parsley	Black pepper

Combine all the ingredients except the mayonnaise in a blender until the mixture is smooth. Add the mayonnaise and blend just long enough to mix thoroughly. Cover and refrigerate at least two hours until well chilled.

CURRY MAYONNAISE

1 1/2 cups mayonnaise	1/2 teaspoon salt
2 teaspoons curry powder	Black pepper
1 tablespoon grated onion	Few drops of Tabasco
1/2 teaspoon dry mustard	

Combine all the ingredients in a bowl and mix them together thoroughly. Add more curry powder if you really like it hot. Cover and chill for at least two hours.

CASSOULET
It will be helpful to get the overall strategy of this dish firmly in mind before you become involved in the tactics. You can see where the whole thing is going to come out if you have the Grand Design in your head all along.

There are basically three areas of operation. You are going to roast the duck and the pork in the oven. You are going to boil the beans. You are going to cook the lamb in a sauce on top of the stove. Finally you are going to put all this together and bake it in the oven.

Plainly you are going to need an array of pots and pans —most of them big. You can serve the cassoulet in two separate casseroles, or in one large one. It won't matter at all to the success of the dish, but sometimes a buffet works more smoothly if there are two serving dishes operating at once.

1 five-pound duck	3 pounds dried white beans,
2 pounds boned pork loin	preferably Great Northern
1/2 cup chicken broth	3 quarts water

1½ quarts chicken broth	3 tablespoons duck fat
1½ pounds Polish sausage ring	3 cups chopped onion
¼ pound lean salt pork	3 cloves garlic, minced
2 whole onions	2 one-pound 13-ounce cans tomatoes, drained and chopped
Bouquet garni made by tying four parsley sprigs, one bay leaf, one cut clove garlic in cheesecloth	1 cup dry white wine
	½ cup chopped fresh parsley
	1 bay leaf
½ teaspoon thyme	2 teaspoons thyme
2 pounds boned lamb shoulder, cubed	Salt and pepper

Preheat the oven to 325°. Place the duck, breast side up, in a shallow roasting pan. Place the pork loin in a small casserole. Insert a meat thermometer into the center of the loin. Cover the bottom of the casserole with one half cup chicken broth, put the lid on and roast the pork until the thermometer reaches 170°, about an hour and a half. Roast the duck at the same time. It will be done in about two and a half hours, or when the legs move easily up and down. Set both roasts aside when finished.

While the meats are roasting, tackle the beans. Rinse them thoroughly and put them in a large pot. Add three quarts of water, cover and bring to a full rolling boil. Remove the pot from the heat and let it stand one hour. Then, when the beans have plumped up, add one and one half quarts chicken broth, the sausage, salt pork, whole onions, bouquet garni and one half teaspoon of thyme. Bring to a boil, spooning off scum as it rises. Reduce the heat and simmer the beans uncovered for 30 minutes. Remove the sausage and set it aside. Continue cooking the beans for another 30 minutes or so, until they are barely tender. They have more cooking to do later and you do not want them to be mushy. Discard the bouquet and onions. Drain the beans, taking care not to throw out the salt pork, and save the liquor.

Now for the lamb and the sauce. While all of this cooking is going on you will have the time for this preparation, but don't forget that you must keep an eye on the pork (which will be done before the duck) and on the beans which will be going on and off the heat. Remove three tablespoons of duck fat from the roasting pan. Put it into a large skillet and add the pieces of lamb to brown. Put in enough pieces to cover the bottom of the pan without crowding. Add extra fat if needed. Remove the pieces as they brown and continue the process until all the lamb is browned. Remove lamb and set it aside. Add the chopped onions and garlic to the pan and cook, stirring, until soft. Add the tomatoes, wine, parsley, bay leaf and two teaspoons of thyme. Put the lamb back in the pan, cover and simmer over low heat for 20 minutes. Then, using a slotted spoon, remove the pieces of lamb from the sauce. Pour the sauce into a bowl and add three cups of bean liquor to it. Save any remaining bean liquor in case the cas-

soulet looks dry during the last baking. Stir the sauce and the liquor together. Add salt and pepper as needed.

All the cooking except the final baking is now done and it is time to cut the meats into the final sizes you want. Slice the pork roast and then cut each slice into bite-size pieces. Remove the legs and wings from the duck. Cut away the skin and fat and then cut the duck meat into bite-size pieces. Slice the sausage.

You are now, at last, ready to put the whole thing together. First spread a thick layer of beans in the bottom of one 10- to 11-quart casserole or two five- to six-quart casseroles. Top with a generous layer of lamb, sausage, pork and duck, saving the legs and wings for garnish. Repeat with another layer of beans and most of the rest of the meat. Finish with the remaining beans. Garnish the top of the cassoulet with the duck legs and wings—and a few pieces of the meats. Pour the bean-tomato liquid over all. It should come nearly to the top, but the dish should not be awash. If you are making it the day before, put it in the refrigerator now. If you are doing it just before serving, bake it, covered, in a 350° oven for two hours. If the cassoulet seems dry, add leftover bean liquor as necessary.

If the cassoulet has been made ahead and refrigerated, it may take more than two hours to heat through.

CHEESECAKE

Cheesecake has as many versions as an old joke. This one, which combines cottage and cream cheese with sour cream, is like New York's Jewish-American style.

You'll need an electric mixer—or a particularly well-developed right arm. You'll also need a spring-form pan. It will allow you to remove a cake from its pan without any worry of damaging it—just undo the clasp and the sides spring apart and can be lifted off the finished cake.

16 ounces cream cheese, softened	3 tablespoons flour
	1½ tablespoons lemon juice
1 pound creamed cottage cheese	1 teaspoon grated lemon rind
1½ cups sugar	1 teaspoon vanilla extract
4 eggs, slightly beaten	½ cup butter, melted
3 tablespoons cornstarch	1 pint sour cream

Heat oven to 325°. Grease a nine-inch spring-form pan. With an electric mixer, beat the cream cheese with cottage cheese at high speed. Gradually beat in the sugar, then the eggs. At low speed, beat in the cornstarch, flour, lemon juice and rind, and vanilla. Beat in the melted butter and sour cream. Pour into the greased pan. Bake one hour and 10 minutes, or until firm around the edges. Turn off the oven. Let the pan stand in the oven for two hours. Then remove and let it cool at least two hours. Refrigerate the cake for three hours, or until well chilled.

To remove the cake from the pan, run a spatula around the sides of the cheesecake and then release the clasp of the spring-form pan. Leave the bottom of the pan in place and put it right on a serving plate.

A Paella from Valencia

Paella is a succulent dish from Spain that combines unexpected yet harmonious ingredients—mussels and sausage, pimiento and shrimp. It takes its name from the shallow open dish in which it is cooked and varies from region to region. In the interior, cooks use meat, chicken and vegetables with rice. On the Mediterranean, seafood is added, but varies with the catch. In Valencia, home of the classic version, the rice is always cooked with saffron to turn it a brilliant yellow.

The rich taste of a paella makes it splendid company fare, but it has other virtues too. If certain ingredients are unavailable, substitutions can be made in a freewheeling way and no hair-raising timing is called for. When served with the menu presented here it can be a feast —for the eye as well as the palate.

Paella still retains its country origins and is best served informally. It should, however, be a sit-down dinner since many ingredients are cooked in their shells and require a certain amount of manipulation. The recipe given here provides generous portions in the expectation that the result will be good enough to warrant seconds all around.

The clear soup is flavored with a touch of sherry, a traditional Spanish wine. The French bread is crusty, a pleasant change in texture. The wine is dry to quench the thirst that is bound to come with eating the paella. The dessert, crème brûlée, is smooth and gentle, suitable at the end of a highly seasoned meal. This menu has also been planned with an eye on the welfare of the cook. The soup and the dessert can be made ahead so that on the day of the party the cook can concentrate on the paella.

Shopping for the paella (and for the salad greens and bread, of course) should be done at the last minute if fresh ingredients are used. When fresh shellfish is available, by all means use it; the flavor is unbeatable. Have the fishman cut up the lobster. If fresh seafood is unavailable, frozen rock lobster tails are a good substitute and frozen shrimp will do fine—canned is less satisfactory since it has already been completely cooked. If fresh clams are unavailable, canned or frozen ones—thawed—can be added during the last few minutes of cooking. They will not look as pretty but the flavor is satisfactory. There is no substitute for mussels but they are not absolutely essential. If the hot, hard Spanish chorizo is not to be had, use Italian pepperoni instead.

What you need, to be both a good cook and a charming hostess on the same evening is good timing. With the proper preparation you can be present—and even serene—during cocktails. The soup must be prepared at least a day ahead of time, and can actually be made a week in advance and frozen. The crème brûlée will have more flavor if made the day before, and refrigerated.

Early on the day of the dinner do the marketing. The clams and mussels should be cleaned as soon as they are brought home. Scrub the mussels with a stiff brush, pull off the "beard." Throw away any that are open. Clams should be cleaned in much the same way. Shrimps can be peeled ahead and then refrigerated. If frozen shellfish is used, thaw it in time.

Many chores can be done well in advance. Washed salad greens will keep perfectly in a dry towel in the refrigerator. Mix the vinaigrette dressing (three parts olive oil, one part wine vinegar, salt and pepper). Set the table, put out serving dishes, allowing a large casserole for the paella. Prepare hors d'oeuvres, which in view of the dinner ahead can be as simple as raw vegetables. Put white wine in refrigerator to chill—allow two bottles for six people, two glasses each. Shortly before the guests are expected, slice the mushrooms for the soup (but not earlier or they will turn brown), spread the brown sugar on the crème brûlée.

There are two schools of thought on how to cope with the timing of the paella. Allow 20 minutes for preparation and 40 minutes in the oven. The safe but sane cook will have the paella assembled before she changes her clothes for dinner. It can wait an hour or so without any effect. But if you want to live dangerously, and be certain that the rice won't be the least bit limp, get an all-enveloping apron and prepare the paella after you have changed.

MENU FOR SIX

SHERRIED CONSOMMÉ WITH MUSHROOMS

Toast triangles

PAELLA
Green salad,
vinaigrette dressing
French bread
Dry white wine

CRÈME BRÛLÉE

RECIPES

SHERRIED CONSOMMÉ WITH MUSHROOMS

Until you eat this, or any other rich broth made from scratch, you will never know how good a home-cooked broth can be. But it is a lot of work and if you are not game for it, a good canned bouillon pepped up with sliced mushrooms and sherry is an adequate and easy way out.

This recipe is not as expensive as it seems since the beef used in it is delicious served cold or cooked up as hash. For the best flavor add sherry to the soup just before it is taken off the heat. But if you prefer to serve with a flourish, add a dollop to each bowl at the table.

2 pounds beef chuck	3 celery stalks, cut up
2 large beef marrow bones, cracked	2 carrots, cut up
	1 bay leaf
2 large onions, quartered	1 large clove garlic, split
4 whole cloves	2 egg whites, lightly beaten
1 tablespoon salt	1 cup very thinly sliced raw mushrooms
15 peppercorns	
4 quarts cold water	2 tablespoons dry sherry

Roast marrow bones and onions in hot oven (450°) for 45 minutes, turning once or twice, until they are browned. (This gives soup a richer flavor and good color.) Remove from oven. Put bones and onions in a large soup kettle with beef, celery, carrots, bay leaf, garlic, cloves, salt and peppercorns. Discard any fat in the pan in which bones and onions were browned, and then deglaze the pan by putting one or two cups of the water into it, bringing the water to a boil, stirring and scraping to remove browned bits from the pan. Add this to the soup kettle along with the rest of the four quarts of water. Bring to a boil, skimming off scum as it rises. When the scum ceases to rise, reduce heat, cover and simmer for two hours. Strain soup and put beef aside for other uses. Chill at least six hours, or overnight. This should make about three quarts of stock. Remove congealed fat from chilled soup. Return soup to pot, stir in egg whites and bring to a boil, stirring constantly. Reduce heat and simmer uncovered for one hour, reducing consommé to about two quarts. Strain through cheesecloth.

Just before serving put mushrooms and two cups of consommé into a large saucepan. Boil for about two minutes. Add the remaining consommé and heat slowly to serving temperature. Stir in sherry.

PAELLA

This dish is open to lots of variation, so do not be discouraged if one or two of the seafood ingredients used here are unavailable. There will still be enough elements in it so that it will be full of delicious and surprising morsels. As you become more familiar with the recipe you may find other things you want to add—cubed pork or a white-meat fish, such as halibut, which make the dish less expensive than this version.

Traditionally in Spain, the paella is cooked over direct heat in a pan so large that it cannot fit into the average oven. Cook the dish that way if you choose but it requires closer watching—the bottom layer is apt to stick. Although this way is more authentic, it does not add enough in flavor to compensate for the added difficulty. In fact you probably could never tell the difference.

6 chicken legs	2 cups long-grain rice
3 one-pound live lobsters	2 teaspoons salt
1½ pounds fresh shrimp	Freshly ground black pepper
24 mussels in shell	4 tomatoes, peeled and
24 hardshell clams in shell	quartered or one 1-
1 pound chorizo, sliced	pound can, drained
1 quart chicken broth	1½ cups peas, fresh or
½ teaspoon saffron	frozen
½ cup olive oil	1 four-ounce can pimientos,
2 cloves garlic, crushed	sliced
1 large onion, chopped	

First prepare the shellfish. Remember to have the lobster cut up at the market. Peel the raw shrimp, leaving the tails on. Large-size shrimp, which run about 15 to the pound, are easier to handle and you won't need to peel as many of them. Clean the clams and mussels thoroughly. About an hour before dinner time, preheat the oven to 325° F. Put chicken broth on to boil. If you have homemade stock, so much the better, but you can use canned chicken broth or broth made from bouillon cubes. When the broth comes to a boil turn off the heat and add saffron.

Meanwhile, sauté chicken legs in olive oil over medium heat until they are golden brown. Then put them aside in a covered dish to keep them warm and juicy. Add garlic and onions to oil and cook over low heat, stirring fre-quently, until the onion is translucent. Add rice and cook until it is translucent and faintly golden (absorbing the oil makes it so), stirring lightly with a fork. Add chicken broth, salt and pepper, and stir to loosen any browned bits at bottom of pan. Cover and simmer 10 minutes so that the rice will absorb some of the broth.

Into the largest casserole you own, or two small ones —rubbed with olive oil beforehand—put half of uncooked shellfish (lobster, shrimp, mussels, clams), chorizo slices, tomatoes, peas, pimiento. Top this with about three quarters of the rice mixture. Arrange the chicken legs and the rest of the shellfish, chorizo, tomatoes, peas and pimiento on top and spoon remaining rice and broth around these. Cover the casserole and bake for 30 minutes. Look in on it once or twice and if it seems too dry add extra liquid. You may use extra broth if you have any or water if you don't but it must be boiling, otherwise the temperature of the mixture will be lowered considerably, cooking time thrown off and rice gummy. Remove cover and bake until rice is fluffy (about 10 minutes).

CRÈME BRÛLÉE

This dessert is neither difficult nor time consuming but it does require constant attention. It must be stirred steadily while it cooks to keep it smooth, and it must be carefully watched as overcooking will make it curdle. It also has a tricky moment when it is put under the broiler: don't leave it—you may be undone in a moment.

2½ cups heavy cream	1 teaspoon cornstarch
6 eggs	1 teaspoon almond extract
6 tablespoons sugar	1 cup light brown sugar

In top of double boiler heat cream slowly just until a light skin forms on top. Remove from heat and set aside to cool. Beat eggs until thick and light-colored. Mix sugar with cornstarch and add to eggs gradually, beating constantly. Add cream to beaten egg mixture very, very slowly, stirring briskly. Return to double boiler and cook over simmering, not boiling, water. Stir constantly until the mixture will coat a metal spoon with a light layer. As soon as the custard coats the spoon take it off the heat. Stir in flavoring. Strain through a sieve into a heatproof serving dish or six individual heatproof dishes. Stir it gently twice during the first 10 minutes of cooling to prevent a surface skin from forming. When it is lukewarm put it in refrigerator to chill. Large dish should be chilled at least six to eight hours, small ones need only three to four hours to chill thoroughly.

Just before serving comes a critical moment. Sprinkle the top of the custard with the brown sugar which has been put through a sieve before measuring to remove any lumps. Set dish into a pan of ice (to avoid the chance of breaking the dish because of a sudden change in temperature) and place it, ice and all, under the broiler for two or three minutes, or until sugar bubbles. This should be watched carefully, as sugar has a tendency to burn. Serve the custard immediately.

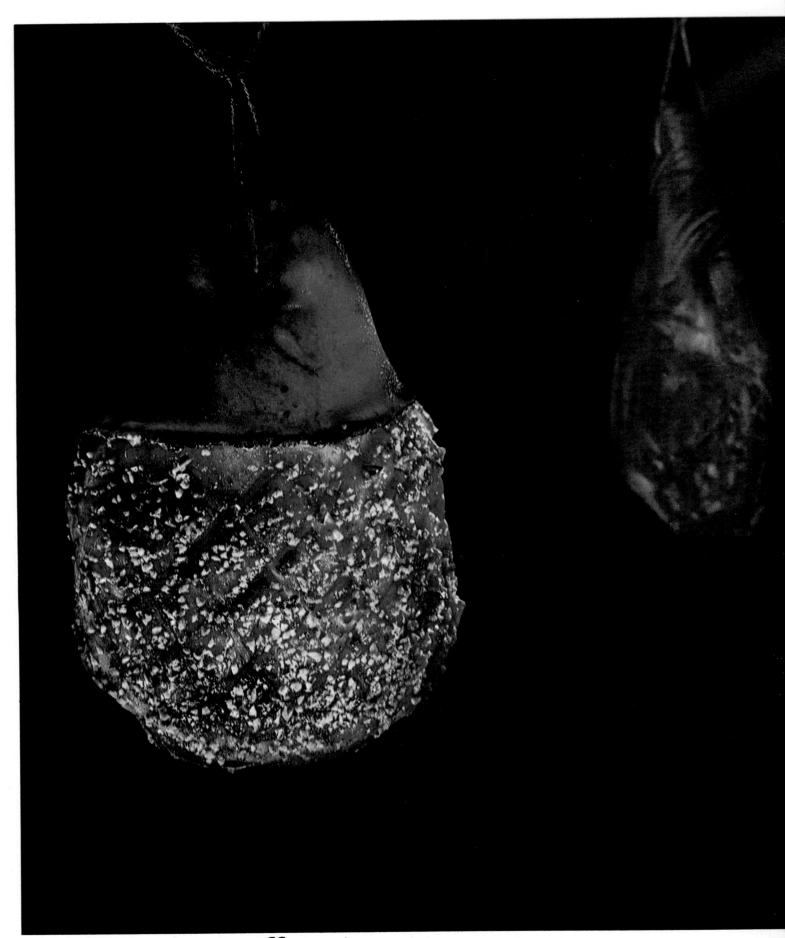

Baked Stuffed Ham

Ham is a natural for entertaining, and its fame has made it such a predictable fixture at the buffet table that many cooks go out of their way to avoid it. This is a mistake; ham became a perennial party

dish with good reason. It has a fine hearty flavor, is easy to prepare for a large group, and is relatively inexpensive. On top of this, ham lends itself to imaginative preparation, as in this ham stuffed with *pâté*.

It is no trick at all to elevate it above the usual sideboard standby.

This stuffing, which combines liver *pâté*, sherry, mushrooms and walnuts, has a smooth rich taste which comple-

ments the salty, smoky tang of the ham. The glaze of nuts and honey also makes a crunchy crust that gives the ham an interesting texture. Hot or cold it is an excellent treatment of an old partygoer.

35

This dinner is a rarity—it is equally attractive served buffet or sit-down. If you choose buffet style, ladle the soup from a tureen into mugs, which can be more easily managed than soup plates or cups and saucers. Carve the ham ahead and let the guests help themselves to everything. But you had better slice the *bombe* yourself rather than let everyone fend for himself.

Decide what you prefer to serve to drink with this dinner. You have lots of options—cider or beer would be good, or if you want to be a little fancier, serve a light red wine. Don't bring out an expensive important wine for this occasion —ham and cabbage will just overpower it.

A couple of days before the party, set the raisins soaking for the *bombe* and order the ham. Tell the butcher you want it boned and that since you plan to stuff it, he should disturb the meat as little as possible. Butcher-

MENU FOR EIGHT
WATERCRESS SOUP

BAKED HAM
WITH PÂTÉ STUFFING
Sweet potato soufflé
Red cabbage and apples

BRANDIED ORANGE BOMBE

ing techniques vary, but it really doesn't matter so long as you end up with a ham that can be stuffed and then skewered, sewn or tied back into shape. You can do a lot of the cooking the day ahead if you prefer: soup, cabbage, stuffing and dessert can all be prepared in advance. Freeze the *bombe*, refrigerate the rest. On the afternoon of the dinner, stuff the ham and start it cooking about three hours before serving time. An hour before dinner glaze the ham, put the soufflé in the oven and the cabbage over a very low heat. Heat the extra stuffing. Unmold the *bombe*, popping it right back into the freezer. Just before dinner time, heat the soup. When it has been served, take the ham out of the oven to "rest." Bring on the ham and cabbage, then take the soufflé out of the oven—at the last minute: the less chance it has to fall the better.

RECIPES

WATERCRESS SOUP

This soup is shamrock green and sure to have everyone guessing what it is before they taste it. Some of your guests may go on wondering even after they've tasted, for its slightly bitter flavor is hard to place. If you like the taste, the soup is no trick to make and will probably become a regular event, served either hot or cold.

3 bunches watercress	2 tablespoons flour
3 tablespoons butter	2 13-ounce cans clear
1/4 cup minced onion	chicken broth
1 1/2 cups water	2 cups milk
1 teaspoon salt	2 egg yolks
1/2 teaspoon white pepper	1 cup heavy cream

Rinse and drain watercress and remove the coarsest stems. Melt one tablespoon butter in a large saucepan, add onion and cook until golden. Add watercress, water, salt and pepper, and cook over high heat for five minutes. Put mixture into a blender at high speed for a few seconds. Melt the remaining two tablespoons of butter in a saucepan, stir in flour. Add the chicken broth and the milk; bring to a boil. Stir in the watercress mixture. Beat egg yolks and the heavy cream together. Stir one cup of the hot soup into the egg-cream mixture, then add this combination to the soup, stirring constantly. Heat thoroughly but do not boil.

BAKED HAM WITH PÂTÉ STUFFING

There is much confusion over what the labels on ham mean. Commercial hams—the kind widely available from butchers and supermarkets—have been cured by injection. Words like "tenderized" don't mean a thing as far

as cooking goes, and the only real distinction is between hams labeled "fully cooked" and "cook before eating." Even "cook before eating" types have been partially cooked by the packer to the point where they can be safely eaten without further cooking. More cooking simply develops flavor. Cook "fully cooked" hams to an internal temperature of 130° on a meat thermometer, others to a temperature of 160°. Commercial hams, as opposed to "country hams," don't need soaking.

It is not very easy to carve a stuffed ham as the stuffing is crumbly and may not be evenly distributed. Tell your husband you don't expect perfect, fully rounded slices. If you don't warn him, he's apt to be furious with the ham, his carving equipment and you.

1 12-to-14-pound fully	1/3 cup honey
cooked ham, boned	3/4 cup chopped walnuts
Pâté stuffing (recipe below)	

Preheat oven to 325°. Trim excess rind off the ham if necessary, leaving some around the shank end. Pack as much stuffing as you can into the opening left by the removal of the bones. Save the rest of the stuffing to heat separately. Insert five or six five-inch skewers through the ham on either side of the opening and then lace the opening together by crisscrossing string around the skewers. If the shape of the hole in your ham doesn't seem to lend itself to lacing, you can either sew the edges together (using string and upholstery needle) or cover the hole with foil and tie it in place. Line a shallow roasting pan with foil to simplify cleanup. Put the ham on a rack in the pan and bake for two hours. Remove ham from oven. Cut the fat into a diamond pattern. Spread half of the honey over the fat area and sprinkle with walnuts. Dribble the rest of the honey over the nuts. Insert a meat thermometer into thickest part of the ham. Return the ham to the oven and cook for an additional hour or until the meat thermometer reaches 130°. Let the ham rest out of the oven for 10 minutes to make carving easier.

PÂTÉ STUFFING

1 pound mushrooms, finely chopped	1 tablespoon dried parsley
½ cup finely chopped onion	Freshly ground black pepper
½ cup butter	2 four-and-a-half-ounce cans liver pâté
2 cups fine dry bread crumbs	1 cup chopped walnuts
	¼ cup dry sherry

Sauté mushrooms and onion in butter, for 10 minutes, or until moisture has evaporated. Stir in crumbs, parsley and pepper. Remove pan from heat and work pâté into mixture with a fork or pastry blender. Add walnuts and sherry. If the mixture seems very dry, add a tablespoon or so of sherry. After packing it into the ham—you will probably use about half—put the rest into the top of a buttered double boiler. Cook over simmering water for an hour. Serve a spoonful with each slice of ham.

SWEET POTATO SOUFFLÉ

Don't expect this dish to be as towering as a dessert soufflé. It won't blow up that much, so you needn't worry that you've done something wrong. The flavor is not as sweet as you might expect it to be either. In fact it's on the spicy side.

3 one-pound two-ounce cans sweet potatoes or four pounds sweet potatoes, cooked	¾ cup sugar
	½ cup milk
	1 tablespoon freshly grated lemon rind
½ cup butter, melted	1 teaspoon ground ginger
6 eggs	½ teaspoon salt

Preheat oven to 325°. Drain canned sweet potatoes, or peel fresh ones. Mash potatoes, then beat, using low speed of electric mixer to make them as lump-free as possible. Beat in melted butter. Separate eggs and add yolks to sweet potato mixture. Beat until well blended. The longer you beat, the smoother the final result. Add sugar, milk, lemon rind, ginger and salt. Beat egg whites separately until stiff but not dry and fold into potato mixture. Turn into a buttered two-quart soufflé dish or casserole. Bake for one hour. Serve immediately.

RED CABBAGE AND APPLES

1 two-pound head red cabbage	Freshly ground black pepper
¼ cup butter	2 cups water
2 medium onions, finely chopped	2 tablespoons cider vinegar
	4 firm apples
½ teaspoon nutmeg	3 tablespoons fresh lemon juice
2 teaspoons salt	

Cut cabbage head into quarters and then into shreds, removing the hard core. Melt the butter in a large pan. Add the onions, nutmeg, salt and pepper, and cook until the onions are golden. Add water and vinegar, and stir in the cabbage. Cover and cook over medium heat for 30 minutes. While the cabbage is cooking, peel and slice the apples. Add them to cabbage, cover, and continue cooking for 30 minutes more, adding a little more water if the cabbage looks dry. Stir in lemon juice.

BRANDIED ORANGE BOMBE

You can create a *bombe maison* by combining any two —or three—flavors of water ice, sherbet or ice cream you want to. Select the combinations for color as well as taste. When serving this particular combination, pour a spoonful or so of brandy over each slice of *bombe*.

1 quart orange water ice	raisins
1½ quarts vanilla ice cream	½ cup brandy
½ cup white seedless	

As long ahead as you think of it—anywhere from three days to the night before—put the raisins in the brandy to soak. Put them in a covered jar and let them sit at room temperature to soften. To make the *bombe*, chill a two-quart mold in the freezer. Spread the inside of the mold with orange ice, which has been softened slightly, pressing the ice against the mold with the back of a spoon so that it will take on the shape of the mold. The layer of orange ice should be about one half inch thick. Put the mold back into the freezer and prepare vanilla ice cream as follows. Drain soaked raisins and stir them quickly into the ice cream without letting the ice cream melt. Pack ice cream into the center of the mold. Cover the mold with its lid, if it has one, or with foil. Return to freezer and freeze for at least six hours. To unmold, remove the cover or foil, then place the mold on a chilled serving plate, wipe the outside of the mold several times with a cloth wrung out in hot water and lift off the mold. The *bombe* can be unmolded ahead and kept frozen until serving time.

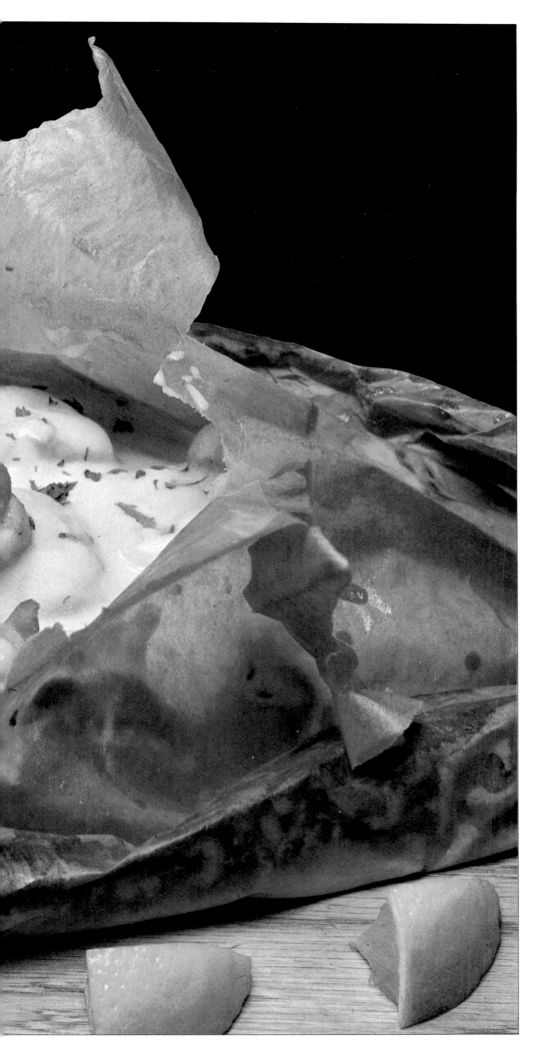

Sole en Papillote

This recipe demands the most elegant ingredients—a delicate fish, sauce made with champagne, tiny mushrooms—and then wraps the whole fancy creation up in plain brown butcher paper. Cooking *en papillote,* in a cocoon of paper, is a practical way to prepare this dish. The subtly flavored juices are held in the paper and, because the fish will not get cold quickly, it can be kept waiting a reasonable amount of time—until the paper is torn open with a flourish to reveal the gastronomic feat and release the fragrance of the food inside.

The cooking of this dinner is not hard but it does require a kind of deftness and artistry that just can't be achieved when you're also making peanut butter sandwiches and trying to feed the dog.

The first thing you must realize when you shop for the sole for this dinner is that there isn't any such fish around. True sole is Dover sole and considered by many food lovers to be the best-tasting fish in the world. A very small quantity is imported from Holland and most of it goes to restaurants. If by chance you have a fish market elegant enough to carry it, you'll be staggered by its price. What Americans commonly sell as sole is flounder, which is about a fourth cousin to the Dover sole, and, like it, has white meat and a delicate flavor. Most flounders belong to one of two main families—right-eyed and left-eyed, according to how the fish looks up from the muddy bottom he calls home. Among the dozens of U.S. flounders, two are most widely used for "filet of sole"—lemon sole and gray sole. Both are members of the right-eyed flounder family. The gray sole, which comes from New England, most closely resembles Dover sole in flavor; lemon sole, caught only off the Georges Banks, is coarser and thicker, with a fishier taste. Settle for whatever type you can get—it won't make much difference in the recipe anyway.

Before you can begin to discuss the sole problem even with the fishman, you should know how to pronounce what you're going to serve. *En Papillote* is easy—on pappy-yutt—it's the other that's hard. People who sell it call it "fillet" (pronounced fill-it), and indeed the dictionary agrees that this is correct. Restaurants with

MENU FOR SIX

ARTICHOKES WITH HERB SAUCE

SOLE EN PAPILLOTE WITH CHAMPAGNE SAUCE
Parsley potatoes
Fresh broccoli
Champagne or dry white wine

POUNDCAKE WITH ORANGE GLAZE

menus in French usually spell it "filet" and pronounce it fee-lay. So take your pick.

There is not too much work to making this dinner, although some fast footwork is required during the last half hour of preparation.

Early on the day of the dinner, cook the artichokes, make the herb sauce. Wash the broccoli, peel the potatoes. Make the poundcake, glaze it and let it sit, covered, until serving time. Chill the wine. Then, if you've never made it before or if you've got more thumbs than fingers, spend a little time practicing how to make the *papillote*—the paper wrapping. It isn't really hard, but you ought not to be doing it for the first time when the paper is filled with sole and champagne sauce and the living room is filled with guests.

The sequence on cooking the sole goes like this: 1) sole in the oven, 2) sole out of the oven, 3) make sauce, 4) combine sole and sauce in the *papillote*, and finally 5) put it back in the oven again. Time things so that step No. 1 takes place when guests arrive. You will have to excuse yourself 20 minutes later for the next three steps—but don't put the fish back in the oven yet, keep it in a warm place. While you are out in the kitchen start the water for the broccoli and potatoes. Before you sit down to the artichokes put the vegetables in to cook. Put the fish back in the oven for final baking while you clear the table. It takes a bare 10 minutes. To cut down on trips to the kitchen, you can cook the potatoes and broccoli before dinner and keep them warm by setting the pans in a large pan of simmering water. They may not taste as perfect, but the saving in harassment may be worth it.

RECIPES

ARTICHOKES

This vegetable is now becoming more widely appreciated in the U.S. although it has been a delicacy in Europe for centuries. Serve the artichokes on a salad-size plate so that there is room for the discarded leaves on the side. Serve the sauce separately in small dishes—one per guest—or fill the inside of the artichoke with the sauce.

6 large artichokes	1 clove garlic, split
Boiling water	2 teaspoons salt
1 lemon, sliced	

Wash artichokes and cut one-half inch from top with sharp knife. Cut off the stem. With scissors, snip the sharp tip from each leaf. Stand artichokes upright in a saucepan, and cover with boiling water. The pan should hold the artichokes snugly, depending on size, you may be able to cook only two or three in one pan. (If so, di-vide lemon and garlic, but use two teaspoons salt in each pan.) Add remaining ingredients, cover and simmer for 45 minutes or until an outside leaf pulls off easily.

Drain the artichokes upside down until cool. Carefully spread leaves apart and use a teaspoon to remove the fuzzy center, or choke. Handle the artichoke gently, but do the job thoroughly and get all the whiskers out. Chill and fill center with herb sauce just before serving.

HERB SAUCE

½ cup wine vinegar	1 teaspoon chervil
½ cup melted butter	1 teaspoon tarragon
1 cup olive oil	1 teaspoon grated onion
1 large clove garlic, crushed	½ teaspoon sugar
1 tablespoon minced pimiento	¼ teaspoon dry mustard
1½ teaspoons salt	Freshly ground black pepper

Combine all ingredients and stir thoroughly. Let stand at least one-half hour at room temperature to blend flavors. Don't refrigerate sauce, even if you make it early in the day. Makes about one third cup of sauce per serving.

SOLE EN PAPILLOTE

This dish tastes too good to pass up just because you may not feel you have the dexterity to cope with the *papillote*. If you do feel this is beyond you, skip it, and serve the fish arranged on a platter and coated with sauce.

There are some things you can do to simplify matters. If you have a suitable platter, of either stainless steel or some other heatproof material, lay the *papillote* on that. It will save one rather precarious transfer after the dish has cooked. If, when folding it, the paper tends to unwind, carefully stick a paper clip where needed—but don't forget to take it out before you serve. There are several kinds of paper you can use. Butchers' paper takes on a pleasant brown color in the oven, but other kinds of parchment paper will work fine. Foil is easy to use, and many good restaurants do use it for dishes served *en papillote*. But it's a bit like wearing pin curls to the table. Foil, marvelous as it is, belongs in the kitchen.

12 small sole fillets	1 cup skimmed, canned
24 small mushroom caps	chicken broth
3/4 cup butter, softened	1/2 cup flour
1/2 cup chopped shallots	1/4 cup heavy cream
(about eight)	2 tablespoons lemon juice
1 teaspoon salt	2 tablespoons chopped
1/8 teaspoon white pepper	fresh parsley
12 slices of carrot	1 egg white, slightly beaten
1 split (6 1/2 ounces) of dry	Lemon wedges
champagne	

Preheat oven to 350°. Put the 12 best-looking mushroom caps aside. Slice the rest of the caps and arrange a few slices on the center of each fish fillet. Fold the ends of the fillets over the mushrooms. Spread one-quarter cup of the butter in a baking pan, sprinkle with shallots, salt and pepper. Then put in the fillets, folded side down. Put the 12 remaining mushroom caps and the carrot in the pan. Pour in the champagne and chicken broth. Cover the pan with foil. Bring to a boil, then immediately place the pan in the oven and bake for 20 minutes. While the fish is baking, prepare *beurre manié* by mixing the remaining one-half cup butter with the flour. Now to the *papillote*. Cut an oval about 20 inches long and 14 inches wide from one large piece of butchers' paper or parchment. From another piece cut another oval one inch bigger all around. Use the bigger oval as the top. Generously butter the bottom sheet of paper to within one inch of the edge and put it on an ovenproof platter or cookie sheet. When the fish is baked, gently lift the fillets, mushroom caps and carrot slices from the baking pan with a slotted spatula and set them on a plate to drain. Cover them with foil to keep warm. Raise the temperature

of the oven to 400°. Drain the broth from the baking pan into a saucepan; there will be about three cups. Place over medium heat and add the *beurre manié* a little at a time, stirring with a whisk until blended, smooth and thick enough to coat the whisk lightly. You may not need all of it. The nice thing about making a sauce by this method is that it is easy to control. Just add more or less *beurre manié* as needed. Stir in cream, then add the lemon juice. Arrange the drained fillets on the buttered bottom piece of paper. Garnish each with a mushroom cap, cut across the top to hold a carrot slice. Spoon about one cup of sauce over the fillets, enough to cover them. Sprinkle with parsley. Set the rest of the sauce aside to keep warm. Brush edges of both pieces of paper with egg white diluted with a little water. Put the second piece of paper on top and fold the bottom edge over the top edge, rolling them together and crimping them to get a tight seal. Brush the edges and the top sheet with egg white. Bake for 10 minutes or until the paper gets crisp, puffs up and begins to brown. Serve with lemon wedges and pass the remaining sauce separately.

Serve with boiled potatoes that have been dusted with parsley, and broccoli.

ORANGE-GLAZED POUNDCAKE

1 cup butter	1/4 teaspoon baking soda
2 1/2 cups sugar	1 cup sour cream
6 large eggs	1 teaspoon grated orange
3 cups sifted flour	rind
1/2 teaspoon salt	1 teapoon vanilla

Preheat the oven to 350°. Grease the bottom of a 10-inch tube pan, and line with wax paper. Using an electric mixer beat the butter until it is soft and fluffy. Add the sugar and beat until blended. Add the eggs, one at a time, beating well after each addition. Sift the flour with the salt and the soda. Then, alternately, add the flour mixture and sour cream to the butter and sugar, starting with the dry ingredients and ending with the dry ingredients. Beat batter until smooth after each addition. Run a spatula around the edge of the bowl occasionally. Stir in the orange rind and the vanilla. This is a fairly thick batter. Spoon the batter into the prepared cake pan. Bake on the oven's center rack for one hour and 30 to 40 minutes, or until a cake-tester inserted in the center comes out clean. Place the cake in the pan on a cake rack; let it stand for five minutes. Then pour the hot orange glaze over the entire cake. The glaze will be absorbed into it. Let the cake sit for one hour before removing it from the pan.

ORANGE GLAZE

1 cup orange juice	1/4 cup butter
3/4 cup sugar	1 tablespoon lemon juice

Combine ingredients in a small saucepan. Bring to a boil, lower heat, simmer for 10 minutes. Pour over the cake.

Grilled Lamb Chops

There are certain things so delectable that to eat a lot of them seems almost immoral. If you happen to be an Arab the eye of a sheep might be one such morsel, but Americans are more likely to think of the mouth-watering qualities of a steak tenderloin or a rib lamb chop. Even the thick double chops shown here are scarcely more than a few succulent bites, and costly ones at that. The French—who have given the matter considerable thought—believe that rib chops are moister than any other cut of lamb, and cook them, seasoned with a hint of herbs, only until they are the palest pink. What the chops lack in substance is more than made up for by the array of vegetables that surrounds them—and by the splendid soup and dusky rich dessert which complete this elegant midwinter menu.

A number of old favorites are done up elegantly for the holidays in this dinner. The chestnuts, which usually appear in stuffing, make an unusual soup, the grilled lamb chops are flavored with a mixture of herbs, baked potatoes sharpened with Roquefort. The dessert is outstandingly rich and chocolaty.

Shop ahead for the raw chestnuts. Although they are at their peak now, you might have to give your store advance notice—canned chestnuts are packed in sweet syrup and won't do. Allow yourself a good hour to peel them. Do this a few days before the dinner, if you like, and keep them wrapped and chilled until ready to use. Make the soup the day before. While it is cooking, make the chocolate mousse. This will leave you very little to do the day of the dinner. Several hours before your guests arrive, put the potatoes in to bake. Prepare but do not cook the vegetables that surround the lamb chops. Chop the parsley for the soup. Finish preparing the potatoes, and keep them loosely covered at room temperature. About a half-hour before the first guest is due, take the soup from the refrigerator. Cook the onions and the mushrooms for the vegetable garland—do not add the cherry tomatoes, though, or the lemon juice. Do that at the last minute. Season the lamb chops. Put the soup on to

MENU FOR SIX

CREAM OF CHESTNUT SOUP

BROILED LAMB CHOPS WITH HERBS
Garland of vegetables
Roquefort-stuffed potatoes
Red wine

BITTER CHOCOLATE MOUSSE

simmer one-half hour before you plan to serve it.

Now comes the juggling part. For this you need to use a timer, or you will have overcooked lamb chops. Allow 15 minutes for your guests to eat the soup course. Just before you sit down to the soup, put the chops on to broil—set your timer for eight minutes. When the bell rings, disappear briefly to turn the chops over, turn off the heat under the vegetables and put the potatoes in the oven. If your oven is the type in which the broiler is a separate unit, place the potatoes in the oven part. If your broiler and oven are all in one, put the potatoes on the rack under the pan with the chops—that way the potatoes will heat but not burn. All this will actually take only a minute to do. Set the timer for an additional eight minutes, and return to your guests. After finishing the soup course try to beat the bell back to the kitchen—it can get tiresome. At this point, put the cherry tomatoes in with the vegetables and add the lemon juice. They just need a minute or so to heat. Transfer the chops to a serving platter and surround them with the vegetables. Leave the potatoes in the oven until the very last minute to be sure they are heated through. The dessert is ready to serve directly from the refrigerator.

RECIPES

CREAM OF CHESTNUT SOUP

Don't avoid this soup because it sounds like work. It won't be tedious if you peel the chestnuts early. Also, if you're lucky enough to find a chestnut vendor you can use roasted ones.

1½ pounds fresh chestnuts	9 cups water
1 veal knuckle	2 cups dry white wine
3 carrots, scraped and chunked	1 tablespoon salt
	2 whole cloves
2 stalks of celery, with leaves coarsely chopped	½ cup heavy cream
	2 tablespoons brandy
3 medium onions, coarsely chopped	Freshly ground black pepper
	Chopped parsley
3 tablespoons butter	

Wash the veal knuckle to remove any small bone chips, pat dry and set aside. In a large kettle or soup pot, cook the carrots, celery and onions in the butter until they are just wilted, not browned—about 10 minutes. Place the veal knuckle on top. Add the water, wine and salt. Cover pot and simmer for two hours. If you haven't done them ahead of time, peel the chestnuts now. With the tip of a pointed knife make a deep crisscross gash on the flat side of each nut. Then place them in a saucepan and

cover with boiling water. Simmer for 20 to 25 minutes. Drain the chestnuts, and when they are still warm, working quickly with your fingers, remove the by-now loosened shells and skins.

When the stock is done, let it cool. Remove the veal knuckle and the meat and skim the fat from the surface. An easy way to do this is to lay a double thickness of paper towels on the surface of the broth. The towels will absorb the fat. Turn the towel over and then discard it. Repeat this once or twice until all visible fat has been removed. Strain the stock, reserving the vegetables. Return the vegetables to the pot along with six cups of the broth, the peeled chestnuts and the cloves. Although it seems troublesome, tie the cloves into a small piece of cheesecloth so they are not lost among the vegetables and can be fished out later. Cover and simmer the broth for 20 minutes. Remove the cloves. Purée the mixture, a little at a time, in a blender or a food mill, until it is smooth. Return the puréed mixture to the pot, and add the cream and brandy. Bring the soup to a simmer and add more salt, if needed, and a grinding or two of black pepper to taste. If the soup is too thick, add a little more veal stock, stirring it in well. Serve it piping hot, lavishly sprinkled with chopped fresh parsley.

BROILED LAMB CHOPS WITH HERBS

6 double-rib lamb chops, 2 inches thick	1 teaspoon marjoram
	½ teaspoon thyme
1 teaspoon basil	1 teaspoon salt

Have your butcher prepare the chops in the French manner. This means that the meat and fat are trimmed from the ends of the bone, and the bone is covered with a paper frill, which should be removed for cooking and can be put back on afterward if you want to dress the chops up. This style of trimming the chops makes no difference, except in appearance. Preheat the broiler. Mix the herbs and salt together and rub the mixture into both sides of the meat. Place the chops on a broiler pan four inches from the heat and broil them eight minutes on each side. Transfer the chops to a heated platter and surround them with small white onions, mushroom caps and cherry tomatoes which have been sautéed in butter, seasoned and sprinkled with a little lemon juice.

ROQUEFORT-STUFFED POTATOES

6 baking potatoes	3 ounces)
4 tablespoons butter	2 tablespoons minced chives
3 tablespoons milk	
1 cup sour cream	1 teaspoon salt
5 tablespoons crumbled Roquefort cheese (about	Freshly ground black pepper

Preheat the oven to 450°. Wash the potatoes, dry them and rub their skins with a little salad oil, and place them in the oven. Bake until they are tender when tested with a fork—about 45 minutes. Remove potatoes from oven at once. Cut a slice from the top of each. Scoop out the pulp, being sure that you do not break the skins, and mash it well. Beat in the butter, milk and the sour cream until the mixture is light and fluffy. Stir in the cheese well, add the chives, salt and a good grating of pepper. Pile the mashed potatoes back into their shells, mounding them slightly. Return the stuffed potatoes to the oven for eight to 10 minutes, making sure that they are thoroughly heated through.

BITTER CHOCOLATE MOUSSE

A dessert mousse can be made in many ways, with egg yolk, egg white or cream. This spectacular one uses all three, and adds a dash of brandy. Needless to say, the results are rich so be sure to make the servings small.

3 eggs, separated	4 tablespoons soft butter
¾ cup superfine sugar	3 tablespoons strong coffee
3 tablespoons brandy	1 tablespoon superfine sugar
1 teaspoon vanilla	
5 ounces unsweetened chocolate	½ cup heavy cream, whipped

In the top of a double boiler, beat the egg yolks with the sugar, brandy and vanilla until the mixture is thick and pale yellow. Use a small electric hand mixer for this. Place over barely simmering water, and continue beating until the mixture is slightly foamy—about five minutes. Remove from the simmering water and let it come to room temperature. In a small saucepan, melt the chocolate. Remove from the heat and gradually stir in the butter. Stir this mixture into the egg yolk-sugar mixture until smooth and creamy. Stir in the coffee. Beat the egg whites until foamy. Sprinkle the additional one tablespoon of sugar over them and continue beating until stiff peaks form. Stir part of this into the chocolate mixture, then fold in the rest until no white streaks remain. Fold in the whipped cream. Spoon the mousse into individual serving dishes or chocolate cups, or into a serving bowl. Chill at least four hours before serving.

Brazil's National Dish

For anyone born north of the equator, *feijoada* (pronounced fay-*zhwah*-dah) is a feat to cook and to eat. For Brazilians this dish—built around the two staples of Brazil, beans and rice—is a way of life and even an inspiration. The Brazilian composer Villa-Lobos was so enraptured

by it that he composed a fugue divided into four movements entitled: "Farina," "Meat," "Rice" and "Black Beans."

Actually *feijoada* may be less of a fugue and more of a culinary Bossa Nova. It is somewhat dissonant, full of contrapuntal textures and temperatures: chilled orange slices offset spicy Portuguese sausages, the blandness of rice neutralizes the Tabasco-soaked onions, and smoky black beans take the edge off bananas sweetened with rum. This recipe calls for the same debonair attitude about meat that you have about a clove of garlic —use for flavoring and discard. A bottle of Tabasco, one that normally lasts a year, is required to provide three tablespoons of sauce. And, finally, after feasting on *feijoada*, you are likely to feel as if you have just scored a fugue or danced the Bossa Nova—or both.

Plan this dinner as a buffet. It involves at least half a dozen separate serving dishes and they are most easily managed at a buffet.

With this meal, organization is everything. There is a lot of work to it—none of it difficult, but it will be less rigorous if the whole production is thought through ahead of time. As a start, be sure you can get black beans. Success depends on being able to do several things at once and, happily, the recipes lend themselves to it. Two nights before the dinner, soak the beans overnight. On the day before the dinner, cook them. While they are simmering, prepare the shrimp, which will improve with marinating, and pack the ice cream into the mold and

MENU FOR EIGHT
SHRIMP IN MUSTARD SAUCE

FEIJOADA
Beer

COCONUT-ALMOND ICE CREAM

put it in the freezer. On the morning of the dinner cook the bananas, and while they are baking prepare the oranges and onions. Three hours before dinner put the pork in the oven. Measure out the ingredients for the rice dish and take the beans and sausages out of the refrigerator. An hour before dinner, put the beans on to heat slowly while you serve the shrimp with cocktails. Half an hour before dinner glaze the roast, cook the rice. Start cooking the sausages. To serve, put the beans in a chafing dish if you have one, put the pork roast and sausages on a large platter—ask your husband to carve the pork while the guests are helping themselves to the other dishes.

RECIPES

SHRIMP IN MUSTARD SAUCE

2 1/2 pounds shrimp, shelled and deveined

1/4 cup finely chopped parsley

1/4 cup finely chopped shallots

1/4 cup tarragon vinegar

1/4 cup wine vinegar

1/2 cup olive oil

4 tablespoons Dijon mustard

2 teaspoons crushed red peppers

2 teaspoons salt

Freshly ground black pepper

Cook the shrimp in boiling salted water to cover just until they turn pink. Drain and transfer to a large bowl. Mix the remaining ingredients together and pour over the warm shrimp. Mix well so every shrimp will be coated. Cover and refrigerate. Serve them in a bowl, passing it along with toothpicks for the guests to help themselves.

FEIJOADA

Like all dishes that are institutions in their native countries, *feijoada* has many variations. Traditionally it is made with dried salted beef, probably because originally that was the only kind available. All the meats are usually cooked in the same pot as the beans, but this turns them an unattractive purple color. So in this recipe the meats are either cooked with the beans only for flavor and then discarded, or they are cooked separately. In Brazil a frequent accompaniment is collards, and the whole is lavishly sprinkled with manioc meal. Manioc, a ubiquitous tropical root which turns up in many guises in South American dishes, is hard to get in this country and can easily be omitted from the *feijoada*.

A serving of *feijoada* should consist of one pork chop, one sausage, a couple of spoonfuls of rice with beans ladled over it, half a banana, onion rings and a slice or two of orange. Obviously, large dinner plates are in order.

BLACK BEANS
This is served as a sauce and will be quite runny.

4 cups black beans

2 pigs' feet, cracked

1/2 pound piece beef chuck

1/2 pound salt pork, sliced

2 teaspoons olive oil

1/2 cup chopped onion

2 cloves garlic, minced

Salt

Freshly ground black pepper

Wash the beans, cover with water and soak overnight. The next day, drain them and transfer to a large, heavy kettle. Add enough cold water to come about two inches above the beans. Bring to a boil, add the pigs' feet, beef, salt pork. Lower the heat and simmer, covered, for three hours, stirring occasionally. The meats, and beans as well, will turn purple, but later the meats are discarded as they serve just to flavor the beans. The beans themselves will eventually become a rich chocolate brown. Cool and discard the meats. Heat the olive oil in a small skillet, add the onion and the garlic and cook just until the onion is tender. Stir into the beans. Cover and refrigerate overnight. To serve, heat for an hour, stirring occasionally. Adjust seasonings, being prepared to add as much as two teaspoons of salt and a generous grinding of pepper.

BRAZILIAN RICE

2 cups long-grain rice

3 tablespoons oil

1 onion, peeled and sliced thinly

1 tomato, peeled and chopped

1 1/2 teaspoons salt

Heat the oil in a medium-sized skillet. Add the rice and onion and cook, stirring, over very low heat until the rice makes a swishing sound—about 10 minutes. Stir in the tomato and salt. Add two cups boiling water. The mixture will spatter, so stand back. Bring the rice to a boil; lower heat, cover and cook for 25 minutes.

ROAST GLAZED LOIN OF PORK

1 4½- to 5-pound loin of
   pork (10 chops)
2 teaspoons salt
Freshly ground black pepper
1 cup orange juice

½ cup light brown sugar
1 tablespoon ginger
¼ teaspoon powdered
   cloves

Preheat the oven to 325°. Place pork, fat side up, in a roasting pan. Insert thermometer; do not let it touch bone. Rub in the salt and pepper. Roast for 35 minutes to the pound, or until it reaches 170°. Meanwhile, in a small saucepan, mix the orange juice, sugar, ginger and cloves together. Simmer for 30 minutes. Brush this glaze generously over the roast, at least twice, during the last hour of roasting time.

SAUSAGES

1½ pounds smoked
   sausages (Portuguese
   linguiça or Spanish

   chorizo)
2 teaspoons oil

Sauté the sausages in the oil over very low heat until they are heated through, about 20 minutes. Turn them often. If you cannot get the Portguese or the Spanish sausages, use the Italian sweet or hot, but since they are not smoked they must be thoroughly cooked.

BAKED BANANAS WITH RUM

1 cup sugar
½ cup fresh lemon juice
1 tablespoon butter

2 tablespoons white rum
6 medium-sized underripe
   bananas

Preheat oven to 400°. In a small saucepan, mix the sugar, lemon juice, butter and rum together and simmer for 10 minutes. Peel the bananas and slice them in half, lengthwise. Place them, cut side down, in a buttered bak-

ing dish. Pour the hot syrup over them. Bake for 30 minutes, turning once after the first 15 minutes. Let cool.

ONIONS IN HOT SAUCE

Unbelievable as it sounds, it is possible to put three tablespoons of Tabasco in something, eat it and live to tell about it. In fact, the onions, while hot, are not searing.

1 large Bermuda onion
3 tablespoons olive oil
3 tablespoons red wine

   vinegar
3 tablespoons Tabasco
¼ teaspoon salt

Peel the onion and slice it very thin. Cover with boiling water, drain and rinse with cold water. Mix the oil, vinegar, Tabasco and salt in a bowl. Add the onion slices, marinate at room temperature for three hours.

COCONUT-ALMOND ICE CREAM

If you like ice cream bars with the toasted coconut coating, you'll be wild for this.

1½ quarts vanilla ice cream
1 cup flaked coconut

¾ cup finely chopped,
   toasted slivered almonds

Stir the ice cream to soften it slightly and pack it into a chilled one-and-one-half-quart mold. Freeze until solid, which may take several hours. Preheat the oven to 350°. Put coconut flakes on a baking sheet and toast 15 minutes until brown, turning occasionally. Cool and mix with the almonds. (If you have not bought almonds already toasted, bake them right along with the coconut.) To unmold the ice cream, dip the mold quickly into very hot water, give it a shake. Loosen it around the edges with a small spatula. Turn the mold upside down onto a small baking sheet or tray. Remove the mold. Quickly pat on a thick coating of the coconut-almond mixture, covering the ice cream completely. Return the ice cream to the freezer. To serve, use a spatula, and transfer to a platter.

Roast Ribs of Beef

There is no more majestic sight nor more robust eating than a standing rib roast of beef. Full of flavor, firm but tender, a standing roast is the finest of meats. In England it is not merely a dinner, it is an institution. "Give them great meals of beef, and iron, and steel," wrote Shakespeare; "they will eat like wolves, and fight like devils." The still active London Beefsteak Society, established in 1635, is dedicated to "Beef and Liberty." But today—and even Englishmen admit this —the world's best beef comes from the U.S. Our way of serving it rare and thickly cut is replacing the British way of serving it rather well done and sliced wafer thin. Rib roast is a costly dish. But properly cooked—a simple but precise operation—it deserves a menu in the grand style, the best red wine and discriminating guests.

This is a dinner to serve on a formal occasion and in your most baronial style. The menu, with all stops pulled, should be served on your best tablecloth and china. For this event, enlist your husband. In fact don't tackle this dinner unless he feels cheerful about helping, for once it is on the table he is going to have to do a lot of work. He must serve the fish deftly. He must pour two wines. He must carve the beef. He should also, if he can manage it, serve the vegetable. So be sure that he has the proper utensils: a knife and serving fork for the fish, a sharp carving knife and a fork for the roast, an oversize platter to work on and a reliable corkscrew.

The fish (it can be any of several kinds) is as handsome to behold as the main course. Its subtle flavor is set off by a lively mayonnaise and enhanced by a dry white wine. Traditional Yorkshire pudding accompanies the beef. It is not nearly so formidable to make as it may sound to someone who has never done it, and when made in your own oven it is like a giant popover and bears no resemblance to the soggy creations that sometimes turn up in restaurants. A familiar vegetable is done with a different touch. At this point many hostesses may feel that they have done enough and think of skipping dessert entirely. But don't stop now: the raspberry ginger is a perfect ending—chilled, light and tangy.

The quality of the meat is every bit as important as the cooking of it. Most beef sold to consumers is "USDA Choice" grade, almost as good as "Prime." (Only 3% of all beef slaughtered is Prime and it goes almost entirely to restaurants.) Look for a thick layer of white fat out-

MENU FOR SIX

POACHED FISH
in aspic with cucumbers
Dill mayonnaise
Dry white wine

STANDING RIB ROAST
Yorkshire pudding
Green beans with onion rings
Red wine

RASPBERRY GINGER

side, abundant marbling, or streaking, of fat through the meat. The first cut, the ribs nearest the rump, is the most desirable because it has the biggest eye. Three or four ribs are ample for six people. If you have the butcher cut off the short ribs to serve braised or boiled as another meal, ask him to tie additional fat on the roast so there is enough for the Yorkshire pudding or for gravy.

Everything on this menu except the main course can be prepared either a day ahead or on the morning of the day of the dinner. Since the roast beef does not need any fussing over, the only things that need attention after guests arrive will be the vegetables, gravy and pudding.

The fish course can be prepared the day before and kept covered in the refrigerator. On the morning of the dinner make the mayonnaise and dessert and refrigerate them. (If you're ambitious, homemade mayonnaise. However, a good prepared mayonnaise will do.) Put white wine in the refrigerator to chill. Use the timetable below to figure out when to put the roast in the oven, allowing half an hour extra after it comes out for it to "rest." When you put in the beef, fix the beans so they are ready to cook and mix the Yorkshire pudding batter.

Your next chores come when the roast is done and you have taken it from the oven. Immediately turn the oven to 450°, beat the pudding vigorously for two minutes. Then put the pudding in the oven. (It will cook while you eat the fish.) Make gravy and keep it warm. Put water on to boil for the beans. Start cooking them when you clear the table of the fish dishes. They will be done when you bring on the beef, pudding and beans.

RECIPES

POACHED FISH IN ASPIC

This dish is the trickiest one on the menu to prepare, so allow yourself a couple of undisturbed hours on the day before you plan to serve it. Select a white meat fish that weighs about three pounds—in the East and South red snapper or striped bass would be a good choice, whitefish would be suitable in the Midwest, rockfish near the Pacific. Have the fish man clean and scale the fish, but leave the skin, head and tail on. If you cook a lot of fish, a special pan called a *poissonnière,* or fish poacher, is a worthwhile investment —it is the proper shape and has a rack to make moving the fish easier. But you can manage perfectly well with a roasting pan.

You must use a light touch on this dish. Handle the fish gently to keep it from breaking, and be careful when removing the cheesecloth that you don't pull off the skin.

When you garnish it you can be as artistic as you want —the aspic coating will keep the cucumber in place, along with anything else you may want to add, like lemon slices.

1 2½- to 3-pound whole fish	1 bay leaf
6 cups water	1 teaspoon tarragon
1 cup dry white wine	1 tablespoon salt
¼ cup wine vinegar	2 unpeeled cucumbers, thinly sliced
1 onion stuck with 2 cloves	1 egg white, lightly beaten
1 lemon, sliced	1 envelope unflavored gelatin
12 peppercorns, cracked	

Wrap the fish in cheesecloth, leaving extra cloth at both ends to serve as handles for lifting the fish. Combine water, wine, vinegar, onion, lemon, peppercorns, bay leaf, tarragon and salt in a large roasting pan—or your new *poissonnière* if you have invested in one. Boil for 10 minutes. Reduce heat and lower the fish gently into the bouillon. Cover and simmer for 10 minutes per pound. Remove the fish from the bouillon, lifting it gently by the ends of cheesecloth. Set it on a rack where it can drain and cool and unfold the cloth so it does not stick to the fish. When cool, lift the fish off the cloth carefully and place it on a serving platter. Garnish with cucumber slices. Chill it in the refrigerator. Meanwhile strain the stock, put it into a three-quart saucepan and boil for 20 minutes. Add egg white and cook five minutes more. Strain the stock through filter paper or a linen towel into a large pot. This may take an hour or more but does not require watching. If you haven't clarified stock before, you will be astonished at what happens: the stock is now clear and golden. There should be about one-and-three-quarters cups. Measure, and if you have less, add some water. Soften gelatin in one-quarter cup cold water. Add to stock, return to pan and bring to a boil. Remove from heat and stir until gelatin is completely dissolved. Set pan in a bowl of ice and stir gently until the stock becomes like heavy syrup. Remove from ice and immediately spoon over fish. Refrigerate at least one hour or until the syrup has jellied into a firm aspic. Carefully cut away aspic that has drained onto the platter from around the fish and dice it. Serve the diced aspic with the fish, along with additional cucumber slices and mayonnaise to which you have added a tablespoonful of chopped fresh dill, two tablespoons of chopped fresh parsley and one teaspoon of minced onion.

STANDING RIB ROAST

There are two schools of thought on how to roast beef. One holds with searing it quickly in a hot oven, then decreasing the temperature. The other believes in roasting at a constant lower temperature. Searing gives a crisper, browner outside. But cooked at a constant temperature the meat is more apt to be an even color throughout. If you feel you must sear, turn up the oven during the last 15 minutes —ovens are so well insulated today that if you do it at the beginning the high heat will be retained too long. Put the meat in the oven directly from the refrigerator—it is unimportant to bring it to room temperature. For cooking time be guided by the weight but use a meat thermometer; it's the surest guide there is. Chefs can tell when meat is done by the feel. It feels soft to the touch when underdone, springy when medium rare, firm when well done. But don't rely on this until you're really expert. Preheat the oven to 325° and place the roast, rib side down, in a shallow pan. Insert a meat thermometer into the thickest part of the roast, making sure the tip does not touch a bone. Cook according to this guide: *Very rare;* allow 15-17 minutes per pound, cook to 130° on the thermometer. *Medium rare;* allow 16-19 minutes per pound, cook to 140° on the thermometer. *Medium;* allow 18-20 minutes

per pound, cook to 150°-160° on the thermometer. *Well done;* allow 20-28 minutes per pound, cook to 165° on the thermometer. When done remove the roast from the oven and let it rest for 20 or 30 minutes. This allows the juices to settle, and makes carving much easier. Less juice will run out onto the platter and the meat will be more succulent. For roast beef *au jus,* pour off fat from the roasting pan (saving one-half cupful for Yorkshire pudding). Add about one cup of beef bouillon or water (enough to cover the bottom of the pan) to the remaining juices. Cook over direct heat, stirring constantly to dissolve the brown bits in the bottom and sides of the pan. To carve, stand the roast on its side so that the ribs are to your left. Thrust a fork between the ribs to hold it firmly. Cut the meat along the bone for a depth of two or three inches, then cut in slices across the top of the roast.

YORKSHIRE PUDDING

3 eggs	1 teaspoon salt
1½ cups milk	½ cup hot beef drippings
1½ cups sifted flour	

Pour one-half cup hot beef drippings into a 13x9x2-inch pan. Place on bottom rack of 450° oven to heat while preparing batter. Add eggs to milk and beat well with rotary beater. Add flour and salt all at once, and continue beating until smooth. Pour into heated drippings and bake for 30 minutes. Serve at once.

At Simpson's, a century-old London restaurant, which made a worldwide reputation on its beef and Yorkshire pudding, the chef recommends rain water, or better yet, melted snow, be used instead of milk in the pudding.

Serve the roast and pudding with fresh green beans that have been cooked with a thinly sliced onion, and a generous amount of butter.

RASPBERRY GINGER

3 10-ounce packages frozen raspberries	1 cup sifted light brown sugar
1½ pints heavy cream	½ teaspoon ginger

Thaw berries and drain them thoroughly. Gently separate berries. Whip the cream until stiff. Mix brown sugar with ginger and fold it into the cream. Fold in berries lightly so as not to crush them. Chill for at least one hour or until ready to serve. Before serving, stir gently to blend in any juices that have come from the berries.

If you are planning this dinner for a historic occasion—at least to you—you may want to serve two wines. Choose a light, dry white wine to go with the fish course, and a resounding red to be served with the beef. If you decide to serve only one wine don't try to be all things at once by choosing a rosé. Select the best red that you can afford. Whatever red wine you pick, the bottle must be opened an hour or so before you serve it.

Squab with Grapes

Squab is a perverse bird. Although expensive and synonymous with formal dining, it scarcely provides enough food for a man-sized appetite and is virtually im-

possible to eat with party manners. Its only excuse, in fact, is that it tastes so good. The meat is dark, velvety and rich. Squab is neither fragile nor hard to cook. Carving problems are eliminated and there is no guesswork about how much to buy—get one apiece. Though the etiquette books are divided on the issue, the only way to enjoy the bony birds properly is with fingers. To satisfy even the hungriest guest, use the French way of serving each squab on toast spread with pâté.

This dinner is the quintessence of holiday elegance. It does indeed require an expenditure of money and effort. You will almost certainly find it worth it.

Start a week ahead of time on this dinner. Choose an afternoon or evening when you're going to be home and make the plum pudding. Putting it together will take less than an hour, but it must cook for four hours with an occasional check. During the week, douse the pudding occasionally with brandy. You will have to buy a pudding mold—it costs a couple of dollars. Order the squabs well ahead of time and make sure the butcher includes the livers. If they are too expensive for you, buy Rock Cornish hens and prepare them as you would the squabs. The night before the dinner, make the bisque and the hard sauce. In the morning make the pâté canapés for the squabs and get the birds ready for roasting. Refrigerate them. An hour and a half before dinner, start reheating the pudding and let squabs and soup come to room temperature. An hour and a quarter be-

MENU FOR SIX
LOBSTER BISQUE

ROAST SQUAB
Rice
Tiny peas with mint
Champagne

PLUM PUDDING
WITH HARD SAUCE

fore you plan to sit down, put the squabs in the oven and measure out the ingredients for the sauce. Whenever you are in the kitchen on another chore, baste the squabs. Twenty-five minutes before dinner, put the soup in a double boiler to heat, add the grapes to the roasting squabs and put the canapés into the oven. Just ahead is the busiest quarter-hour of your kitchen life, and you should plan ahead of time exactly how you will operate. Have all ingredients measured out beforehand. Fifteen minutes before dinner put each squab on top of a pâté canapé on the serving platter, garnish with the grapes and return to the oven (turned down to low) to stay warm. Put two cups of rice on to cook—it will take about 15 minutes, about the time it takes to eat the soup course. Prepare the sauce for the squabs. Put the peas on. After eating the soup course, fluff the rice, add butter and transfer to a serving dish. Drain the peas, add butter and a teaspoon of dried mint. Pour the sauce over the squabs and serve.

RECIPES

LOBSTER BISQUE

2 9-ounce packages frozen South African rock lobster tails, thawed	1/8 teaspoon marjoram
	1/4 cup dry white wine
	3 tablespoons butter
2 3/4 cups chicken broth	3 tablespoons flour
1 tablespoon Madeira	2 cups milk
1/4 cup chopped carrot	1 teaspoon tomato paste
1/4 cup chopped onion	1/4 cup heavy cream
1/2 bay leaf	

Parboil lobster tails by dropping them into boiling chicken broth and cooking them for two minutes. Remove from the broth, set the broth aside and douse the tails with cold water to prevent further cooking. With kitchen shears, cut the membrane away from the underside of the lobster and remove the meat. Put the shells back into the pot with the broth. Cut the meat into bite-size pieces, put them in a small bowl and sprinkle them with Madeira. Set aside. Add the carrot, onion, bay leaf, marjoram and white wine to the broth and shells. Bring to a boil, cover and simmer for 30 minutes. Line a colander with several layers of cheesecloth, place it over a bowl and strain the broth mixture through it. Let it stand a few minutes to be sure you get all the liquid out of the shells. Melt butter in a large saucepan. Stir in the flour, mixing until smooth, then add the lobster broth, milk and tomato paste. Simmer, stirring until smooth and thickened, about 10 minutes. Remove from the heat, add the lobster meat with the Madeira, and the heavy cream.

Taste for seasoning, adding salt and a dash of pepper if it seems necessary.

ROAST SQUAB

6 squabs	1/2 cup softened butter
1 1/2 teaspoons salt	6 slices blanched bacon
Freshly ground black pepper	3/4 pound green grapes
1 teaspoon tarragon	

Preheat oven to 400°. Wash squabs and pat dry. Sprinkle cavity of each one with salt, pepper and tarragon. Put one teaspoon butter inside each bird. Truss birds and rub skin with remaining butter. Cut the blanched bacon slices in half, and tie two pieces over the breast of each bird. (You blanch bacon by simmering it in water for 10 minutes.) Place birds in a roasting pan and put on middle rack in the oven. Roast until browned and tender, about one hour, basting often with the drippings. During final 10 minutes of cooking place grapes, cut in six clusters, around squabs and baste. Open the foil-wrapped canapés and place, on the foil, in the oven. When squabs are done, cut off strings and remove bacon.

PÂTÉ CANAPÉS

6 slices white bread	1 tablespoon Madeira
1/2 cup clarified butter	1/4 teaspoon salt
6 squab livers	1/4 teaspoon freshly ground
4 tablespoons canned liver pâté	black pepper

Cut the bread into 2x3-inch rectangles. Heat the clarified butter in a skillet, add bread and sauté on both sides until lightly browned. (To clarify, which prevents burning, melt butter and pour off the clear liquid, discarding the white residue.) Drain the bread on paper towels. Add the livers to the butter in the skillet and sauté gently until they are lightly browned, about two minutes. Transfer livers and pan drippings to a small bowl; mash well with a fork. Blend in pâté, Madeira and seasonings. Spread the mixture on one side of the sautéed bread. Cover loosely with foil and set aside. Place the canapés, with foil opened, in the oven for the lst 10 minutes of the squabs' cooking time to heat up.

MADEIRA SAUCE

1 10½-ounce can beef bouillon	1 tablespoon brandy
⅓ cup water	1 tablespoon softened butter
⅓ cup Madeira	1 tablespoon flour

Make the sauce in the squab roasting pan. First pour off the fat, then add bouillon, water, Madeira and brandy to the pan. Bring to a boil and, stirring occasionally, cook until the sauce has been reduced to about a cup. Work the softened butter and flour together with your fingers, add the combination to the sauce and cook, stirring, two to three minutes, until slightly thickened. To serve the squabs, place a hot pâté canapé under each bird, garnish the platter with small clusters of grapes and spoon the sauce over all.

PLUM PUDDING

¼ pound suet, finely chopped	1 tablespoon cinnamon
½ cup pared, chopped green apple	1½ teaspoons ginger
¾ cup diced mixed candied fruits	½ teaspoon nutmeg
	¼ teaspoon salt
¼ cup finely chopped dates	1½ cups dark brown sugar
1½ cups raisins	6 eggs
1 cup currants	6 tablespoons brandy
3 cups packaged bread crumbs	6 tablespoons red wine
	¼ cup milk
	¼ cup brandy

In a large bowl, mix together all the ingredients listed above down through the brown sugar. In a separate bowl, beat eggs until foamy and stir brandy, wine and milk into them. With a rubber spatula or wooden spoon combine contents of both bowls, mix well and spoon the batter into a well-buttered two-quart pudding mold and cover with the mold's tight-fitting lid. Place the mold on a rack in a large pot. Add boiling water halfway up the sides of the mold. Cover the pot and steam the pudding for four hours, adding more water as needed. Gently boiling water should always be halfway up sides of mold. When done, place pudding on wire rack, remove lid and

let stand for five minutes. Invert onto rack and lift off mold. Wrap in several thicknesses of brandy-soaked cheesecloth. Wrap tightly in foil and store at room temperature. Moisten cheesecloth every third day with two tablespoons brandy. To serve, remove cheesecloth, put pudding back into the buttered mold and steam for two hours. Unmold onto serving platter, decorate with sprigs of holly, pour one-quarter cup heated brandy over it, ignite and serve, passing the hard sauce separately.

BRANDIED HARD SAUCE

½ cup softened butter	2 tablespoons brandy
2 cups confectioners' sugar	1 teaspoon vanilla

With electric mixer, whip butter until creamy; then gradually add the sugar and continue beating until light and fluffy. Add the brandy and vanilla to the mixture and beat at low speed. Pile into small serving dish, twirling the top of the hard sauce with the back of a spoon. Cover and refrigerate at least three hours before serving.

A Belgian Beer Stew

Into this stew go three he-man ingredients—beef, onions and beer. Out of the pot, after cooking, comes a dish that is neither harsh nor heavy, but lightly and pleasantly flavored. Called *carbonades à la flamande,* it is an invention of the Belgians, who drink more beer than anyone else in the world and also cook a lot with beer. As happens when liquor is used in cooking, the alcohol in the beer evaporates but the flavor remains, in this case, to give the stew a suggestion of sweetness. The onions, steeped in beer, become a gentle-tasting sauce. The dish is a hearty one, fine for a mid-winter meal, and when the lid of the big *carbonades* pot is lifted, an aroma wafts across the table that will tempt any appetite.

This dinner needs lively appetites and it is better to serve on a weekend, when your guests are more likely to have spent some of the day in the open, rather than on a week night, when they have probably been cooped up in home or office.

Most of the ingredients of this dinner are very humble—pork and salt pork for the pâté, the simple ingredients of the carbonades, which is accompanied by carrots, a plain vegetable. The dinner is finished off with a kind of apple pie. However, every one of these dishes is treated with a light touch, or combined with other ingredients in such a way as to turn the ordinary into something special.

This is not a hard meal to get together. The pâté should be made at least 2 days ahead and its flavor will actually improve with 48 hours in the refrigerator. It must be thoroughly chilled so it will slice cleanly without crumbling.

MENU FOR SIX

COUNTRY PÂTÉ

CARBONADES À LA FLAMANDE
Dumplings
Glazed carrots
Romaine salad, vinaigrette dressing
Beer

APPLE FLAN

The main dish is a casserole, which can be assembled, then left to cook unattended. The apple flan, or pie, can be made the day before and then put in the refrigerator. The crust is firm and crisp enough so that it will not get soggy. Or you can do it in an hour or so on the morning of the day of the party. You can wash the salad greens, make the vinaigrette dressing, prepare the carrots and cut up the meat and onions for the stew anytime during the day. Set the table, put the beer that you're going to drink in the refrigerator to chill. About three hours before serving time make the carbonades. Cook the carrots. Before you sit down to eat the pâté, stir up the dumplings and add them to the carbonades. Between courses toss the salad, and reheat the carrots—which takes only a minute or two—but be sure to keep an eye on them as you go in and out of the kitchen.

RECIPES

COUNTRY PÂTÉ

The very idea of serving homemade pâté is so unusual that until you actually do it you will not believe how easy and how good it can be. There is no limit to the possible variations, and after becoming familiar with the technique you may want to develop your own pâté *maison*. It can be expensive, if you use goose liver and truffles, or it can be inexpensive, if you use ground meat, as in the one given here. This recipe calls for wrapping the pâté in fat, a perfectly acceptable and easy way to do it. If you prefer you may make a pâté *en croute,* cooked in a crust. Either way, serve the pâté as a loaf at the table, cut in fairly thick slices. Tiny sour pickles and radishes go well with it as a garnish, and be sure that there is plenty of French bread to eat with it.

1 pound boneless veal	2 tablespoons oil
1½ pounds boneless pork	2 teaspoons salt
1 pound fresh pork fat	Freshly ground black pepper
¾ cup dry white wine	2 large onions, sliced
2 tablespoons brandy	2 small cloves of garlic, split

Two days before your dinner cut veal and pork in pieces and put through a food grinder twice, using finest blade —or ask the butcher to do it for you. Put in bowl and mix well. Combine wine, brandy, oil, salt and pepper and mix well. Pour this marinade over the meat. Put onions and garlic on top. Cover bowl tightly and refrigerate at least a full day. Preheat oven to 375°. Remove meat from refrigerator and discard onion. Put garlic through a garlic press. Stir marinade and garlic into meat. Cut pork fat into thinnest possible slices, and use most of them to line bottom and sides of a 7½ x 3½ x 2½-inch loaf pan or a two-quart

mold, overlapping them slightly. Pack meat into the pan. Arrange the remaining slices of pork fat on top of meat. Fit foil over the pan or mold. Put the mold in a shallow pan of boiling water—the water should come about halfway up the outside of the mold. Bake for two hours or until the pâté shrinks slightly from the sides, and the surrounding fat and juices are clear yellowish white with no traces of pink. Remove from oven. Loosen the foil but leave it over the pan. Set it on a rack to cool to room temperature. Then put another pan with heavy cans in it, or a plate—or a brick if you happen to have one—on top of the pâté to push it down. Chill thoroughly (overnight is best) before serving. It keeps about a week.

CARBONADES À LA FLAMANDE

This dish is a relatively inexpensive one to make since the best cuts of beef to use for it are the less costly ones like rump or round. These have excellent flavor and will be properly tender when they are through cooking because in the carbonades they are simmered gently—always below the boiling point. This is an ideal method for these less tender cuts, but there are a few tricks to doing it successfully. In order to have the sauce properly dark and rich, brown the meat. First coat it evenly with flour by putting the flour in a large paper bag, adding a few pieces of meat at a time, and shaking well. Put a small amount of the fat in a skillet. When it is very hot, drop meat in a few pieces at a time and cook until browned. If you try to brown all the meat at once it gets crowded; the meat steams rather than sears and ends up gray rather than the rich brown color you're after. The casserole in which you cook the carbonades must be the right size to hold the meat and onions comfortably, with a little extra space for cooking the dumplings later. Its lid is at least as important as its size. It must fit snugly so the carbonades can be tightly covered and not lose either flavor or moisture.

Carbonades is a stew but it does not have several kinds of vegetables and a starch cooked in it as stews usually do. The vegetable dish is done separately and the dumplings are cooked in the carbonades only at the very end.

4 pounds lean beef, cut into ½-inch slices	2 small bay leaves
2 pounds large onions, thickly sliced	2 teaspoons thyme leaves
	1 tablespoon salt
½ cup flour	Freshly ground black pepper
½ cup cooking oil	2 10½-ounce cans beef broth
6 cloves garlic, crushed	
3 tablespoons brown sugar	24 ounces beer
¼ cup red wine vinegar	Dumpling batter (recipe below)
½ cup chopped parsley	

Preheat oven to 325°. Cut the beef slices into pieces about one inch by two inches. Flour them lightly, brown them a few at a time in hot oil and put them into a large ovenproof casserole. (A deep six- or eight-quart size is about right.) Add onions and garlic to oil in pan and brown them lightly, adding more oil if necessary. Put them in the casserole, then add sugar, two tablespoons of the vinegar, parsley, bay leaves, thyme, salt and pepper. Stir once or twice. Pour off any oil remaining in the skillet. Put in the broth and heat over low flame, stirring to loosen all browned bits. Pour over meat mixture in casserole. Add the beer. Cover casserole and bake for two hours. Transfer the casserole to the top of the stove. Stir in the remaining vinegar. Cook over medium heat until the sauce bubbles. Drop dumpling batter by teaspoonfuls on top of the hot stew, cover, reduce heat and cook for 15 minutes. Do not remove cover during these 15 minutes.

DUMPLINGS

To achieve light fluffy dumplings instead of solid hunks of cementlike dough remember two rules: no matter how curious you are, don't take the cover off the pot while the dumplings are cooking. If you do, the steam escapes and the dumplings will boil rather than steam. The other command is not to allow the stew to boil furiously, but only to simmer. Otherwise the dumplings will cook too quickly and break apart. After 15 minutes test them with a toothpick. If it emerges clean, they are done.

2 cups sifted self-rising cake flour	¾ cup milk
	2 tablespoons melted butter

Combine all ingredients, mixing lightly. Drop batter by teaspoonfuls into simmering stew or stock, cover and cook for 15 minutes or until fluffy.

Serve the carbonades with carrots that have been simmered until tender, then glazed with butter and sugar.

APPLE FLAN

A flan is an open tart. It is very popular in Europe and although it is not any harder to make than an ordinary pie it looks quite special. You will need a flan ring—a straight-sided frame which has no bottom or top and, in baking, sits on a cookie sheet. It will be a very inexpensive addition to your kitchen equipment if you don't already have it. The crust of this flan is quite rich and tastes like shortbread. It is sticky so you cannot roll it easily. Instead you press it into the ring to form sides and bottom. When you select apples get firm, fresh ones; otherwise they will become mushy—McIntoshes or Rome Beauties.

2 pounds apples	almonds, chopped
1 cup maple flavored syrup	Baked 8-inch pastry flan (recipe below)
½ cup dark brown sugar	
2 tablespoons lemon juice	Crème pâtissière (recipe below)
1 six-ounce can shelled	

Cut apples into eighths, pare and core. Bring syrup, sugar and lemon juice to a boil in a large skillet. Add apples, reduce heat, cover and simmer for 15 minutes—until the apples are just tender. Remove from heat and let cool. Drain apples and arrange them in the cooked flan. Sprinkle half the almonds over the apples. Pour *crème pâtissière* over them and sprinkle with remaining almonds. Chill well.

PASTRY

2 cups sifted flour	½ cup butter
¼ cup sugar	1 egg, beaten
¼ teaspoon salt	

Combine flour, sugar and salt in a bowl. Add butter and cut in with a pastry blender until the pieces are the size of small peas. Make a well in the center of the mixture and add the beaten egg. Mix with a fork, then work with fingers until everything is blended together. Place an eight-inch flan ring on a cookie sheet and press the dough into the bottom and around the sides of the ring. Make the sides slightly thicker than the bottom. If you don't have a flan ring, use a 10-inch pie plate. Flute the edges of the pastry. Prick the bottom with a fork. Chill pastry for 10 minutes. Preheat oven to 425°. Bake pastry 10 minutes, reduce heat to 375°, prick the bottom again if it has puffed up, and bake 15 minutes longer. Cool pastry on the cookie sheet before removing the ring.

CRÈME PÂTISSIÈRE

3 egg yolks	1½ cups milk
¾ cup sugar	2 tablespoons apple jack, Calvados or brandy
3 tablespoons flour	
¼ teaspoon salt	

Beat egg yolks lightly. Combine sugar, flour and salt and add to egg yolks, mixing thoroughly. Stir in the milk. Put the pan over moderate heat and cook, stirring constantly, until the mixture boils and thickens. Reduce heat, cook two minutes more. Remove from heat and stir in apple jack.

Crepes Suzette

Nothing nicer can happen to a pancake than to turn into crepes Suzette—and what better time for it to happen than during the Christmas holidays. The most famous of all French desserts, it is the ultimate achievement in flapjack-griddle-cake-tortilla-blini cuisine. The wafer-thin crepes are flamed in liqueurs for an effect that is as theatrical as the result is delectable. Indeed, the presentation of crepes Suzette requires more showmanship than cookery, and in recognition of the fact, Antoine's of New Orleans always dims the lights.

The dessert is put together in a chafing dish in full view of your guests. An array of ingredients is at your fingertips. The butter sizzles in the pan. You stir in sugar, splash in orange liqueur, add a spiral of orange peel. Then come the crepes, each one folded into quarters with a well-brandished fork and spoon. A dash more liqueur—and then you ignite it. Flames dance over the dish, then die away. The performance is over at last and only marvelous eating remains.

The preparation of a holiday feast is an undertaking of importance, and one must begin by facing up to certain facts: feasts are work, feasts are expensive and feasts are fattening. They are worth it all.

In the best tradition of fine eating, this dinner is French—including the provincial potato pie—from *coquilles* to *crepes*.

Don't expect to create a work of art overnight—even if it is going to be devoured in a couple of happy hours. Order the filet and scallops ahead and try to find scallop shells to serve the *coquilles* in. They are inexpensive and usually sold by food specialty shops. You can easily do all the preliminaries the day before, or can get started a week ahead. Whichever you choose, the *crepes* are the first order of business. Make them, place them between layers of wax paper, cover with foil. If you make them more than 48 hours early, freeze them. Otherwise, they will keep in the refrigerator. At this point there is nothing more to do about dessert until you get behind the chafing dish. The morning of the dinner, make the potato pie shell and refrigerate it. Prepare the scallops, mushrooms and sauce and refrigerate them separately. Make the potato pie filling and refrigerate it. Grate the Swiss cheese. Trim the celery. Make the wine sauce, leaving out the last dab of butter. Assemble the dessert ingredients on a side ta-

MENU FOR EIGHT

COQUILLES ST. JACQUES
Dry white wine

ROAST FILET OF BEEF WITH WINE SAUCE
Potato pie
Braised celery
Red wine

CREPES SUZETTE

Cordials

ble. Chill the white wine, but if the dinner seems too alcoholic to you, this is the beverage to leave out. The red wine enriches the meat course, and the cordials are a finish with flourish.

There is crucial work to be done an hour before dinner. If you fluster easily, make yourself a time chart, tape it above the stove and keep an eye on the clock. An hour-and-a-quarter before dinner remove the *crepes* from the freezer. Preheat the oven. Fill the pie shell and bake it 50 minutes. Heat the *coquilles* sauce, remove the mushrooms and scallops from the refrigerator. By now 10 minutes should have elapsed and you can roast the beef 40 minutes and take it out at the same time as the potato pie. It is now dinner hour minus 40 and you can rejoin your guests. After 25 minutes you must duck into the kitchen again to start the celery—and make sure that the *coquilles* sauce is hot but not boiling. Back to the guests until just before dinner. Remove the filet and pie from the oven. Let both rest in a warm place. Assemble the *coquilles* and put under the broiler for a minute. Let the celery continue simmering. Heat the wine sauce while clearing away the *coquilles*. While the main course is being cleared put the *crepes* into a low oven for a few minutes to warm up. They will be thoroughly heated when they cook in the sauce. Offer cordials after the coffee.

RECIPES

COQUILLES ST. JACQUES

Coquilles St. Jacques is the French name for scallops, but it is also the name of this dish, which combines the shellfish with mushrooms in a white wine sauce. Scallops got this odd name because pilgrims to the shrine of St. James of Compostela in Spain found the handsome shells nearby and brought them home to use as plates.

1½ pounds scallops	7 tablespoons butter
1½ cups dry white wine	½ pound mushrooms,
1 teaspoon salt	chopped
6 peppercorns	¼ cup flour
3 sprigs parsley	¾ cup milk
1 small bay leaf	3 egg yolks
¼ teaspoon thyme	½ cup heavy cream
4 tablespoons shallots,	1 teaspoon lemon juice
chopped	Cayenne
½ cup water	½ cup grated Swiss cheese

Combine scallops, wine, salt, peppercorns, parsley, bay leaf, thyme, shallots and water in saucepan. Bring to a boil, then cover and simmer for five minutes. Remove from heat and strain off liquid; there will be about two cups. Put the liquid back on the heat and boil it rapidly for about 10 minutes or until it has reduced to one cup. Pick scallops out from among the herbs, cut them in small pieces and set them aside. Heat two tablespoons of the butter in a skillet. Add the mushrooms and sauté over low heat about eight minutes. Drain mushrooms and set them aside. To make the sauce, melt three tablespoons of the butter in a saucepan, blend in the flour. Gradually add milk, stirring constantly, until the mixture is thick and smooth. Add reduced cooking liquid and cook, stirring, for one minute. Beat egg yolks with cream in a bowl. Beat in the hot sauce, a little at a time. Put the sauce back in the pan and cook, stirring, about two minutes until slightly thickened. Remove from heat and add lemon juice and a dash of cayenne. Refrigerate sauce, scallops and mushrooms separately. Before serving, let the scallops and mushrooms come to room temperature. Heat the sauce in a double boiler. Remove one cup of sauce and set it aside. Add the scallops and mushrooms to the sauce in the double boiler and heat. Spoon the scallop mixture into eight buttered scallop shells or individual casseroles. Spoon two tablespoons of the extra sauce into each shell.

Sprinkle with Swiss cheese and dot with the remaining butter. Broil six to eight inches from the heat, three minutes or just until lightly browned and bubbly.

ROAST FILET OF BEEF

This is the world's most tender cut of meat. It is the whole tenderloin—a roll-shaped piece, about four inches in diameter and 12 inches long. It comprises what you see on menus as chateaubriands (the thickest slices from the middle), filets mignon (approaching the end) and tournedos (at the narrow end).

You have two shocks in store when you buy a tenderloin. The first is when you ask the price, the second when you find that a 10-pound tenderloin becomes a five-pound tenderloin when trimmed for the oven. Some butchers quote the price for a trimmed filet so you get the bad news all at once. Since it is solid meat, a four-and-a-half-pound trimmed roast will feed eight generously.

About the only way to ruin this investment is by overcooking. If you wish to serve the tenderloin rare—as you should—allow nine to 10 minutes per pound or until you estimate the roast has an internal temperature of 120°. Meat thermometers don't go below 130°, so using one involves some guesswork.

4- to 4½-pound filet	Suet
Salt	

Preheat oven to 425°. Salt meat lightly. If your butcher hasn't, place a piece of suet under filet and top it with a narrow ribbon of fat. Roast about 40 minutes.

WINE SAUCE

2 carrots, coarsely chopped	¼ teaspoon pepper
2 stalks celery, chopped	2 cups red wine
¼ cup chopped shallots	1 cup beef broth
½ teaspoon thyme	2 tablespoons butter
½ teaspoon salt	1 tablespoon flour

Combine carrots, celery, shallots, thyme, salt, pepper and red wine in saucepan. Bring to a boil. Cook, uncovered, over low heat 10 minutes. Add broth and cook 10 minutes longer. Strain the sauce. Knead one tablespoon of butter and the flour together to make *beurre manié*. Stir it into the sauce a little at a time. At the last minute, stir in the other tablespoon of butter and taste for seasoning.

POTATO PIE

This is a favorite in the French provinces, where it is usually served hot the first day, cold the next. Chances are you won't have any left to serve cold.

Make your own mashed potatoes if you like, but instant mashed potatoes will work perfectly well.

1 10-inch unbaked pastry shell	½ cup sour cream
	2 eggs
1 pound cottage cheese	2 teaspoons salt
2 cups mashed potatoes	⅛ teaspoon cayenne
½ cup scallions, sliced	Parmesan cheese
3 tablespoons grated	

Put the cottage cheese through a food mill to make it smooth. Beat the mashed potatoes into the cottage cheese. Beat in sour cream, eggs, salt and cayenne. Stir in scallions. Spoon into pastry shell. Sprinkle with grated cheese. Bake at 425° for 50 minutes until golden brown.

BRAISED CELERY

4 bunches celery	1 cup beef broth
4 tablespoons butter	½ cup sherry

Select four young bunches celery, strip away the outer stalks, split the heads in half from top to bottom and trim them to seven- or eight-inch lengths. Wash, then cook in two large skillets—cut side down—in melted butter until golden, about eight to 10 minutes. Turn the celery once. Add broth and sherry (half in each skillet), cover and simmer about 30 minutes or until tender. The sauce will reduce considerably. Arrange celery on a hot platter and moisten it with the extra sauce.

CREPES SUZETTE

You should practice if you haven't made *crepes* before. However, this amount of batter, which will make about 30 *crepes,* provides for some mistakes and when the *crepes* are folded, slight imperfections won't show.

6 eggs	¾ teaspoon salt
1 cup plus two tablespoons flour	3 cups milk
	Melted butter
1½ tablespoons sugar	

Beat the eggs. Add flour, sugar and salt and beat until smooth. Gradually add milk, beating constantly. Melt one teaspoon melted butter in a seven-inch frying pan and add additional butter as needed. Add about two tablespoons of batter, quickly tilting the pan to cover the bottom with the batter. Cook until golden on bottom, then turn with a spatula and cook the other side until light brown. Repeat until all *crepes* are made.

SAUCE FOR CREPES

¾ cup butter	Sugar
⅓ cup sugar	3 tablespoons orange
¾ cup orange juice	liqueur
⅓ cup orange liqueur	6 tablespoons cognac
3-inch strip orange peel	

Melt butter in chafing dish. Add sugar, orange juice, the liqueur and orange peel. Cook until mixture bubbles and reduces a little. Take out orange peel. Dip *crepes* in this hot mixture. Fold *crepes* in quarters. When all the *crepes* are folded, sprinkle with a little sugar, add remaining orange liqueur and cognac. To ignite, take a spoonful of sauce, light it and pour into the dish. Spoon sauce over *crepes,* serve three per person.

A Golden Goose

The goose is a noble bird, famed in history, fable and rhyme. Sacred to the Egyptians, guardian to the Romans (cackling geese warned of approaching

Gauls), the goose honking high in a clear sky bespoke good omens. As festive fare, goose was written about by Dickens. In 20th Century calorie-conscious America, however, the fattened goose fell from favor. Now, at last, the goose is back and is even to be found in the supermarket freezer. With proper cooking the bird bastes itself to a golden turn. Underneath the crackling crisp skin is superb dark meat that sets any holiday feaster to thinking of Christmases past.

This menu has such a lip-smacking, old-fashioned ring to it that the mere reading of it may bring on visions of after-dinner stupor. But this need not be the case. Although it is a full-scale formal dinner, it is happily balanced. Provided you keep your head about second helpings, none of your satisfied guests will doze off in the living room.

Although the goose is hearty, the stuffing is the only starch, and the vegetables are light and highly seasoned. Dessert is rich but frothy.

Don't plan to have this dinner on Christmas Day if you have youngsters. In many ways it is much too good for them—and to them the idea of fish eggs, onions and *spinach,* of all things, on Christmas would be as bad as not having a tree. Serve this meal instead at your most festive holiday dinner party.

You cannot turn out a feast without effort, but at least with this one there is no short-order cookery. Everything can be done before you dress, except warming up the vegetables and the sauce. Even these have been cooked ahead. Once you leave the kitchen to dress, you don't have to go back until you announce dinner.

The least arduous way of preparing this meal is to do everything on the day of the dinner. There are a few chores that can be done the day before, but it will seem like less of a production if you just give over the morning of your dinner party to cooking.

Although goose is more plentiful than it used to be, don't wait until the day before the dinner to be sure that your supermarket is one of the enlightened ones. In the morning of the day of the dinner, cube the bread for the stuffing so it will have time to dry out. Then make the mousse and refrigerate it, giving it plenty of time to set. Make the sauce for the goose next—the longer it sits the better it will taste. Cook the spinach and the onions, which should also be stored in the refrigerator until they are heated up before serving. Stuff and truss the goose, refrigerating it until you have the oven warmed up. (You needn't worry about bringing the bird to room temperature before you put it in the oven.) Drain the frozen fruits and make the custard for the trifle. At this point the only remaining task is to whip the cream and assemble the trifle, which you should do just before you dress for dinner. Set the table at your convenience and an hour or so before the guests arrive open the wine.

MENU FOR EIGHT

CAVIAR MOUSSE

ROAST GOOSE
with orange stuffing
and Cumberland sauce
Glazed onions
Puréed spinach
Red wine

TRIFLE

RECIPES

CAVIAR MOUSSE

The appetizer is very much like a canapé of red caviar and sour cream, with a dash of chopped onion—only in this dish the ingredients are combined into a mousse. The mousse is attractive-looking, faintly pink with flecks of parsley in it. And you needn't feel extravagant serving it—six ounces of red caviar isn't expensive. You would not be improving the dish to substitute black caviar; it would be much too delicate to give the mousse flavor—and besides it would turn out gray.

6 ounces red caviar	1 pint sour cream
1/4 cup chopped parsley	1 cup heavy cream
1 tablespoon grated onion	1 envelope gelatin
1 teaspoon grated lemon rind	1/4 cup water
	Freshly ground pepper

In a large bowl combine caviar, parsley, onion and lemon peel. Stir the sour cream into this mixture. In a separate bowl, whip the heavy cream. Sprinkle gelatin over the water in a saucepan and cook over low heat, stirring constantly, until the gelatin is completely dissolved. This takes only a minute or two. Stir gelatin into the caviar and sour cream mixture. Fold in whipped cream and add pepper to taste. Spoon into eight small simple molds—individual soufflé dishes or custard cups are perfect. Chill until set. To serve, unmold onto lettuce, or if you're nervous about the unmolding and your ramekins are suitable, serve the mousse in them, without lettuce. The easiest way to unmold the mousse is to run a sharp knife around the edge of the mold, turn it upside down, and shake the mousse loose. Serve with small squares of thin pumpernickel bread spread lightly with sweet butter.

ROAST GOOSE

The goose has had a poor reputation among cooks. It is indeed a very fatty bird, and the shame of serving a greasy goose was such that strong measures were urged to prevent this catastrophe. As a result the poor goose was often jabbed and pricked until it was dry, and was overcooked until it was tough. Pull out all the fat inside the body cavity (render it and you will have superb cooking fat for weeks to come), and be sure that you cook the goose only three to three-and-a-half hours.

In the days when most geese weren't sold frozen, the way to tell a young one—and goose is good eating only when it's under six months old—was to pinch its beak. Soft beak, young goose. Today your frozen goose won't have a beak for you to pinch. But you don't run much risk of getting an old bird. A 12-pound goose will look big and serve eight well, but don't expect to have any left over. A goose is a far less meaty bird than turkey. In fact your husband should be warned that he may have to get all the meat there is off the bones. And carving a goose is different from carving a turkey. The leg joint is much farther down under the bird and harder to get at. The wings are constructed differently, too, and must be taken off in order to carve the breast. Don't serve the wings—they have no meat on them. Slice the drumsticks —the bird will go much further. The crisp skin is choice, so see that everyone has a piece.

12-pound goose	Celery leaves
Orange stuffing (recipe below)	3 oranges

Preheat oven to 325°. Rinse the goose inside and out with cold water and dry thoroughly. Cut away any large fat layers remaining in the body cavity and remove any stray pinfeathers. Fasten neck skin to back with skewer. Spoon the orange stuffing into the body cavity, packing it lightly. Truss the goose and place it on a rack in a shallow roasting pan. Roast three to three-and-a-half hours (allow 16 minutes a pound) or until drumstick meat feels soft to the touch and the joint moves easily. As the goose roasts, spoon off fat as it accumulates. Don't do anything else to the bird. Don't prick it, don't jab it, don't baste it. But don't forget it. Overcooking is the only way you can hurt it.

If you want to dress up the platter, prepare this garnish: cut long strips of peel from three oranges, using a vegetable peeler or sharp knife. Arrange the orange strips in coils around it. Tuck celery leaves between the coils.

ORANGE STUFFING

8 cups fresh bread cubes	shredded orange rind
1/2 cup chopped onion	1 cup chopped fresh parsley
1/2 cup chopped celery	1/2 teaspoon thyme leaves
2 tablespoons butter	1/2 teaspoon ground sage
1 cup fresh orange juice	2 teaspoons salt
2 tablespoons coarsely	Freshly ground black pepper

Spread bread cubes out for an hour or so before starting stuffing. Sauté the onion and celery in butter until soft. Mix with bread cubes in a large bowl. Add the rest of the ingredients, tossing them together lightly but thoroughly.

CUMBERLAND SAUCE

This is a traditional port wine sauce that is often served with game and that goes equally well with goose. It is sweet and spicy, and a deep red. It can be thickened with cornstarch, which makes a less transparent sauce, if you can't get, or don't want to trouble with, arrowroot.

1/2 cup port	Few drops of Tabasco
1 cup orange juice	1 1/2 tablespoons arrowroot
1/2 cup lemon juice	1 tablespoon coarsely
1 cup red currant jelly	shredded orange rind
1/2 cup chopped onion	1 tablespoon coarsely
1 teaspoon dry mustard	shredded lemon rind
1/4 teaspoon ground ginger	

Combine the port, orange and lemon juices, jelly, onion, mustard, ginger and Tabasco in a saucepan. Bring to a boil, stirring occasionally. Be careful as this may foam up and over the pan. Strain the sauce. Combine arrowroot with a little hot sauce in a cup and mix together well. Stir this back into the rest of the sauce and cook over low heat, stirring constantly, until slightly thickened. Do not allow to boil. Add orange and lemon rind.

Serve the goose with onions that have been simmered in beef stock, then glazed in butter and sugar, and with puréed spinach seasoned with a pinch of nutmeg.

TRIFLE

This is a venerable English dessert consisting essentially of sponge cake, custard and fruit. There are many versions ranging from one, destined for the nursery, that is primarily intended to use up stale cake. But in a more elaborate form, redolent with sherry, it becomes a truly baroque creation.

9-inch sponge cake layer	(recipe below)
3/4 cup dry sherry	2 egg whites
2 packages frozen raspberries	1 cup heavy cream
	1 tablespoon sugar
2 packages frozen peaches	1/2 cup toasted slivered
Chilled custard sauce	almonds

Thaw and drain fruit. Slice sponge cake into three thin layers. Place one layer in the bottom of a serving bowl. It should be flat-bottomed and about 10 inches across and five inches deep. If you have one of glass use it because the layers of the trifle look very pretty. Sprinkle the cake layer with one-quarter cup sherry. Spread about a third of the raspberries and peach slices on top. Pour one-third of the custard over the fruit. Repeat cake, sherry, fruit and custard for two additional layers, saving a dozen or so of the choicest raspberries for garnish. To make the topping, beat egg white until stiff and, in a separate bowl, whip cream. Stir sugar into cream and gently fold in beaten egg white. Mound cream-and-egg-white mixture over the top of the trifle. Garnish with raspberries and toasted almonds. Refrigerate until ready to serve.

CUSTARD SAUCE

Scald milk in a double boiler. Meanwhile, beat egg yolks and add sugar and salt. Pour a little hot milk into the egg-yolk mixture, beating with a fork, and then stir into the rest of the milk. Place over simmering, not boiling, water and cook—stirring until the mixture coats a metal spoon. Pour the custard into a bowl and stir in the vanilla. Cover and refrigerate for one hour or until thickened before adding to the trifle.

2 cups milk	Pinch of salt
6 egg yolks	1 teaspoon vanilla extract
1/4 cup sugar	

There is scarcely time to sample all the delicacies of the season. The first asparagus, no thicker than a finger, the early pale greens for salad, young lamb for roasting or for a navarin printanier (whose very name means springtime) and strawberries, the most brilliant of springtime's fleeting bounty.

spring

Roast Leg of Lamb

So much marvelous food is suddenly available in spring that the only way to cope with it is to start eating as early as possible. Young lamb is one of the season's tenderest arrivals. To cook the delicious roasts, you must throw the book away—in fact, you should with any lamb. Most cookbooks are full of bad advice to roast legs of lamb until they are uniformly brown and well done. Lamb must be cooked only until it is pink and juicy on the inside, crisp on the outside. This state of perfection will be reached in far less time and at a far lower internal temperature than called for in American cookbooks—the French know better. A touch of garlic (a French standby), a light brush of lemon juice (a Greek notion) and a moistening with mint sauce (an English tradition) completes the job.

This is a robust meal—a rich soup, a succulent roast, a sturdy vegetable and a creamy custardy windup.

Many of the dishes are familiar but on this menu they are treated in ways that may be unfamiliar to you. You may have eaten many onion soups but chances are you've never had one as deliciously oniony as this before. The lamb is served pink and juicy. The white beans are cooked here with scallions and chicken stock. *Oeufs à la neige* is a formal adult version of a dessert you probably remember from childhood as floating island.

All the things that require much work on this menu can be done ahead of time. The main course must be cooked just before serving but it requires little effort on your part, except keeping an eye on it. For the soup, you will have to slice what may seem like a mountain of onions and it is a good idea to allow time for the smell of the onions to wear off your hands and disappear from the kitchen. So make the soup that morning or even the day before—it improves with a little aging. In the morning prepare the three dessert ingredients but do not put them together. Chill the custard, keep the meringues and

caramel at room temperature. This dessert involves the most work of any item on the entire dinner and will take you about an hour. Well before dinner, precook the beans, toast bread for the soup. The toast goes back in the oven just before serving. An hour before your guests are due, put the lamb in the oven, start the beans and make the mint sauce. On the assumption that your leg of lamb will weigh about six pounds, this schedule allows two hours for it to cook, but since there are so many variables and this is a critical matter, check the roast after an hour and a half. Open the wine. Cut the tomatoes in halves, drain them, then dust with crumbs, a little dried basil, and dot with butter. Fifteen minutes before starting to serve dinner reheat the soup in the oven alongside the lamb. When you serve the soup, the lamb should be ready to take out of the oven to rest. If it isn't quite done, let it cook while you eat soup. Just before you serve the soup add the scallions and parsley to the beans. Put the tomatoes in the broiler. Heat the mint sauce as you clear soup dishes. Assemble the dessert just before you serve it—it won't take a minute.

RECIPES

ONION SOUP

There is one secret to this soup: use plenty of onions and cook them a long time. The other main ingredient is beef stock and you are best off if you have rich homemade stock on hand. You can still make a fine onion soup with canned stock but you must doctor it a little. Dilute three cans of condensed bouillon with only one cup of water, and add a quarter of a cup of dry white wine. This cuts the sweet taste common to many canned stocks.

6 cups thinly sliced onions	Freshly ground black pepper
½ cup butter	6 one-inch-thick slices
5 cups strong beef stock	French bread
1 teaspoon salt	Grated Parmesan cheese

Sauté the onions in butter in a large saucepan over low heat for 30 minutes or until they are soft and golden. Stir often to prevent them from burning. The onions should be completely limp before you add the broth. Add the beef stock, salt and pepper and bring to a boil. Reduce heat, cover and simmer for 30 minutes. Taste and correct the seasoning. Meanwhile toast the bread slices on a cookie sheet in a 325° oven for 20 minutes. Just before serving sprinkle each slice with a teaspoon or so of the grated Parmesan cheese and put the toast back in the oven for five minutes more. To serve, float the toast, cheese side up, on the soup. Pass additional Parmesan cheese at the table for guests to help themselves.

ROAST LEG OF LAMB

Don't try to cook this roast without a meat thermometer. It will eliminate a lot of guesswork, for although an "average" six-pound leg should be just about right when cooked for two hours, a chunky leg will require longer cooking than a thin one. You can be sure that you are getting real spring lamb by watching the butcher scale. A spring (five-to-eight-month-old) leg will generally weigh no more than seven pounds with all the sirloin chops left on, or five pounds with the chops removed.

Leg of lamb	½ teaspoon rosemary
1 clove garlic	Salt
Juice of one lemon	Freshly ground black pepper

Preheat oven to 325°. Cut the garlic into eight slivers, then cut eight shallow slits in the surface of the lamb, and insert a slice of garlic in each slit. Brush the lamb with lemon juice, sprinkle with rosemary, salt and pepper. Insert a meat thermometer into the thickest part of the roast so the bulb reaches the center but does not touch a bone. Place the lamb on a rack in a roasting pan and roast for about 20 minutes a pound or until the thermometer reaches 150°. Remove from oven, and let the leg stand uncovered for 10 to 15 minutes. There are two schools of thought on how to carve lamb. The standard technique is to cut the lamb across the grain like a ham, then free the slices by cutting along the bone. Another is to carve along the leg with the grain, getting longer and thinner slices. This is easier to do and the thin slices are more attractive.

MINT SAUCE

The recipe below is for fresh mint only. Dried mint is much stronger and more bitter. (If that's all you can get, use one quarter of the mint, and twice the sugar.) Don't brew the sauce too far in advance. If it steeps more than a couple of hours the color will darken from the attractive amber gold it should be.

1/4 cup chopped fresh mint	1/4 cup boiling water
2 tablespoons sugar	3/4 cup cider vinegar

Put the mint in a bowl and sprinkle the sugar over it. Crush mint and sugar together with the back of a spoon. Pour in boiling water and let mint steep for five minutes. Add vinegar to mint and water mixture. Taste the sauce and add more sugar if needed. Heat before serving.

WHITE BEANS

Dried beans are the traditional French accompaniment to lamb. Although in France they would use green beans or *flageolets,* virtually unavailable in this country, white beans make a very acceptable substitute. There are many varieties—navy, marrow, Great Northern, kidney, large and small Limas—all of which have a slightly different size or shape. All of them have slightly different cooking times as well. This recipe is for marrow beans, but if you switch to another type you can always tell when the beans are done by taking one or two out and blowing on them. If the skin splits, the beans are cooked.

1 pound dried marrow beans	3 cups chicken broth
1 teaspoon salt	Freshly ground pepper
1 cup chopped onion	1 cup chopped fresh parsley
1/2 cup butter	1/2 cup chopped scallions

Put the beans in a large saucepan and add cold water to one inch above the level of the beans. Each cup of dried beans will blow up into about two cups when soaked, so be sure to use a big enough pot. Add salt. Bring to a boil, cover, reduce heat and simmer 45 minutes. Drain the beans. Up to this point you have been precooking the beans; now, to make the finished dish, sauté the onion in butter just until translucent. Add onion and butter, chicken broth and pepper to the beans. Stir well. Cover and simmer two hours until the beans are barely tender. Taste and add more salt and pepper if needed. Stir in parsley and scallions and cook uncovered 15 minutes more.

OEUFS À LA NEIGE

This dessert, which under the name of floating island you will associate with the nursery, is a light and elegant concoction. The brandy gives it an unexpected richness that takes it a long way from any children's party.

Custards and many sauces that contain eggs are prone to curdle and are most safely cooked in a double boiler over hot, but not boiling, water. However, this can be a rather long process, requiring tedious stirring. If you want to be daring, cook the custard over direct heat, lifting the pot off the burner from time to time, to make sure that the bottom of the pot never gets too hot to touch with your hand. This is riskier, but it is a lot quicker, and you will get the hang of it easily, but be sure to use a heavy saucepan and low heat. If the worst should happen and the custard does curdle, add a teaspoon of ice water and beat vigorously with a rotary beater until it becomes smooth again.

2 cups heavy cream	3 tablespoons brandy
2 cups milk	1 teaspoon vanilla extract
1/2 cup sugar	Caramel sauce (recipe
2 egg whites	below)
6 egg yolks	

Bring cream, milk and one quarter cup sugar to a boil in a large skillet, stirring constantly to dissolve sugar. Reduce heat to lowest possible point. Beat the egg whites until they form soft peaks. Then gradually add the remaining one quarter cup of sugar, beating until stiff. To make the *oeufs* fill one tablespoon with the egg white meringue and use another to shape it like an egg. Drop gently into the simmering cream-milk mixture. Repeat this until the skillet is full. Have a cup of cold water handy so you can dip the spoons in it to keep them unsticky. Poach the *oeufs* for two minutes on each side, turning them gently. Remove and drain them on cheesecloth draped over a cake rack. In all, this will make about a dozen *oeufs*. Strain the cream-milk mixture into a bowl. Beat the egg yolks thoroughly in the top of a double boiler. Slowly pour the cream-milk mixture into the yolks, beating constantly. Put over hot, not boiling, water and stir constantly until the mixture thickens enough to coat a spoon. It should have the consistency of a light cream sauce. Remove from heat, stir in brandy and vanilla. Cool to room temperature, stirring occasionally to prevent a skin from forming. Put in serving bowl and chill for at least two hours. To serve, float the snow-white *oeufs* on top of the ivory custard and spoon a little caramel sauce over each one.

CARAMEL SAUCE

1 cup sugar	1/2 cup boiling water

Put the sugar in a small heavy saucepan. Cook over low heat, stirring constantly and breaking up little lumps as they form, until the sugar turns to a golden brown liquid caramel. Gradually stir in the water. It will spatter and sputter when it hits the sugar, but in a few seconds it will blend in. Stand at arm's length as you do this, as it is very easy to get burned. Cook, stirring occasionally, for 10 minutes. Remove from heat and cool.

Shrimp-Stuffed Artichoke

The globe artichoke is surely the engineering marvel of the vegetable world. It is so formidably constructed that one wonders what inquisitive Italian first thought that the bud of the thistle plant would be good to eat. Layers of leaves must be pulled off with the fingers, then scraped between the teeth. The fuzzy choke must be carefully removed. At last the prize is finally revealed—the heart, or bottom. The artichoke is trouble to eat, but worth it—hot or cold, as an appetizer or a vegetable course, with a sauce or stuffed. Here it is presented as an appetizer extravaganza, filled with puréed shrimp blended with an herb mayonnaise. In eating it, each leaf is dipped in the shrimp sauce, and then finally the bottom, coated with the sauce, is cut up and eaten with a fork.

This dinner is meant to be enjoyed on a spring evening. It has a warm-weather mood about it. Because there is quite a lot to eat at each course, don't serve large helpings. Limit yourself to medium, rather than giant, artichokes and one portion of chicken breast per person.

This dinner requires some manual dexterity. If you have never boned a chicken breast before, you should practice and serve the results to your family before attempting the feat for guests. Putting the collar on the soufflé dish also requires being a bit deft. Early on the day of the dinner cook the artichokes and shrimp, refrigerate them separately. Bone the chicken and refrigerate it. An hour and a half before the guests are due, chill the wine, prepare the soufflé dish and make the basic soufflé mixture. Make the sauce for the chicken up to the point where you add the cream. Fill the artichokes with the shrimp and return them to the refrigerator. Near the end of the cocktail hour start the water for the rice

MENU FOR SIX

ARTICHOKES STUFFED WITH SHRIMP

CHICKEN BREASTS SUPRÊME
Rice
Green beans with lemon
Dry white wine

GRAND MARNIER SOUFFLÉ

and beans, sauté the chicken and keep it warm. Just before you sit down, beat the egg whites for the soufflé, combine them with the sauce and put the soufflé in the preheated oven. As you serve the artichokes add the rice and the beans to the boiling water. Don't serve the wine with the artichoke course, they do not go well together. After eating the artichokes, add the cream to the sauce, heat and pour it over the chicken breasts. The rice and beans will be done. The soufflé will take an hour to bake and it must be eaten at once, so during dinner gauge the flow of things so that the dessert dishes are in place when the hour is up. But it isn't necessary to keep looking at your watch during dinner. If you're through with the main course a little early, give your guests another glass of wine. And there won't be a disaster if the soufflé sits five extra minutes in the oven, providing you've turned the oven down as far as it will go —but don't try to hold it longer than that.

RECIPES

ARTICHOKES STUFFED WITH SHRIMP

To insure that this dish looks as attractive as it should, you must remove the chokes of the artichokes very carefully. If you don't, you may inadvertently knock off some of the leaves. After you have spread out the center leaves, pull out the very innermost ones—they will be pale in color and rather thorny—then scrape away the fuzzy choke with a spoon. If it doesn't come easily, cut around it with a grapefruit knife. A word of caution: don't overcook the artichoke, lest it fall apart when you handle it.

6 medium artichokes (about 3 inches across the base)	4¾ teaspoons salt
1½ pounds raw small shrimp	½ teaspoon tarragon
	¼ teaspoon ground black pepper
8 tablespoons lemon juice	1 cup mayonnaise

To prepare the artichokes, remove the stems, cut one-half inch off the tops and snip off the sharp tips of each leaf. Then cook, tightly covered, in plenty of boiling water to which you have added two tablespoons of the lemon juice and two teaspoons of salt, until the base can be pierced with a fork, 30 to 40 minutes. Drain well.

To cook shrimp, bring one quart water to a boil, add one tablespoon lemon juice and two teaspoons salt. Add shrimp and bring the water to a boil again. Reduce heat and simmer, covered, three to five minutes or until shrimp have turned pink. Reserve one-half cup of the water the shrimp were cooked in. Then drain, peel and clean the shrimp. Reserve 18 shrimp for garnish. Place remaining shrimp in a blender with the reserved liquid, the remaining five tablespoons of lemon juice, seasonings, including the remaining three-quarter teaspoon of salt, and one cup of mayonnaise. Blend until the shrimp are broken up. Chill the mixture in the refrigerator, where it will become considerably thicker, until ready to fill artichokes.

CHICKEN BREASTS SUPRÊME

Boneless chicken breasts are often used in French cooking, where they are known by the elegant name of *suprêmes de volaille*. The bones are not removed just for cosmetic purposes: with bones out and the meat lightly flattened, the breasts will cook very quickly so that the result is juicier than most chicken dishes, which must cook longer.

Boning is not difficult. After you've practiced you will find that it won't take you more than five minutes to do a whole breast. It gives a sense of accomplishment, and is a good skill to have since boneless breasts can be used in many recipes. Chicken is such a gelatinous, malleable meat that even if you haven't done a perfect job you can easily pat it back into shape again. There won't be any waste when the job is properly done. Of course, you can always ask your butcher to do it for you. Use breasts that weigh 12 to 16 ounces before boning—the equivalent of a breast from a three- to three-and-one-half-pound chicken. Then you can serve half a breast to each person.

Work on a cutting board, if you have one, and use a pointed knife, four to six inches long—and very sharp. Begin by removing the skin, which you can do easily with your fingers. Then turn the breast over, rib side up, neck end toward the top of the cutting board. Take a firm hold on each side of the breast and bend it backwards until the keel bone, which runs down the center, pops up. Work it completely loose and remove it. You can use your fingers to do this, or the tip of the knife. Then cut the breast in half. Find the long rib bone and slip the point of the knife under it. Free this bone and then, using it as a handle, with a cutting and scraping motion loosen the rib cage. Hold the knife blade flat against the rib cage as you work and keep pressing up against it to lose as little meat as possible. The ribs should all lift out in one piece. With your fingers work out the wishbone and any other bones buried in the meat. Flatten the breast lightly with the side of a heavy knife. Repeat this procedure with the remaining breasts.

In this recipe the breasts are served with a classic creamy sauce based on stock and wine.

3 whole chicken breasts, boned to make 6 pieces	1/4 teaspoon salt
Salt	White pepper
7 tablespoons butter	1/2 cup chicken stock
2 tablespoons flour	1/4 cup white wine
	1/4 cup heavy cream

Sprinkle boned breasts lightly with salt. Heat five tablespoons of the butter in a 12-inch skillet. Add chicken breasts and cook four minutes over medium heat. Turn breasts and cook another four minutes or so or until done. Test with your finger to see that they are springy. Remove chicken breasts from skillet and keep them warm.

In a separate saucepan, melt the two remaining tablespoons of butter. Blend in flour, one-quarter teaspoon salt and white pepper. Stir in chicken stock and cook over medium heat, stirring until thickened. Add wine and simmer two minutes. Just before serving stir in the heavy cream and heat. Pour sauce over the chicken. Serve with rice sprinkled with parsley, and green beans.

GRAND MARNIER SOUFFLÉ

If you have never made a soufflé before, try one—of any kind—before you prepare it for company. If nothing else, experience will make you less nervous. Also you may be the kind who would feel easier with a bowl of fruit or some cheeses on hand, in case something goes terribly wrong. Chances are it won't, particularly if you have the assurance that comes with an ace in the hole.

Any kind of fruit liqueur or brandy or rum can be substituted for Grand Marnier. A wire whisk is the preferred tool of most chefs when they are trying to get an absolutely smooth sauce, and it is recommended in this recipe that you blend the cream sauce with one. However, beating eight egg whites into a meringue is a tiresome chore when done by hand, particularly while your guests are in the living room. Use an electric beater if you have one. Egg whites will whip up more quickly and produce more volume if they are brought to room temperature first. Remove them from the refrigerator half an hour beforehand. Be sure to prepare the soufflé baking dish ahead

of time, and to grease the "collar" enough. It would be a pity to tear a hole in the side of the soufflé at the very end as you remove the collar. This recipe calls for more flour than most. It does not affect taste or texture and it does give it more staying power, the quality needed most in the triumphant march from stove to table.

1/3 cup butter	1 cup sugar
3/4 cup flour	2 tablespoons lemon juice
1/2 teaspoon salt	1 teaspoon grated lemon rind
1 1/2 cups milk	
5 eggs, separated	1/2 cup Grand Marnier
3 egg whites	

You can't use just any baking dish for a proper soufflé. Buy the special soufflé dish, straight-sided and made of china, two-quart size. Grease it lightly with butter, then sprinkle with granulated sugar. (Sugar helps prevent sticking.) Cut a strip of waxed or brown paper or foil about 30 inches long and six inches wide—long enough to overlap itself by at least two inches when placed around the outside of the dish. Fold it in half lengthwise, then grease one side with butter and sprinkle with sugar. Tie the paper as a collar around soufflé dish, sugared side in, so that it extends at least two inches above dish. Secure ends of collar with paper clips or straight pins so that it will hold firm when the soufflé rises. This may seem like fussy work, but it protects the soufflé from overflowing in the oven and makes it rise to glorious proportions.

Melt butter over low heat in saucepan—don't let it brown. Remove from heat, add flour and salt, and mix until smooth. Add the milk, a little at a time, stirring constantly. Return to heat and cook, stirring constantly until thickened and smooth. (This is best done with a wire whisk which tends to keep the sauce smooth.) Remove from heat. Separate the eggs. Set egg whites aside. Beat the five egg yolks until thick. Add hot cream sauce a small amount at a time, beating constantly until all the sauce has been added and the mixture is a creamy custard. Set aside to cool. If you make the sauce ahead of time keep it covered and at room temperature. When hot weather dictates refrigerating the sauce, remove it from the refrigerator at least 30 minutes before proceeding with recipe.

Preheat oven to 350°. Beat all eight egg whites until soft peaks form when the beater is lifted gently. Use a rubber spatula to keep returning the whites to the center of the bowl as you beat them to guarantee that all of them are properly beaten. Add sugar gradually, beating constantly until a stiff meringue is formed. Gradually beat in the lemon juice, a few drops at a time. Stir the lemon rind and Grand Marnier into the egg yolk mixture, mixing well. Add, all at once, to the egg whites and fold in thoroughly using quick, light strokes. Pour into the soufflé dish and set dish in a pan containing one inch of hot water. Bake in a moderate oven (350°) for one hour. Remove from oven and carefully remove paper collar. Serve at once, dishing it out with a large spoon.

Steak and Kidney Pie

In the taverns of old London so beloved by Dr. Johnson and Sir Arthur Conan Doyle, no fare was relished more heartily than the crusty pastries filled with meats, and the celebrated favorite was a steak and kidney pie. As unusual as this combination may seem to modern Americans, it is a satisfying dish full of textures and flavors that are, well, surprising and stimulating. Chunks of round steak, tender veal kidneys, smooth fresh mushrooms, all simmered in herbs and wine, then baked under a pastry top, give a blend of succulent tidbits spiked with pungent aromas that is something to bite into.

The accompaniments to this dish —which of course is a meal in itself —place the accent on unexpected combinations in the same way. Prefaced with a delicate vegetable broth, served with a tart orange and onion salad and washed down with a tall cold glass of half stout, half champagne, this cherished bit of old England can be a spring tonic to wake up tired winter appetites.

This dinner may be the last chance you'll have to serve a robust dinner until the cool and crisp days return. From now on most menus will probably be summery so make the most of the occasion by serving a lusty meat pie—but surround it with light dishes that offer a hint of the weather ahead.

There is a fair amount of work to this dinner but the saving grace is that there will be no last-minute flurry. Make the soup any time you feel like it—you can even freeze it. Prepare the steak and kidney pie the day before, up to the point of adding the crust. Like all stews, its flavor will improve with a day of rest. On the morning of the dinner make the cake

MENU FOR SIX

SPRING TONIC WITH CHEESE CROUTONS

STEAK AND KIDNEY PIE
Orange and onion salad
Black velvet

DOUBLE CHOCOLATE ROLL

for the chocolate roll, keep it rolled and covered. Chill the champagne and the stout. In the late afternoon make the pastry for the meat pie. Prepare the salad ingredients and the salad dressing. Remove the steak and kidney mixture from the refrigerator and put the pastry crust on. Fill the chocolate roll and refrigerate it. Three quarters of an hour before announcing dinner, put the pie in the oven. Heat up the soup just before serving. At that time turn down the oven heat; the pie should be nicely browned by the time you have finished the soup. Combine the stout and champagne at the last minute. Dust the chocolate roll with sugar before serving.

RECIPES

SPRING TONIC

This vegetable bouillon, which is equally good served hot or cold, is very easy to make, with no fussing, since the vegetables are simply cut into chunks. The result is a bright clear red—made extra rich both in taste and appearance by a splash of port.

3 one-pound cans tomatoes	1/2 teaspoon basil
2 stalks celery, with leaves	1/2 teaspoon sugar
2 carrots, scraped	1/4 cup port
1 green pepper, seeded	1 tablespoon fresh lemon
1 large onion	juice
3 peppercorns	Cheese croutons (recipe
2 whole cloves	below)
1 teaspoon salt	

Put the contents of the cans of tomatoes, juice and all, in a large saucepan, breaking the solid chunks up with a fork. Cut the vegetables into chunks and add them to the pot. Stir in peppercorns, cloves, salt, basil and sugar. Cover the saucepan tightly and bring it to a boil, then lower the heat and simmer for one hour, stirring once or twice. Cool. Strain the soup through a fine sieve or through several thicknesses of cheesecloth, squeezing all the juices out of the vegetables. Return the bouillon to the saucepan and add the port and lemon juice. Add more salt and pepper, if desired. Bring to a boil and serve, adding a few cheese croutons to each serving.

CHEESE CROUTONS

2 slices day-old white bread	1 tablespoon grated
3 tablespoons butter	Parmesan cheese

Use a firm rather than spongy type bread. Trim the crusts and cut the bread into one-quarter-inch cubes. Heat the butter in a skillet until it is hot and bubbly; add the bread cubes. Cook and toss over low heat until the crou-

tons are crisp and well browned. Drain them on paper towels, then place them in a small bowl and sprinkle with the cheese while still warm.

STEAK AND KIDNEY PIE

Don't attempt to improve on this recipe by upgrading the quality of the meat. Bottom round is the right texture and has a rich, full flavor. Cook the dish in two stages: the stew the day before, to let the flavors blend, and to make it easy to remove any fat; then add the crust and bake the pie just before serving. You can bake it in any shallow two-quart dish. A round one is more pie-like, and it will be easier to handle the crust for a circular dish, but an oblong one will provide more crust with each serving. Use any favorite crust recipe.

2 1/2 pounds bottom round	Freshly ground black pepper
3 veal kidneys (1 pound)	1/2 teaspoon crushed
1/2 cup flour	rosemary leaves
6 tablespoons cooking oil	1/2 teaspoon tarragon
2 medium onions, thinly	1 tablespoon tomato paste
sliced	2 teaspoons Worcestershire
1/2 pound mushrooms,	sauce
sliced	1 cup beef broth
1 teaspoon salt	1 cup dry red wine

Cut the beef into pieces slightly larger than bite-size. Trim fat from the kidneys and cut into small cubes. Put flour into a large bowl, add the beef and the kidneys and toss until all the pieces are well coated with the flour. Heat the oil in a large frying pan or Dutch oven. When it is very hot, add the meat and sear quickly on all sides. It is best to do this in several stages so as not to crowd the meat. Remove meat as it is browned. When all the meat has been browned, add the onions and mushrooms to the drippings, with an additional tablespoon of oil if necessary. Sauté about five minutes, until the mushrooms are lightly browned, turning them often. Return the meat to the Dutch oven, if that's what you've been using. If not, transfer vegetables from skillet to casserole and add meat. Add remaining ingredients. Cover and simmer until meat is tender, about two hours, stirring from time to time. Remove from heat and cool. Refrigerate overnight. Remove fat from surface. Preheat oven to 400°. Put the steak and kidney stew into a shallow two-quart casserole, at least 10″ in diameter. It is better if the casserole has an edge for the pastry to adhere to. On a lightly floured board or pastry cloth, roll out the chilled pastry until it is about two inches larger all around than the top of the casserole. Do not try to roll it too thin. The pastry should be thicker than it would be for a dessert pie. Place dough on top of casserole, turning it under at the edges so there is a double thickness. Press dough over the edges of casserole and to the sides. Cut four gashes for steam in the center of the pastry. Bake in 400° oven for 30 minutes; lower heat to 350° and continue baking 15 to 20 minutes until the pastry is golden and the stew bubbles.

ORANGE AND ONION SALAD

Oranges and onions may seem like an odd marriage, but in a salad they are made for each other. Their sweet-tart flavor is an excellent contrast with the meat pie. Pour the dressing over it at the table so that your guests can admire it before it is tossed.

6 cups assorted salad greens, washed and torn into bite-size pieces	Freshly ground black pepper
	5 tablespoons olive oil
2 large red Italian onions	1 tablespoon fresh orange juice
3 large seedless oranges	
1/2 teaspoon salt	1 tablespoon fresh lemon juice

Arrange chilled salad greens in a large salad bowl. Peel the onions and slice them very thin. Peel oranges, removing all the white membrane. Do this over a bowl to save the juice—they should give one to two tablespoons which will be used in the dressing. Cut oranges into thin slices. Sprinkle salt and pepper over greens, toss gently. Arrange alternate slices of onion and orange on top of the greens. Mix olive oil, orange and lemon juices together. Sprinkle the dressing over the salad, toss and serve.

BLACK VELVET

This is a smooth Edwardian mixture of stout and champagne. But don't use a vintage champagne—it is totally wasted in a concoction like this. Chill equal amounts of champagne and stout thoroughly. Pour both into a large pitcher, give the mixture a swirl and serve in either mugs or tall glasses.

DOUBLE CHOCOLATE ROLL

This dessert is a chocolate sponge cake, which is wrapped around a chocolate-cream filling. It is not frosted, but dusted lightly with confectioner's sugar. It is bound to develop a crack or two in the rolling process, which the drift of sugar easily disguises.

3 ounces semisweet chocolate	1/4 teaspoon salt
	3 tablespoons cold coffee
4 eggs	1 teaspoon vanilla
3/4 cup sugar	1/4 teaspoon baking soda
1/2 cup sifted cake flour	Confectioner's sugar
1/2 tablespoon baking powder	Chocolate cream filling (recipe below)

Preheat the oven to 375°. Grease the bottom of a jelly-roll pan (15x10x1); line the bottom with waxed paper. Grease this also. Melt the chocolate in the top of a double boiler over hot, not boiling, water. Remove from the heat. In a large bowl, beat the eggs with the sugar until thick and light, about 10 minutes. Sift the flour with the baking powder and salt over the surface of the egg-sugar mixture. Fold in gently, using a rubber spatula, until no trace of the flour remains. Stir the coffee, vanilla and the baking soda into the melted chocolate; stir until blended. Quickly fold this mixture into the batter, and keep folding until all streaks of chocolate have disappeared. Spread the batter evenly in the prepared cake pan. Bake 15 to 20 minutes, until cake pulls away from the sides of the pan, and springs back when touched lightly with a finger. While the cake is baking, sift a thick layer of the confectioner's sugar over the surface of a dish towel. When cake is done, loosen it from the sides of the pan, using a small spatula. Turn out onto the towel and carefully peel off the waxed paper. At once cut along the edges of the cake with a serrated knife, to remove the crisp sides. This makes the cake easier to roll. Working from the narrow end, roll the cake up, gently but quickly. The towel will be rolled up with the cake and prevents it from sticking to itself. Transfer it to a cake rack to cool, about one hour. Just before serving, or up to an hour or so before, unroll the cake, still leaving it on the towel, and spread with the filling. Roll cake up, this time without the towel, extra gently, being careful not to squeeze the filling out the ends. Using two spatulas, transfer it to a good-sized serving platter. Cover with foil and refrigerate. Sift additional confectioner's sugar over the top just before serving.

CHOCOLATE CREAM FILLING

1 1/2 cups heavy cream	1/2 cup confectioner's sugar
6 tablespoons cocoa	1 teaspoon vanilla

In a medium-sized bowl, mix the cream with the cocoa and sugar—just enough to moisten the dry ingredients. Refrigerate for two to three hours. Beat until very thick and creamy. Stir in the vanilla.

Red Snapper

The red snapper is a very handsome fish. The ichthyologist who named it, in fact, waxed unscientifically lyrical and called snappers "the tanagers and grosbeaks of the coral reefs." It loses none of its good

looks when it is ready for the table, swimming in a steaming wine broth, its skin delicately traced with red. When cut, its flesh shows up white, firm and succulent. Whole snapper can be bought in most of the U.S.; on the West Coast red rockfish makes an agreeable substitute. The snapper is a fish for a small, elegant dinner, poached with rosé wine and shallots. Rosé is the ideal wine for snapper—it won't darken the meat as a red might, yet gives the fish a winier flavor than most white ones would. The ideal poacher is this French kettle, not an extravagance since it insures years of finely cooked fish.

This is a dinner of delicately flavored dishes, each one of which has a lightness and freshness particularly suited to warm weather. The menu is impressive enough for a dressy party and simple enough for cooks with spring fever.

This will surely be one of the best-looking dinners you will ever serve. Not only is the fish a handsome platterful, but everything that goes before, after or with it is exceptionally good to look at. The *quiche* is a puffy pie, rich golden brown. The new potatoes and the bright-green bean salad are attractive accompaniments. Dessert, a properly spectacular finale, is a trembling tower of pink froth.

This dinner, for all its festivity, makes only one serious demand on the cook. She must do some fast footwork in the kitchen about three quarters of an hour before dinner. Everything else is simple and straightforward; no special shopping trips are required.

But be sure that you have the proper kitchenware. A fish poacher, though expensive to buy and awkward to store, is a beautiful and satisfying object. If you don't own one and don't want to buy one, use a roasting pan. Be sure it has a rack that lifts out so that the fish can be easily removed. Measure your roaster before you buy the fish, so that you can get a snapper that will not have to be jammed into the pan. Make certain you have a soufflé dish for the dessert. Make the dessert early on the day of

MENU FOR SIX

MUSHROOM QUICHE

POACHED RED SNAPPER
Boiled new potatoes
Green bean salad
Rosé or white wine

COLD STRAWBERRY SOUFFLÉ

the dinner: it needs at least four hours to achieve a firm consistency in the refrigerator. Prepare the bean salad any time during the afternoon and refrigerate it. Make the pie shell ahead if you wish. About an hour before the guests are due make the filling for the *quiche* and set it aside in the refrigerator. Cook up the court bouillon for the fish and let it sit on the stove in the poaching pan until you are ready to begin cooking the fish. Refrigerate the wine you are going to serve at the table. Lastly, make the hollandaise sauce and let it sit over warm water. Don't turn on the heat under the water—the sauce may curdle. Turn on the oven for the *quiche*. Forty-five minutes before serving you will have to get very busy and work fast. When you go out into the kitchen at that time, know exactly what you have to do and have the dishes and utensils set out to work with. Pour the *quiche* filling into the pie shell, dust the top with the already grated cheese and put it into the oven. Put the fish in the poacher and start it simmering. You can and should do all this in 10 minutes at the most. The *quiche* will be done in about a half hour. Put the small new potatoes into boiling water just before you are ready to serve the *quiche*. When you have finished eating the *quiche,* the potatoes and fish will both be cooked, and the hollandaise can be warmed and whisked in a minute.

RECIPES

MUSHROOM QUICHE

This *quiche*—a name which applies to any savory pie or tart made with an egg custard base—is a change from the more usual bacon-flavored *quiche lorraine*. This version is chock full of mushrooms, set off by a dash of cheese and a sprinkling of shallots.

Make the pie shell ahead of time if you wish, using your own recipe, a mix, or a frozen shell. If you use a mix, prepare the whole box and use what you need. Half, which most directions say is enough for a bottom crust, will make too thin a crust for this *quiche*. Whatever your shell, prick it well with a fork before you bake it. This will prevent it from buckling and blistering. Prebake the shell until it is pleasantly light brown. Don't be afraid of letting it cook a few extra minutes, as this preliminary baking keeps the crust from getting soggy when the mushroom mixture is added.

Don't be too zealous about cleaning mushrooms. If you soak them, they will get too watery and lose much of their flavor. Do not peel or scrub them since a lot of their taste is in the skin. Instead wash them quickly under running water or wipe them with a damp cloth.

10-inch pastry shell	1 teaspoon lemon juice
4 tablespoons butter	4 eggs
2 tablespoons minced shallots	1 cup heavy cream
1 pound fresh mushrooms, thinly sliced	1/8 teaspoon pepper
	1/8 teaspoon nutmeg
1 1/2 teaspoons salt	1/2 cup grated Swiss cheese (about two ounces)

Preheat oven to 450°. Bake the pastry shell for 10 minutes or until it is lightly browned. Set it aside to cool. Reduce the oven temperature to 350°. Melt three tablespoons of the butter in a large skillet. Add the shallots and cook them for a minute or so, stirring constantly. Stir in the mushrooms, one teaspoon of the salt and lemon juice. Cover pan and simmer over low heat for 10 minutes. Uncover, increase heat and boil for five to 10 minutes until the liquid is completely evaporated and the mushrooms begin to sauté in the butter. Stir to prevent scorching. Beat the eggs and cream together, add the remaining one-half teaspoon of salt, pepper and nutmeg. Stir in the mushrooms. Pour this mixture into the prebaked pastry shell. Sprinkle the top with grated cheese and dot with the remaining tablespoon of butter. Bake at 350° for 35 minutes or until the *quiche* is puffy and browned and a knife inserted in it comes out clean.

POACHED RED SNAPPER

Poaching is a very delicate form of cookery. It does not mean boiling, but rather keeping the liquid just below the boiling point, so that it seems to shiver rather than bubble. If you cook the fish faster than this it is apt to fall apart, so keep the heat as low as possible. The poacher or roaster will probably stretch across two burners. Do *not* overcook the fish—a common occurrence.

4- to 5-pound whole red snapper	1 bunch of parsley
	1 tablespoon salt
1/4 cup chopped shallots	4 cups water
1 stalk celery with leaves, cut up	2 1/2 cups rosé wine
	2 lemons, cut in wedges
1 carrot, cut up	

Combine shallots, celery, carrot, four sprigs of parsley, salt and water in a saucepan. Bring to a boil, reduce heat, and simmer uncovered for 20 minutes. Strain through a double thickness of cheesecloth and discard vegetables. Pour this stock, or court bouillon as it is properly called, into a fish poacher or large roasting pan. Add the rosé. Wash the fish inside and out with cold running water. Pat it dry with a paper towel. Place the fish on a rack and put it into the pan. If you're using a roaster and don't have a rack, wrap cheesecloth around the fish first, leaving long ends to act as tabs to help with lifting it. If the fish is not at least half-covered by the bouillon —and this varies with the size of pan you use—add up to one cup of extra water. Bring stock just to the boil, cover and poach over lowest heat for 45 minutes or just until the fish flakes easily with a fork. Carefully lift the rack with the fish on it from the pan. Drain well. (Strain the bouillon and save it for soups or aspics.) Place the fish on a platter and garnish it with lemon wedges and the rest of the parsley. Serve it with hollandaise sauce and with small new potatoes boiled in their jackets.

GREEN BEAN SALAD

Use fresh beans for this salad. They are at their best this time of year and are firmer than frozen beans—and in a salad it is particularly important that beans be served *al dente*. Cook them only briefly, part of the time with the top of the pot off so they keep their bright-green color. If you insist on using frozen beans get the kind that are left whole; they will look more attractive.

1 pound green beans	Freshly ground pepper
2 teaspoons salt	Few grains cayenne pepper
1/2 cup salad oil	1 hard-cooked egg yolk, sieved
1/2 cup lemon juice	
1 teaspoon dry mustard	2 tablespoons capers

Wash the beans and snap off the ends, pulling away any strings that may be there. Leave the beans whole. Bring one inch of water to a brisk boil in a large saucepan, add the beans and one teaspoon of the salt. Boil uncovered for five minutes. Cover and simmer for 10 minutes or just until the beans are tender. Meanwhile combine oil, lemon juice, remaining teaspoon salt, mustard, pepper and cayenne. When the beans are cooked, drain them and put them in a bowl. Pour the dressing over the hot beans. Mix lightly, let cool. Cover and marinate in the refrigerator for at least two hours. To serve, drain beans and arrange them in neat bundles on salad plates. Garnish with sieved egg yolk and capers.

COLD STRAWBERRY SOUFFLÉ

This dessert is called a soufflé only because it looks like one. It isn't cooked like one. It is a froth of strawberries, stiffened slightly with gelatin. It has all the lightness and airiness of a hot soufflé, with none of the split-second timing. It is chilled in a soufflé dish with a paper collar, which when removed leaves the dessert showing well above the rim of the dish.

2 pints fresh strawberries	1 tablespoon lemon juice
2 envelopes gelatin	2 tablespoons kirsch
3/4 cup sugar	3 egg whites
1/2 cup water	1 cup heavy cream

To prepare the collar for the soufflé dish cut a four-inch strip of brown or waxed paper or foil, long enough to fit around the outside of a one-quart dish. Brush the inside of the paper with oil. Fasten the strip in place with cellophane tape or paper clips, allowing it to extend about two inches above the top of the dish. Set the dish aside.

Sort and hull the berries and set aside the eight prettiest to use for garnish. Purée the rest in a blender, sieve or food mill. Mix the gelatin and one-half cup of the sugar in a saucepan. Stir in the water and cook over low heat, stirring until the gelatin dissolves. Stir this mixture into the puréed strawberries. Add the lemon juice and kirsch. Refrigerate, stirring occasionally, until the mixture thickens slightly. This will take about half an hour, and is crucial to making the soufflé stiff enough to stand up. Beat the egg whites until frothy; gradually beat in the remaining one-quarter cup sugar and beat until stiff. Fold the egg whites into the strawberry mixture. Whip the cream until stiff and fold it in too. Gently pour the mixture into the prepared soufflé dish and refrigerate until firm—about four hours. To serve, loosen tape and gently peel off the paper collar. Garnish the soufflé with whole strawberries.

Perfect Pasta Sauce

Almost everyone who goes into the kitchen thinks he knows how to make a great spaghetti sauce. The man of the house who won't cope with Corn Flakes is proud of his way with pasta. Travelers cook up recipes from Palermo to Pisa—in

Italy there are as many ways to make a sauce as there are to phrase an insult.

But the amateurs are kidding themselves. Spaghetti sauce is no mere matter of combining tomatoes, garlic and herbs and letting them cook forever. Really good sauce requires culinary skill and the one described here requires more than usual. It is a basic meat and tomato combination—with no anchovies or spicy sausage to disguise the shortcomings. This sauce must be tasted and seasoned, retasted and reseasoned and in the end it can only be as good as your own palate. But if your palate is sensitive and you follow the recipe on the next page —you are now about to embark on the best spaghetti sauce in the world.

A spaghetti dinner may not sound like a gastronomic treat, but the version of meat sauce given in the recipe below will make this a very special dinner, indeed.

It's just as easy to boil two pots of water as one, so if you're serving spaghetti you might as well have a party. The celery root remoulade and dessert are also easy to prepare in generous quantities, and these are dishes that you can organize well in advance of the first ring of the doorbell.

Though these foods are simple enough to serve buffet style, they aren't meant to be eaten from a plate perched on the knee. If you have an oversized dining table, there's no problem. But if your table barely stretches for eight, round up one or two bridge tables so guests can sit down to dinner comfortably.

The spaghetti sauce will taste better if it mellows in the refrigerator overnight. Make the lemon snow and its sauce on the morning of the dinner. If you do all of this in ad-

MENU FOR TWELVE
CELERY ROOT REMOULADE
SPAGHETTI WITH MEAT SAUCE

Spring green salad, oil and lemon dressing
Italian bread
Red wine

LEMON SNOW WITH GRAND MARNIER SAUCE

vance, you'll have almost all the cooking out of the way.

Two hours before the guests arrive, make the remoulade and wash the salad greens. Make the dressing. Let the spaghetti sauce come to room temperature. Half an hour after the guests show, start the spaghetti water and warm up the sauce. Put the spaghetti into the boiling water when you clear away after the first course. Stir extra herbs and wine into the sauce then, and toss the salad. There may be a slight delay between courses, but pasta *must* be cooked at the last minute.

One word of caution about seasonings, a lavish use of which is called for here. Whole spices like cloves or peppercorns will keep indefinitely, but ground spices and dried herbs lose their strength after a few months, and should be replaced once a year. Keep them on a darkish shelf away from sun and heat and be sure the jars are tightly closed. Since herbs do lose their strength, taste as you cook—and correct seasonings.

RECIPES

CELERY ROOT REMOULADE

Celery root, sometimes called celeriac, is not the root of a celery. It is a cousin to the ordinary kind of celery but bred for the root rather than the stalk. It is a round, brown knob, rather bumpy and quite possibly the world's ugliest vegetable. It tastes very much like the usual celery, with the crunch missing.

In Europe where it is widely eaten, it is cooked in various styles. But it is most popular served raw with a remoulade sauce as an appetizer. Though the basis of the sauce is mayonnaise, that flavor should not be recognizable in the finished sauce. Since prepared mayonnaises vary considerably, and since you probably won't bother to make your own, be sure that the mayonnaise taste is completely buried. If it isn't, add more seasoning.

6 celery roots	scallions
2 cups mayonnaise	2 tablespoons prepared
4 tablespoons tarragon vinegar	Dijon-style mustard
	1 teaspoon tarragon
4 tablespoons chopped fresh parsley	1 teaspoon salt
	Freshly ground black pepper
4 tablespoons chopped	

Peel the celery roots and cut them into julienne strips about the size of matchsticks. Combine all the remaining ingredients and mix them together thoroughly. Mix the celery root julienne with the remoulade sauce. Correct the seasoning if necessary. Chill, covered, for at least one hour before serving.

SPAGHETTI WITH MEAT SAUCE

Producing a perfect spaghetti sauce is no small feat. The ingredients must harmonize and their proportions suit. The sauce must be cooked just long enough—but no longer—for all the flavors to blend. The pot needs watching. Stirring helps, and frequent tasting is advisable.

The basis of this version is Italian plum tomatoes, which cook into a thicker sauce, better suited to coating strands of spaghetti. Along with the ground beef you would expect to use, there's enough bacon to give the dish a faintly smoky flavor. And in addition to the usual onion and garlic there's some green pepper to sharpen the taste. Red wine and an array of herbs season the sauce, but the real trick is to add a little extra oregano and basil, plus a soupçon more of wine, at the last minute. This accentuates the flavors and gives the sauce a distinctive zest.

The blending of flavors requires a long cooking time, but if you leave the sauce too long on the range it will taste dead. The secret is to let the sauce simmer until it is smooth and rich, the flavors just intermingled. Your own taste buds are your best guide. The recipe demands some chopping, but it's the cooking that takes the time. You won't be letting yourself in for much more work if you decide to double this recipe—and if you do, you will have the makings of another dinner or two in the freezer.

½ pound bacon, chopped	1 cup finely chopped green pepper
2½ pounds ground beef	
2 cups finely chopped onion	6 cloves garlic, finely

chopped	¾ cup water
3 2-pound 3-ounce cans Italian plum tomatoes	½ cup chopped fresh parsley
3 6-ounce cans tomato paste	2 teaspoons thyme
1½ cups dry red wine	1 bay leaf, crumbled
5 teaspoons oregano	2 tablespoons salt
5 teaspoons basil	Freshly ground pepper

Fry bacon until crisp in a wide six-quart pot. Remove bacon and all but two tablespoons of fat. Save both bacon and extra fat. Add ground beef, breaking it up with a spoon, and cook until brown, stirring occasionally. Stir in onion, green pepper and garlic and cook for 10 minutes. Add more bacon fat if needed. Mash plum tomatoes with a spoon. Stir the tomatoes and tomato paste, bacon, one cup of wine, four teaspoons each of oregano and basil and all remaining ingredients into the sauce. Bring to a boil, reduce heat and simmer uncovered for three hours, stirring occasionally. Taste after an hour of cooking and correct the seasoning; herbs vary and so do personal notions of flavor. If you make the sauce early, cool and refrigerate it until an hour or two before dinner. Let it warm to room temperature before you reheat it. Ten or 15 minutes before serving, blend in one teaspoon each of oregano and basil and one half cup of wine. Serve the sauce in a tureen and let everyone ladle it out onto plates of spaghetti. Be sure to provide plenty of grated Parmesan cheese to sprinkle on top.

Part of the success of a sauce depends on what's underneath it. The spaghetti should be cooked *al dente* —just on the chewy side, which means boiled eight to 10 minutes—drained well, and eaten while it's still piping hot. Allow three pounds of pasta for 12 people and cook it in plenty of rapidly boiling water. You will need two enormous pots—the 10-quart size if you can get them. One handy trick when you're trying to get a lot of pasta into pots quickly is to float a spoonful of oil in the water. When you stir in the spaghetti, the oil will help keep the strands from cooking in clumps and stop the water from boiling over. "Spaghetti" comes in many sizes, from fine vermicelli to wide linguine, but the thinner the pasta the easier it is to maneuver and twist around a fork.

SPRING GREEN SALAD

From young spinach to radish leaves, there are dozens of greens to choose. For tartness there is mustard or arugola; for a touch of bitterness, field salad or dandelion leaves; for pungency, Italian parsley or chicory; for a peppery tang, watercress or nasturtium leaves. Which you use depends on your taste and where you shop—different regions and nationalities have their own specialties.

To make enough salad for a dozen people, plan to have about 12 cups of coarsely torn leaves. Allowing six cups of that for a basic green like romaine, buy quantities of the others accordingly. Ideally you should have three or four kinds. If you use more than that, no one of them will be plentiful enough to retain its flavor, and if you use fewer, there won't be much variety to the salad. Wash everything well in cool water. Tear, don't cut, into bite-size pieces. Mix well, wrap loosely and put them in the refrigerator to crisp. For the dressing, mix two thirds cup of oil with one third cup of lemon juice or wine vinegar. Add salt and pepper and a little mustard. Taste the mixture and correct the seasoning. Toss the salad at the last minute, but do this job in the kitchen. The lavish quantity of greens is likely to be hard to handle.

LEMON SNOW WITH GRAND MARNIER SAUCE

This is a gelatin-based dessert which requires time to reach the syrupy stage and still more time to set. To hurry this up, place the bowl that holds the gelatin mixture inside a larger ice-filled bowl. Keep the bowl in this ice bath as you whip the mixture.

2 envelopes unflavored gelatin	½ teaspoon finely grated lemon peel
1⅓ cups sugar	⅔ cup fresh lemon juice
3 cups boiling water	6 egg whites

In a large bowl, mix the gelatin and sugar. Add the boiling water and stir well until the gelatin is completely dissolved. Add the lemon peel and juice. Chill until the mixture is syrupy, about one half hour in the ice bath or refrigerate one hour. Beat the egg whites until stiff. Add them to the lemon mixture and beat until it begins to thicken slightly, about five minutes. Pour into a serving dish and chill at least two hours until set.

SAUCE

1 cup heavy cream	juice
6 egg yolks	6 tablespoons Grand Marnier
½ cup sugar	
⅔ cup butter, melted	2 teaspoons finely grated lemon peel
6 tablespoons fresh lemon	

Pour cream into a bowl, set the bowl in an ice bath and beat the cream until it is thick and glossy but not stiff. Refrigerate. Using the same beaters (to save the trouble of washing them), beat egg yolks until thick and lemon-colored, gradually adding the sugar. Slowly beat in the butter, lemon juice and liqueur. Fold in the lemon peel and whipped cream. Chill thoroughly. Ladle some over each portion of lemon snow as you spoon it out.

Spinach Soufflé

Of all the changes the French can ring on cooking an egg—the *haute cuisine* is credited with 500 or so egg recipes—none is a greater feat than the soufflé. A soufflé can do almost anything any other dish can do—and often do it better. Combined with meat or fish it serves as a main course. With sweet flavorings it is a dessert. And here, seasoned with spinach, it is an appetizer. The spinach flecks the dish prettily with green and gives it a slightly dry flavor. The soufflé's airy ways disguise its down-to-earth economy, and make it an appropriate start for the spring-like menu that follows.

The soufflé is the only part of this dinner that is not made ahead of time. Since it is the first course, not dessert, you do not have to keep one eye on the clock all through dinner to be sure that everything comes out on time.

Make the navarin the day before the dinner except for the last-minute addition of the vegetables. This gives the flavors a chance to meld, and, as important, it is easier to remove the fat which will form a top layer after the stew has been refrigerated overnight. Make the pie early in the day. Mid-afternoon on the day of the dinner, set the spinach out to thaw in a colander so that it will be thoroughly drained by the time you are ready to use it in the soufflé. Take the eggs for the soufflé out of the refrigerator so they will

be at room temperature (they will whip much higher) when you are ready to use them. Prepare the vegetables for the navarin. Two hours before the guests are due—and be sure it is also before you change for dinner—prepare the soufflé up to the point of beating the egg whites: that will have to be done at the last minute. Just before your guests arrive put the defatted stew over low heat. Forty-five minutes before dinner, you will have to turn on the oven for the soufflé, whip the egg whites and combine them with the soufflé mixture. Thirty-five minutes before you want to announce dinner put it in the oven. Since soufflés won't wait, you are now committed to moving everyone to the dining room at a given time.

RECIPES

SPINACH SOUFFLÉ

Don't hesitate to use frozen chopped spinach in this recipe—all the chopping has been done for you and the flavor will be fine. One package is just the right amount, and the spinach has been frozen raw so that you will not be cooking it for the second time. If you are making a major effort to keep costs down and you don't have shallots in the house, substitute two tablespoons of minced onions or scallions instead. Shallots have a more delicate flavor but they are a good deal more expensive than the lowly onion.

1 package chopped frozen spinach (one cup)	5 tablespoons flour
	1½ cups milk
1 tablespoon grated Parmesan cheese	1 teaspoon salt
	Freshly ground black pepper
2-3 shallots, minced	6 eggs
2 tablespoons lemon juice	1 egg white
7 tablespoons butter	

Preheat oven to 400°. Butter a two-quart soufflé dish and sprinkle the sides and bottom lightly with Parmesan cheese. Melt one tablespoon of butter in a heavy saucepan and add the shallots. Cook for about three minutes, stirring once or twice. Add the thoroughly drained spinach and lemon juice and cook over a very low heat, stirring frequently until all the liquid has evaporated, which will take about 10 minutes. Set aside. Melt the remaining six tablespoons of butter in a heavy saucepan and over low heat stir in the flour with a wire whisk; remove from heat. Meanwhile bring the milk to the boiling point and add it to the butter-flour mixture, beating vigorously with a wire whisk until smooth. Add the salt and pepper and continue whisking until blended. Let this white sauce cool a little. Meanwhile separate the eggs. Beat the yolks into the sauce one at a time. Stir in the spinach, and set the

mixture aside. Beat the egg whites, including the extra white, in a large bowl until they hold soft peaks. Stir a little of the whites into the sauce to make it easier to manage, then gently fold in the remainder. Pour the mixture into the prepared soufflé dish. Place in oven, turn heat down to 375° immediately and bake for 35 to 40 minutes until the top is well puffed up and lightly browned.

NAVARIN PRINTANIER

This is a lamb stew—but a special kind. As its name indicates it is a spring stew. The lamb should be genuine spring lamb, only three to five months old, which is most plentiful from April through July. The vegetables are also young and tender—early peas and beans, small carrots, little white onions and new potatoes, cooked in their jackets. These are the simplest ingredients, but they must be cooked with considerable care. The lamb is browned and the glaze transferred to the casserole. The vegetables are glazed separately. The fat must be completely skimmed off the stew. It is not difficult, but it does take more time than the usual way of putting everything in a pot to cook.

Because of the number of fresh vegetables used you may feel in the early stages of preparation that a cook's best friend is a scullery maid. Try to do all the peeling, scraping, shelling and snapping when someone in the family has time to sit and chat in the kitchen. But don't let this prospect keep you from trying the dish at all—frozen peas and beans are good substitutes for fresh, and remember the cheerful fact that the potatoes don't have to be peeled at all.

4 pounds lamb	Freshly ground black pepper
6 tablespoons flour	6 tablespoons butter
1 tablespoon salt	1 tablespoon minced onion

½ cup dry white wine	12 small carrots, cut in
2 cups drained canned	chunks
tomatoes	3 teaspoons sugar
2 cups water	24 small white onions,
1 celery stalk with leaves,	peeled
cut in 3 pieces	12-18 small new potatoes,
1 clove garlic, crushed	scrubbed
4 sprigs parsley	1 cup green beans, cut in 1-
1 small bay leaf	inch pieces
1 teaspoon rosemary	1 cup green peas

Preheat oven to 350°. Cut the lamb into good-size pieces —larger than bite-size—removing as much of the fat as possible. Sprinkle the chunks with flour, salt and pepper. Brown the meat in three tablespoons butter, adding more if necessary. As the pieces brown, remove them from the skillet to a large ovenproof casserole. Add minced onion to the skillet and cook it until golden, then add it to the meat in the casserole. Pour off all fat from the skillet and discard it. Add wine to the skillet and cook over low heat for a few minutes, stirring up all the brown glaze and meat bits. Pour over meat in the casserole. Add tomatoes, water, celery, garlic, parsley, bay leaf and rosemary. Cover casserole, set in oven and cook for one hour. Remove from oven and discard the celery, parsley and bay leaf. Set the casserole aside uncovered to cool. Cover carrots with boiling salted water, boil rapidly for three minutes, then drain them well in a colander, shaking it frequently to speed cooling and drying. Melt the remaining three tablespoons butter in a skillet, add the white onions and shake skillet over medium heat until they are coated with butter. Sprinkle the onions with one teaspoon sugar and continue cooking, shaking the pan until onions are golden brown. Remove onions and set aside. Put carrots into the same skillet, sprinkle them with the remaining two teaspoons sugar, and continue cooking, shaking skillet, until the carrots are lightly browned and glazed. Set them aside with the onions. Skim fat off the cooled casserole. Taste the stew and add salt and pepper if necessary. Add the carrots and onions to casserole. Put potatoes on top. Cover and return to oven for 30 minutes. Meanwhile cover the beans with boiling salted water and boil for five minutes. Drain well. Add the peas and parboiled beans to the casserole, cover and cook in 350° oven for 30 minutes or until all the vegetables are done. Everything except cooking the peas and beans and final assembly can be done the day before. If you do cook the stew ahead of time, heat it in a 350° oven for 20 minutes before adding the vegetables so that the gravy and meat will not be icy cold.

ORANGE PIE

Use large seedless oranges when you make this dessert. It will make peeling them less of a chore and they are easier to arrange attractively in the pie shell. But navel oranges, although easy to handle, yield very little juice for the cornstarch mixture. Therefore, if you are using navels, also buy enough juice oranges to produce one- and one-half cups of juice. Before you peel and segment the oranges grate one teaspoon of rind for the pie shell.

1 10-inch pie shell, baked	Fresh orange juice
and cooled (recipe	3 tablespoons cornstarch
below)	⅛ teaspoon salt
4 cups fresh orange	¾ teaspoon vanilla extract
segments (4 or 5 large	⅔ cup apricot jam
oranges)	½ cup toasted coconut
½ cup sugar	

Combine the orange segments with the sugar and let them stand 30 minutes, then turn them into a sieve over a bowl to drain the juice. Measure the juice and, if necessary, add enough fresh orange juice to make one- and one-half cups. Blend the juice with the cornstarch and salt in a saucepan. Cook, stirring, until thickened to the consistency of molasses. Add the vanilla extract. Let stand at room temperature. Spread the apricot jam over the baked pie shell. Arrange the orange segments in the shell and pour the cooled, thickened juice over them, letting the juice seep down between the segments. Chill for at least an hour. Garnish with toasted coconut.

SHELL FOR ORANGE PIE

1⅓ cups flour, sifted	rind
½ teaspoon salt	½ cup shortening
1 teaspoon grated orange	3 tablespoons cold water

Preheat oven to 425°. Stir the flour, salt and grated orange rind together in a large bowl. Add the shortening and, using a pastry blender, mix together until it resembles coarse meal. Stir in the water, until mixture is moistened and begins to cling together. Press into a ball and turn out onto a lightly floured board. Flatten dough, then roll out into a circle about an inch larger than your pie plate. Transfer dough to pie plate, and crimp the edges. Prick the shell with a fork. Chill for 10 minutes. Bake for 10 to 12 minutes until golden. Set aside to cool.

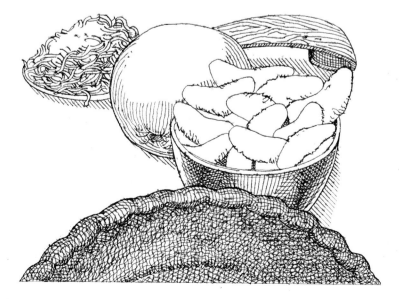

Beef Fondue

Do-it-yourself cookery comes to a delectable boil with Fondue Bourguignonne. For this dish each diner plunges his own bite-size cubes of beef into a communal pot of bubbling oil, and then dips them into an array of sauces—one sweet, one spicy, one sour, one hot or any combination of them.

The dish is a gastronomic misnomer invented relatively recently by a Swiss restaurateur with a high regard for eating and none at all for etymology. It was inspired by traditional cheese fondue, but in this case nothing is *fondu*, or melted, and it has no discernible connection with Burgundy. No matter—the beef is succulent, the flavor combinations interesting, and each cook has a lively time.

The elements of this dinner go happily together despite the fact that the soup is American, the meat dish is a Swiss invention and the dessert owes a bow, at least, to Hawaii. They are an ideal combination for a warm weather backyard supper.

The meal is relatively easy to manage on a terrace or patio but keep the number of diners to six so that everyone can comfortably serve themselves from the communal pot. The hot soup that starts things off can be ladled into mugs from a steaming tureen. There is nothing to get cold as the meal progresses. The fondue keeps itself hot all during dinner and the pineapple should be served frosty—straight from the refrigerator.

The best beef you can buy—tenderloin—is a must for the fondue. Since the meat cooks only a matter of seconds, anything else will be tough and chewy. This cut is expensive but there is no waste, so that for six you will not need more than four pounds. Buy fresh corn, if you can, and keep it in its husks until the last minute. This vegetable loses its freshness particularly fast. Be sure the pineapple is ripe—your nose is your best guide.

The fondue calls for special equipment. Unless you already own it, decide whether to buy it or to organize some

MENU FOR SIX

CORN CHOWDER

FONDUE BOURGUIGNONNE
Béarnaise sauce
Tomato and caper sauce
Mustard sauce
Herb sauce
Horseradish sauce
Barbecue sauce
Red wine

FROSTED PINEAPPLE

substitutes. A Fondue Bourguignonne pot is narrow-necked which keeps the oil from spattering. But a cast iron pot will do. Like a chafing dish, a fondue pot sits over an alcohol burner or a Sterno. You also need a long fork with an insulated handle for each guest. And be careful when you move the pot; a splash of its sizzling contents can produce a nasty burn. The day ahead make five of the six sauces—the barbecue, tomato and caper, mustard, herb and horseradish. Store them in covered containers in the refrigerator. During the day of the dinner make the basic chowder mixture. Prepare the pineapple. Wrap it and let it chill until you are ready to serve it. Set your table on the terrace, being sure that all six diners are within arm's length of the fondue pot. Set up a buffet or side table from which to serve the soup, and from which the guests can help themselves to the sauces. Make the béarnaise sauce and keep it warm in a double boiler. Open the wine so that it can "breathe." Cube the steak, put it on a platter and cover tightly until dinner time. (Don't cube the meat earlier or it will darken and get hard at the edges.) Just before you announce dinner, heat the fondue oil. Add the cream to the chowder base and heat to serving temperature.

RECIPES

CORN CHOWDER

By far the best way to make this is to use fresh corn. There are special gadgets made to scrape the kernels off the cob, but a sharp knife will do as well. If you use a knife take care not to cut too deep. If you cannot get fresh corn, use frozen cut corn. If you do not have homemade stock handy, canned chicken broth with the fat skimmed off will do fine.

2 cups fresh raw corn kernels (about 4 ears of corn)	1 teaspoon sugar
	1 teaspoon salt
	Freshly ground black pepper
1/4 cup butter	2 cups chicken stock
1/4 cup minced onion	2 cups light cream
1 tablespoon lemon juice	Tabasco sauce
1/2 teaspoon dry mustard	

Sauté onion in butter until translucent but not browned. Stir in lemon juice, mustard, sugar, salt and pepper. Add corn and chicken stock. Bring to a boil, cover, reduce heat and simmer for 10 minutes. Just before serving add cream and a dash of Tabasco, mix well and bring to serving temperature over low heat. Do not let chowder boil after the cream is added.

FONDUE BOURGUIGNONNE

4 pounds beef tenderloin   Vegetable oil

Cut beef into three-quarter-inch cubes. Half fill the fondue pot with oil (this will take about a quart but depends on the size of your pot) and heat on the stove until the oil bubbles. Carefully, transfer the pot to the alcohol burner and serve each guest several cubes of meat. Each guest spears a cube with his fondue fork and plunges it into the bubbling oil. How long to leave the meat in the pot will depend on how well done you like it. It will be browned through in about a minute, but it would be a shame not to eat meat of this quality rare, and rare meat lovers will only want to cook their cubes half that time at most. Be sure to warn your guests to transfer the meat to a dinner fork, the fondue fork will be very hot.

Each guest should help himself to a generous dab of each sauce. The meat is then dipped into the sauces, giving each bite a distinctive flavor. You can vary or omit any of the sauces except béarnaise; it is a must. The six sauces given here are an excellent combination and not an outrageous amount of work, since most of them make use of prepared ingredients. Each recipe makes about two cups of sauce.

BÉARNAISE SAUCE

¼ cup dry white wine	Freshly ground black pepper
¼ cup wine vinegar	3 egg yolks
1 tablespoon minced shallots or onions	1 cup butter, melted
1 teaspoon tarragon	1 tablespoon fresh minced tarragon or parsley
1 teaspoon chervil	

Combine wine, vinegar, shallots, dried herbs and pepper in a small saucepan. Cook over low heat until the liquid has reduced to about half. Strain and cool. Now put the egg yolks into the double boiler. Beat until frothy. Beat in vinegar mixture. Place pan over hot but not boiling water, and do not let water touch top pan. Add the butter slowly, about a teaspoonful at a time, beating constantly. Add additional pepper and a pinch of salt if desired. Stir in the fresh tarragon if you have been able to get it, or parsley before serving.

TOMATO AND CAPER SAUCE

2 6-ounce cans tomato paste	Worcestershire sauce
1 cup beef broth	1 teaspoon salt
1 teaspoon caper juice	Freshly ground black pepper
1 tablespoon	Dash of cayenne pepper
	2 tablespoons capers

Combine all ingredients except the capers in a saucepan. Bring to a boil over moderate heat stirring constantly. Reduce heat and simmer for 10 minutes. Stir in capers. Serve hot or cold.

MUSTARD SAUCE

1½ cups prepared mustard	1 teaspoon salt
½ cup dry white wine	2 tablespoons flour
2 tablespoons sugar	¼ cup water

Combine mustard, wine, sugar and salt in a saucepan. Bring to a boil over moderate heat, stirring constantly. Mix flour in water and stir into mustard mixture. Reduce heat and simmer for 10 minutes or until thickened, stirring constantly. Serve hot or cold.

HERB SAUCE

2 egg yolks	1½ cups salad oil
2 tablespoons lemon juice	½ cup chopped chives
1 teaspoon salt	½ cup chopped fresh parsley
Freshly ground black pepper	1 tablespoon grated onion

Beat egg yolks until frothy. Beat in lemon juice, salt and pepper. Beat in the oil, about a teaspoonful at a time, until about one half cup has been added. Then add the rest of the oil more quickly, about a tablespoonful at a time, beating until the mayonnaise is thick. You may not need all of the oil. Stir in chives, parsley and onion. Chill until ready to serve.

HORSERADISH SAUCE

¼ cup prepared horseradish	Dash of Tabasco sauce
1 pint sour cream	1 teaspoon salt
2 tablespoons lemon juice	

Combine all ingredients stirring until thoroughly mixed. Chill until ready to serve.

BARBECUE SAUCE

2 cups tomato catsup	1 tablespoon brown sugar
2 tablespoons wine vinegar	Dash of Tabasco sauce
2 tablespoons soy sauce	

Combine ingredients in a saucepan. Bring to a boil over moderate heat, stirring constantly. Reduce heat and simmer for 10 minutes. Serve hot or cold.

FROSTED PINEAPPLE

This native American fruit, which Columbus discovered here on his second trip, came to be so beloved in the South that it was carved over the door and on furniture as a symbol of hospitality. Picking a perfect one must be done carefully. The inner leaves should pull off easily and the whole fruit should smell as delicious as it tastes.

1 large ripe pineapple	Confectioners' sugar

Cut the pineapple into six lengthwise wedges, cutting down through the top and leaving the top leaves intact. Slice the core off the top of each wedge. Carefully cut the fruit itself away from the rind. Then slice downward to cut the wedge of fruit into bite-size sections. When you're done you'll have a wedge-like "boat" of rind holding thin slices of fruit. Place each finished wedge on a dessert plate and sprinkle it liberally with sugar. Chill at least one hour or until the sugar looks frosty.

Trout Amandine

Just as a fisherman's heart beats faster at the sight of a trout splashing in a mountain stream, a food lover happily anticipates a well-cooked trout—which in this photographic fantasy is leaping

from a pool of lightly browned almonds. The flavor of trout is so delicate that as a rule the less fancy you are in cooking it the better the fish will be. Most trout that you will find in the market are rainbow trout—which swim in both brooks and lakes. The dish shown here is classic trout amandine, which calls for sautéing the fish in butter and garnishing it with sautéed almonds. The almonds add a touch of sweetness—but do not dominate. The trout, in season in spring throughout most of the U.S., is part of a menu *(next page)* full of things that are never better than they are right now.

Springtime eating is so good that it is a pity to have to cram it into a few weeks. This menu makes the most of spring's offerings and will be a special treat to everyone who feels that at this time of year a dinner of anything except the freshest things that come out of the ground —or streams—is a dinner wasted. The only item on this bill of fare which could just as easily be served any time of year is the Quiche Lorraine, a cheese custard pie.

The cooking of this dinner forces you to choose between convenience and perfection—between spending time with your guests or sticking to your job in the kitchen. But the extra half hour you spend in the kitchen will earn you compliments all evening.

This dinner also has some special requirements: two big skillets, a short-sleeved dress, a butcher's apron. And, if you have managed it absolutely right, a husband who is an expert fisherman.

You must schedule your time so that you can do quite a few chores on the day of the dinner. To take advantage of the tastiest fresh foods available, you should not shop ahead. Unless you are using frozen trout, which of course you can buy early, or have had your husband catch them for you, buy the fish the morning of the dinner. A truly fresh fish can be recognized by bulging eyes, bright scales and firm flesh. Its smell should not have the slightest trace of unpleasantness. The best asparagus has straight green stalks, compact tips. It should never be limp. If you buy loose asparagus rather than bunches you will be able to examine each spear and buy them of uniform size. Fat spears are generally considered more choice, but the thin ones are every bit as flavorful. Look for crisp, tender rhubarb. The strawberries should also be bought on dinner day. If local berries are available choose them

---

MENU FOR SIX

QUICHE LORRAINE

TROUT AMANDINE

New potatoes in their jackets
Asparagus hollandaise
Dry white wine

RHUBARB RING WITH STRAWBERRIES

—they are apt to have more taste than berries which have been picked green and shipped.

You must face up to the fact that most of the cooking for the main course has to be short order. But there are things you can do to relieve the last-minute flurry. On the day before, you can make the pie crust for the quiche and refrigerate it. On the morning of the dinner chill the wine, wash the asparagus, scrub the potatoes, rinse the strawberries and put them in the refrigerator in a colander with a dish under it to drain completely. Make the rhubarb ring. This won't take you more than half an hour. The quiche can be served either piping hot or lukewarm. Fry the bacon ahead of time, assemble the remaining ingredients, and put it in the oven 45 minutes before you plan to sit down. At this time you also make the hollandaise and unmold the rhubarb. Be sure early in the day that you have the pots and pans you are going to need: a good-sized skillet for the trout (if you have two of them you can cook all the trout at once); still another skillet or an electric frying pan for the asparagus; a saucepan for the potatoes; a double boiler for the hollandaise sauce. You are also going to need an all-enveloping apron which will cover as much of you as possible while you do the last-minute cooking.

You are going to have to devote either part of the cocktail hour or part of the first course to sautéing the trout. You have to choose between convenience and haute cuisine. You can duck out during cocktails, cook the trout and keep it warm in a very low oven while you eat the quiche. But the trout will inevitably taste better if you cook it just before serving.

Put the potatoes and the asparagus on 15 minutes before deadline. Brown the almonds at the last minute.

RECIPES

QUICHE LORRAINE

This custard pie, smooth in texture and tangy in flavor, originated in the French province of Lorraine. Ham can be substituted for the bacon, onions can be added and Gruyère, which has a stronger flavor, can be used instead of or in combination with Swiss cheese. Whichever way you make it, the pie will probably taste better in homemade crust, but if you have doubts about your skill as a baker, use a prepared mix or a frozen unbaked shell.

6 slices bacon	¼ teaspoon nutmeg
6 thin slices Swiss cheese, about 2 by 3 inches	½ teaspoon salt
4 eggs	Freshly ground black pepper
2 cups light cream	Few grains cayenne pepper
1 tablespoon flour	1 unbaked 9-inch pie shell

Preheat oven to 400°. Fry bacon until crisp. Drain well and crumble it. Sprinkle into pie shell. Arrange cheese slices over the bacon. Combine eggs, cream, flour, nutmeg, salt, pepper and cayenne in a mixing bowl and beat briskly with wire whisk or rotary beater for at least one minute. Pour into pie shell. Bake on the lowest rack of the oven for 15 minutes. Reduce heat to 325° and bake about 30 minutes longer, or until a knife gently inserted into the center of the custard comes out clean. The pie will be slightly puffed and a pretty golden brown. Serve cut in wedges like any pie.

TROUT AMANDINE

The main—in fact the only—trick about cooking this dish is not to cook it too much. The fish will dry out if it is cooked more than about five minutes on each side. Don't try to scale trout—the scales are so delicate it is not necessary. Leave the head and tail on. They keep the fish from breaking.

If you are lucky enough to have a husband who catches these for you, suggest that he clean the fish as soon as it's taken from the water—this keeps the flavor fresh —and you won't have to do it yourself.

6 fresh or thawed frozen trout	1 cup butter
¼ cup flour	1 cup sliced blanched almonds
1 teaspoon salt	1 tablespoon lemon juice
Freshly ground black pepper	Lemon wedges

Combine flour, salt and pepper and roll cleaned trout in this seasoned flour until they are thoroughly coated. You can sauté three trout at a time in a 12-inch skillet. Use one-quarter cup butter for each batch you cook. Sauté trout over medium heat for about five minutes on each side. Carefully remove the cooked fish to a heated platter and cover to keep them warm. When all the fish are cooked, discard browned butter and wipe out skillet. Then add the remaining one-half cup butter and the almonds to the skillet. Cook over lowest possible heat, stirring frequently, until the almonds become a pale golden color. Be careful to do this over low heat or else the butter will brown too quickly and smoke. Remove from heat and stir in lemon juice. Pour almonds with the butter over cooked trout. Serve immediately with lemon wedges.

NEW POTATOES IN THEIR JACKETS

3 pounds small new
   potatoes

Scrub potatoes well. Put into saucepan with barely enough boiling salted water to cover. Cover and cook for 15-20 minutes or until just tender. Drain thoroughly. Return, covered, to low heat for two or three minutes to dry potatoes thoroughly, shaking the pan gently to avoid scorching them. If this last step makes you feel that you need at least four arms, in view of the other last minute activities going on, just skip it this time but remember it for more leisurely cooking.

ASPARAGUS

3 pounds fresh asparagus

Break off tough ends of asparagus by bending the stalks. They will snap at the point where they become tender. Wash asparagus well with cold water. Remove large scales from lower part of stalks. Place the cleaned asparagus in a large skillet with enough boiling salted water to barely cover stalks. Cover and cook rapidly about 15 minutes or until lower part of the stalk is just tender when pierced with a fork. Drain and serve immediately. Do not allow asparagus to sit in the cooking water, as this tends to overcook it, and it will lose its color and crispness.

HOLLANDAISE SAUCE

This is one of the great sauces—with an equally great reputation for being temperamental. It need not be, provided you keep two general principles firmly in mind when making it by the classic double-boiler method. The first is that hollandaise is meant to be warm, not hot. Trying to get it hot can only lead to trouble. The second is to add the butter slowly enough. The trick is to get the egg yolks to incorporate as much butter as possible without curdling. Even if the worst happens there are remedies. If the sauce is too thick, whip in a tablespoon or two of hot water. If, on the other hand, it won't thicken at all, transfer a tablespoon of it to a mixing bowl and whip with a teaspoon of lemon juice until it becomes creamy. Keep adding sauce and whipping until each addition is smooth. If the sauce curdles while waiting, whip in a tablespoon of cold water. The job will take about 10 minutes. And you can do it up to an hour before dinner.

4 egg yolks	1 cup butter, melted
½ teaspoon salt	2 tablespoons lemon juice
Few grains cayenne pepper	⅓ cup boiling water

Combine egg yolks, salt and cayenne in the top of a double boiler over hot, but not boiling, water. Be sure the water does not touch the top pan. Put the double boiler over moderate heat and beat egg yolk mixture with a wire whisk until it is fluffy. Add the melted butter very slowly, about one teaspoon at a time, beating constantly. Slowly add boiling water and lemon juice, still beating, and continue to beat until the sauce thickens. Be sure the water in the bottom of the boiler does not boil.

RHUBARB RING WITH STRAWBERRIES

1½ pounds fresh rhubarb	¼ cup orange juice
1 cup sugar	1 tablespoon lemon juice
1¼ cups water	2 cups washed, hulled strawberries
2 envelopes unflavored gelatin	Sifted confectioners' sugar

Wash rhubarb; cut off root and leaf ends, being sure to discard all the leaves, as they are inedible. Do not peel the rhubarb stalks. Cut into one-inch pieces and combine in saucepan with sugar and three-quarters cup of the water. Bring to a boil and simmer for five to 10 minutes or until rhubarb is tender, stirring gently once or twice. Sprinkle gelatin over remaining one-half cup of water, then stir into the hot rhubarb to dissolve gelatin. Add orange and lemon juices and pour into five-cup, eight-inch ring mold. Let cool to room temperature. Chill several hours or until firm. Unmold onto chilled serving plate by running a knife around the edges and then dipping the ring for a second into hot water. Arrange berries in center of the ring and sprinkle them with confectioners' sugar.

Coq au Vin

Coq au vin, a perennial on the menu of French restaurants, is a classic dish that is all too often turned out in less than classic style. A proper *coq au vin*, which is the only kind worth cooking, requires a

little something extra in work, attention and ingredients—as is described on the following pages.

Originally the dish called for a cock or hen that simmered for hours in red wine, slowly taking on a rich and pungent flavor. Today chickens are tender young things that need far less cooking, but, as a consequence, need more flavoring help in this dish. A dollop of brandy, flamed as it is added to the pot, adds body to the stew. A lot of wine is used and it must be a good, full-bodied dry red. Don't economize here—a wine not good enough to drink is not good enough to eat.

This menu will convince you that spring is really here. Although *coq au vin* can be prepared in any season, most of the other ingredients in the dinner are early spring arrivals—delicious in themselves and harbingers of the magnificent warm-weather fruits and vegetables that are still to come.

You will need to lavish attention only on the *coq au vin*. Everything else on the menu can be pretty easily tossed off. To make matters even simpler, most of the dinner can be prepared well ahead of time, with only a little reheating to do after your guests have arrived.

Make the soup the day ahead. You may either cook

MENU FOR SIX

VEGETABLE SOUP

COQ AU VIN

Rice
Braised endive
Red wine

DEEP-DISH RHUBARB PIE

the *coq au vin* completely the day before or just get the tedious browning of the fowl and vegetables out of the way. Make the pie pastry. On the morning of the dinner put together the pie, blanch the endive and whip the cream. If you are going to make the *coq au vin* just in time for dinner, allow about two hours. Uncork the wine then too. An hour before dinner put the pie in the oven; let it stand on the back of the range after it has baked to keep warm. Before dinner heat the soup, sauté the endive and put the rice in boiling water. By the time you have eaten the first course the rice and endive should be ready to serve.

RECIPES

VEGETABLE SOUP

This contains a galaxy of vegetables and if the recipe includes one of your pet hates you are free to make a few substitutions. But certain ones are essential—carrots, onions, celery, tomatoes, at least one green vegetable, and turnip. The turnip, a much maligned vegetable, here adds body and a peppery flavor. If you are adding new vegetables remember that anything in the cabbage family is apt to take over and dominate the whole dish. You can use frozen vegetables if you want to spare yourself shelling time. Be choosy about the size of the fresh vegetables. Select small-size, firm ones. Then you can cut quite thick slices that will hold together during the cooking. Large vegetables will be unattractive if cut thick, and thin slices tend to fall apart. The quantity given in this recipe will make more soup than any six people could eat, but once you've done all this peeling and slicing you will certainly welcome leftovers. If you plan to keep the soup more than a week, boil it up every couple of days, or freeze it.

4 quarts beef stock (recipe below)	1 cup shelled lima beans
Salt and pepper	1 cup shelled peas
18 whole baby carrots, or one bunch carrots cut in two-inch lengths	1 cup zucchini, sliced but not peeled
3 medium onions, sliced	1 cup white turnip, peeled and cubed
2 leeks, sliced	4 tomatoes, peeled and sliced
1 cup sliced celery	1 clove garlic, crushed
1 cup cut green beans	1/2 cup chopped fresh parsley
1 cup green and red pepper, cut in strips	1 teaspoon basil
1 cup cut corn	1 teaspoon oregano

Measure the stock into a large pot—it should hold at least 10 quarts. If it has two handles it will be much easier to lift. Season to taste with salt and pepper—how much you

want depends on the basic stock flavoring. Canned stock is apt to be saltier than homemade. If you are using canned beef consommé or bouillon, dilute six 10½-ounce cans with an equal amount of water. If you have homemade stock on hand, but not enough of it, supplement it with diluted canned consommé. Add all the vegetables and herbs to the kettle. Stir very gently to mix. Bring to the boiling point, cover and reduce heat. Simmer without stirring—which may break up the more fragile vegetables—for one hour or until the largest pieces, especially the carrots, are tender and cooked through. Taste, add more salt and pepper if necessary.

BEEF STOCK

4 pounds shin and marrow bones, cracked	1 package fresh soup greens
2 large onions, quartered	1 bay leaf
3 pounds chuck, in one piece	2 tablespoons salt
6 quarts of water	15 peppercorns, cracked

Brown the bones and onions in a 450° oven for 45 minutes. This is the key to a good dark, flavorful stock. Transfer these to a large pot, adding the meat and the other ingredients, and bring to a boil. Skim off scum as it rises. When it stops rising, turn down the heat, cover the pot and simmer for two hours.

Remove the beef chunk for future use, strain the stock and let it cool for half an hour. Refrigerate for two hours, then take off the fat that has accumulated on top.

COQ AU VIN

The extra steps that make this version so good include browning the chicken and vegetables, adding brandy (flamed as it is put into the stew) and, most crucial of all, removing the finished chicken and vegetables from the sauce, and reducing the sauce to about half its former quantity by a quick boil. This last intensifies the flavor of the sauce immeasurably. *Beurre manié* is added to make the sauce a little richer and thicken it slightly.

3 chicken breasts, halved	1/4 cup brandy
6 chicken legs	2 cups dry red wine
Salt and pepper	2 cups chicken broth
24 medium mushrooms	1/2 teaspoon thyme leaves
24 tiny white onions	1 bay leaf
1/4 cup butter	1 tablespoon fresh parsley
1/4 pound thick-sliced bacon	1 tablespoon butter
1 teaspoon sugar	1 tablespoon flour
1 clove garlic, minced	

Dry the chicken pieces thoroughly and sprinkle them with salt and pepper. Wipe off the mushrooms and remove the stems. Peel the onions—to do this effortlessly, drop them into a pot of boiling water. Count to 10 slowly (count higher for bigger onions), then drain the onions and run under cold water. The skin will slip off between your fingers. Cut bacon into half-inch pieces and cook in butter in a large Dutch oven or casserole until lightly browned. Remove bacon and drain. Pour half of the accumulated fat into a second large pan or skillet so you can use two pans for browning the chicken. Add the chicken to fat, skin side down, without crowding. Cook it over medium heat until lightly browned on both sides. As pieces brown, remove them and add more. When all are browned, set aside. From now on you will work only with the heavy casserole. Put the onions into it, add sugar and cook, stirring until onions are lightly browned. Then brown mushrooms and garlic. Put the chicken back in the pot and pour most of the brandy in over it. Retain about one tablespoonful and put it into a ladle. Light the brandy in the ladle and pour it, flaming, into the casserole to ignite the rest. When you do this, stand back, as the whole casserole will flame up instantly. When the flame dies, add the wine, broth and herbs. Cover pan and simmer for 30 minutes or until the chicken is tender. Remove chicken, bacon, mushrooms and onions. Bring stock left in pan to a boil, skimming off fat. Boil stock rapidly for about five minutes or until liquid is reduced to about two cups. Mix one tablespoon butter and flour together and stir this *beurre manié* into the sauce. Cook until the sauce thickens. Strain and pour over chicken. If you are making the *coq au vin* ahead, strain the sauce into a separate container and store it in the refrigerator. To reheat, place covered chicken in 325° oven for about 30 minutes. Arrange on platter. Meanwhile, reheat sauce separately and pour over chicken. Serve with rice that has been fluffed up with butter and parsley.

BRAISED ENDIVE

There is considerable confusion about the name endive in the U.S. This recipe calls for Belgian or French endive —a whitish stalk that is a special type of chicory plant grown in the dark. Another form of chicory, sometimes also called endive, is a curly salad green.

6 medium-size endive	1/8 teaspoon white pepper
1/4 cup butter	1 tablespoon lemon juice
1 teaspoon salt	2 tablespoons water

Wash endive and trim base of each stalk. Cut in half lengthwise. Put one inch of water in a 10- or 12-inch skillet; bring to a boil. Add endive, cover and simmer for 10 minutes. Remove endive and pour off water. Wipe pan dry. Melt butter in the same skillet. Add endive, cut side down, and sauté until lightly browned, about two minutes. Sprinkle with salt, pepper, lemon juice and water. Cover the pan and cook over very low heat for about 15 minutes or until the endive is tender, adding a little extra water if needed.

DEEP DISH RHUBARB PIE

This delightful dessert could never be confused with store-bought pastry. This crust is very short, which means handling it with care, but it is especially good with the rhubarb. Serve the steaming pie with a large spoon, and have at your elbow a large bowl of whipped cream. Top each serving with a generous amount.

2 pounds rhubarb	Cream cheese pastry (recipe
1/2 cup flour	below)
1 cup sugar	1 pint heavy cream,
1/2 cup light corn syrup	whipped and sweetened
1 tablespoon butter	

Prepare cream cheese pastry and chill. Preheat oven to 425°. Wash rhubarb. Trim ends and cut into one-inch pieces. There should be about six cups. Toss the rhubarb with flour and turn into an 8x2-inch round cake pan or an 8x8x2-inch square pan. Sprinkle any leftover flour over rhubarb. Mix sugar and corn syrup, bring to a boil over medium heat, stirring constantly. Pour over rhubarb and dot with butter. Roll out pastry between two pieces of wax paper to a size one inch larger than baking pan. Remove top piece of wax paper. Cut several small gashes in center of pastry to let steam escape. Place pastry over rhubarb with wax-paper side up. Remove wax paper. Fold edge under and flute double-thickness pastry against the inside edge of pan. Bake in a 425° F. (hot) oven 25 minutes. Remove from oven and let cool slightly before serving. Spoon into bowls and serve with whipped cream.

CREAM CHEESE PASTRY

1 three-ounce package	softened
cream cheese, softened	3/4 cup sifted flour
6 tablespoons butter,	1/2 teaspoon salt

Mix cream cheese and butter until fluffy. Add flour and mix with a fork until well blended. Form into a ball with hands. Wrap in wax paper and chill before rolling.

Fettuccine all' Alfredo

Pasta is as noble an Italian institution as grand opera. There are as many noodle shapes and sauces with their claques of supporters as there are tenors. The pasta repast shown at right is fettuccine all' Alfredo, one of the most delicious and subtly flavored as well as one of the simplest to make. Fettuccine, a flat ribbon-like noodle, can be either green or white. The rich sauce consists of butter, cream and freshly grated Parmesan cheese. They are added to the cooked noodles at the table, and the tossing that accompanies the cooking makes the dish an entertainment to watch as well as an enjoyment to eat. At dinner in Italy fettuccine is usually served as a small but separate pasta course preceding the meat or fish. But most American appetites will be satisfied with a good-sized portion for the main course, as given in the menu on the following pages.

Chances are that, on the full menu for this fettuccine dinner, there is at least one dish you've never eaten before—or your guests either. The appetizer is a raw seafood mixture which comes from South America but which you might suspect was Oriental. The pasta is a rich Italian delicacy. And the dessert is a creamy concoction that presumably traces its origin to Bavaria.

The *seviche* of shrimp and scallops is a substantial first course. In fact it is so filling that you should not offer second helpings if you want your guests to appreciate the rest of the menu. The fettuccine is a delicately flavored main course, complemented by a tart salad and Italian bread. The dessert is admittedly rich. A dry white wine goes with the entire meal and should be opened with the *seviche*. Although this is not an occasion to count the calories, the meal is not as rich as it at first seems because all the food is

MENU FOR SIX

SHRIMP AND SCALLOP SEVICHE

FETTUCCINE ALL' ALFREDO

Escarole and chicory salad, vinaigrette dressing
Italian bread
Dry white wine

MOCHA BAVARIAN CREAM

light. And this makes it especially suitable for a warm spring night.

The shrimp may be boiled a day early. But marinating them and the scallops and putting them in the sauce must be done the day of the dinner. The dessert can also be made the day ahead.

On the day of the dinner, wash the salad greens, wrap them in a towel and refrigerate them. Make the vinaigrette dressing. In setting the table make sure that you allow plenty of elbow room for fettucine-tossing. If you are the kind that tosses pasta with abandon, protect your table linen by setting the chafing dish on a large tray. Just before the guests arrive set eight quarts of water on to boil in your largest pot, or pots if one is not big enough. It may take a good half hour for the water to come to a rolling boil. When you sit down to eat the *seviche* put the pasta in the boiling water to cook.

RECIPES

SHRIMP AND SCALLOP SEVICHE

This is the South American method of "cooking" fish by pickling, similar to the method of pickling raw herring in vinegar. Almost any white fish or shellfish can be prepared in this manner. This recipe calls for shrimp, our most popular shellfish, combined with scallops, a delicacy that can be eaten raw like clams or oysters—but rarely is in the U.S. The shrimp should be boiled quickly—not more than three or four minutes—and only for color and texture. If you are upset at the idea of eating fish raw, don't be put off. The *seviche* does not taste or even feel raw at all. If you are afraid that the notion would bother your guests, say nothing and they will never know.

There are two kinds of scallops, bay scallops and sea scallops. Bay scallops, which come from inshore waters, are smaller, sweeter, harder to find and much more expensive. Sea scallops, which are dredged from deeper waters, are larger, less delicate and a good deal less expensive. By all means use them if bay scallops are unavailable or too steep for your budget.

2 pounds shrimp, cooked and peeled	2 tablespoons finely chopped green pepper
1 pound raw scallops, thinly sliced	½ cup olive oil
1 cup fresh lime juice (about 6 limes)	½ teaspoon oregano
	Dash of Tabasco
	1 teaspoon salt
6 tablespoons finely chopped red onion	Freshly ground black pepper
4 tablespoons chopped fresh parsley	2 avocados, peeled and and sliced

Cut the shrimp into thirds and mix with the sliced scallops in a bowl. Add lime juice to marinate the mixture. Do this three or four hours before dinner. Cover, let stand at room temperature for one hour, stirring once or twice (marinating should always be done at room temperature for the most flavor). Drain and discard the juice. Add all remaining ingredients, except the avocados, to seafood and toss lightly. Chill for an hour. Arrange on plates with avocado slices. If you have them, scallop shells make a particularly attractive plate for this appetizer.

FETTUCCINE ALL' ALFREDO

Two Roman restaurants, both named Alfredo, regard this dish as their claim to fame. Neither of them serves it exactly the same way and neither serves this precise version. But the combination of fettuccine, butter and Parmesan cheese has come to be known as fettuccine all'Alfredo all over the world.

Fettuccine is a flat egg noodle about a quarter-inch wide. It is called fettuccine in Rome and southern Italy. In the north, it is called *tagliatelle*. It is available as a white noodle or one that has been made green by the addition of spinach. The green noodle is slightly heavier, and not as traditional, but it is much more festive looking. Any flat ribbonlike egg noodle will do if you cannot locate the genuine Italian article. And, if you are a perfectionist with time on your hands, you can make your own. It is a fair amount of work, but the flavor is fresher.

All good Italian cooks have their own answer to how long pasta should be cooked. Most connoisseurs have come to believe passionately in cooking "al dente"—a phrase that raises as many questions as it answers. It literally means "to the tooth," or just to the point at which it can be bitten easily. Getting it to this point of perfection takes about 10 minutes (it varies of course with the shape and thickness of the pasta) and can generally be successfully tested with a fork. But there are other methods. Some Italian cooks supposedly consider this test infallible: take a few lengths of pasta from the pot and hurl them hard at the wall over the sink. If they stick, it's done. A 16th Century gourmet, Cristoforo de Messisburgo, advised that pasta be cooked "just long enough to say a short prayer."

There is no argument at all about the cheese. You must use Parmesan, which comes from the hills around Parma. It is one of the hardest of all cheeses, and has its own distinctive sharpness. It is at its best when freshly grated, so buy it by the piece if you can. (You can safely buy quite a lot. It keeps well indefinitely. In fact, aging enhances it and usually makes it more expensive.) It is not very hard work to grate the cheese, but if you want to save time, you can grate it in the electric blender. Another solution is to bring hunks of the cheese to the table and grate it into the fettuccine with a mill-type grater.

The final cooking of the fettuccine is done at the table. The whole trick of cooking in the public eye is offhandedness. You can feel perfectly confident. Nothing can go far wrong with this dish since you are dealing with very few ingredients and there is no trick at all to combining them. Before you start, be sure you have everything you need at hand—butter, cream, cheese, in attractive containers, a big spoon and a fork to toss with, a grater if you plan to use one, and a pepper mill.

The amount given here is enough for six average servings and it is all you can comfortably handle at one time. If you think that you are going to want second helpings, have another pot of water boiling, and midway through the first serving put more fettuccine on to cook. You will have to start from scratch on the sauce, but by now you will have realized how little time it takes to produce and the very fact there was the demand for an encore should give you all the confidence you need.

1 pound fettuccine noodles	1 cup heavy cream
(recipe below)	Freshly ground black pepper
Boiling salted water	1/4 pound Parmesan cheese,
1/2 cup soft butter	grated

Cook noodles in a large pot of boiling salted water—use two tablespoons of salt—for about 8 to 10 minutes, or until they are just tender when tested with a fork. Drain them well and put them immediately into a chafing dish. If you have an electric frying pan, you can use that. There will be about eight cups of slippery, evasive noodles so it is important that the dish be large enough not only to hold them but to permit tossing without accident.

Up to this point the fettuccine has been cooked in the kitchen. Now you proceed to the dining room. Put fet-

tuccine over low heat from an alcohol burner or Sterno, or set the electric skillet as low as it can go. Add butter in several hunks to the noodles and stir gently until it melts and coats them well. Add the cream and grind in a generous amount of black pepper. Continue stirring and tossing the noodles gently until the cream thickens and clings to the noodles. Add the cheese and stir to mix well. Serve immediately.

FETTUCCINE GREEN NOODLES

3 cups sifted flour	1/2 cup spinach purée baby
1 teaspoon salt	food
2 eggs	

Place two cups of the flour in a bowl. Sprinkle in salt. Combine eggs and spinach purée in another bowl and mix well. Add all at once to the flour, mixing with a fork and then with the hands until flour is incorporated. Place remaining one cup of flour on a board and turn the dough out of the bowl onto this flour. Knead dough until all the flour on the board has been kneaded in. Form into two balls and wrap in waxed paper. Let stand for at least one hour at room temperature. Now on a very lightly floured board roll out one ball of dough into a rectangle about 14 by 16 inches. This will take a few minutes to do as the dough is quite firm. Roll up tightly as you would a jelly roll, starting from the 14-inch side. Cut rolls into slices about one-quarter-inch wide. Repeat with other ball of dough. Unroll slices and place strips on towels to dry for several hours. Makes about one pound. For white noodles, add two more eggs and omit the spinach purée.

MOCHA BAVARIAN CREAM
This dessert is unashamedly rich and gooey, but it is truly worth every calorie.

4 egg yolks	2 squares unsweetened
2 cups light cream	chocolate
1 envelope unflavored	1 tablespoon instant coffee
gelatin	1/4 cup brandy
1/2 cup sugar	1 cup heavy cream,
1/4 teaspoon salt	whipped

Beat egg yolks and light cream until well mixed. Stir gelatin, sugar and salt together in the top of a double boiler. Stir in the yolk and cream mixture. Put the pan over boiling water and stir in the chocolate and coffee. Cook, stirring constantly, until the chocolate is melted and the coffee dissolved. Don't worry about the chocolate flecks. Remove top of double boiler from stove and add the brandy. Beat with a rotary beater until the chocolate is well blended. Chill, stirring occasionally, until the mixture begins to thicken and is about the consistency of cream sauce. (Allow at least an hour for this process.) Fold in the whipped cream. Ladle the mousse into a serving bowl or six individual dessert dishes. Chill for another two hours or until firm.

Straw-
berry
Shortcake

Strawberry shortcake is more American than apple pie and twice as good. Its superiority is no more arguable than its native heritage; New England Indians made an early version of it with wild berries and cornmeal. A proper shortcake today is guaranteed to bring out the greedy schoolboy in anyone—all restraint melting before the rosy tower of berries resting on a buttery biscuit under billows of whipped cream.

This king of deserts has produced some pretenders, like the spongecake version and the one made with ice cream. The only shortcake that's worth the trouble and the calories must have a biscuit base that will stay flaky under the cream and juice. The cream must be freshly whipped and the strawberries so ripe that they deserve the praise given by Izaak Walton who, with his mind off fish for once, cited an authority on the strawberry: "Doubtless God could have made a better berry, but doubtless God never did."

With strawberry shortcake as dessert, you have to plan the meal backward, making sure that it will leave the guests both willing and able to take on all that rich biscuit, berry and cream. This menu does just that with its tart cold soup, delicate veal and rice, and crisp salad.

The meal is a Technicolor spectacular—bright red soup, vivid yellow rice and sumptuous strawberry dessert. But everything is simple and quick to make.

In shopping for the dinner, show special care in choosing berries. They should be firm, shiny red and not necessarily jumbo size. Usually the flavor is better in smaller berries, but this depends on variety—ask your vegetable man. Make sure they have green hulls; this means they were properly picked. And watch out for a stained box; it betrays damage or over-age. If you don't see leaf lettuce at the market, ask a gardener guest if he can bring some along. Otherwise, use Boston or Bibb.

The cooking can be done on the day of the party. In the morning make the gazpacho and chop up the vegetable garnishes. Cover and refrigerate them. Sauté the croutons and set them aside. Better cover them or you

MENU FOR SIX

GAZPACHO WITH GARLIC CROUTONS

VEAL PICCATA
Risotto alla Milanese
Loose leaf lettuce and chive salad
with vinaigrette dressing
White wine

STRAWBERRY SHORTCAKE

will keep nibbling at them. Pound the veal flat, if the butcher didn't do it. Grate the cheese. Prepare the salad greens.

Strawberries should be cleaned and sweetened at least three hours before dinner. The longer they sit, the juicier they will be. Some strawberry addicts like them well chilled, but they have more flavor if they are served at room temperature. Make the biscuits late in the afternoon, and cool them on a rack. Put them back on the baking sheet and wrap snugly in foil. Pour the cream into a bowl and chill it along with the beater. It will speed the whipping. Remember to chill the wine.

Half an hour before dinner, start the veal. When it is done, put it back in the skillet it was cooked in, and cover it. Start the risotto cooking before you serve the gazpacho. After you have eaten the soup course, toss the salad. Add lemon and parsley to the veal and heat it, and whisk cheese and butter into the risotto. Set the oven to 300° and pop in the biscuits in their foil. (They will be nicely warm by the time you are ready for them.) After the main course, whip the cream and assemble the shortcake.

RECIPES

GAZPACHO

An old Spanish dish with a hundred variations, gazpacho is a cold soup that seems a little like a salad because it is made of fresh vegetables and flavored with oil and vinegar. If you want to make it the traditional way, rub tomatoes to a pulp by hand; it takes a big bowl, a huge pestle and a lot of energy. But today's blender is better. Or use a food grinder and be certain to save all the juices. Notice that in this recipe some of the vegetables are cut in chunks; some are finely chopped. Be sure to buy enough of all of them.

3 pounds tomatoes, peeled and cut up (6 cups)	1/4 cup white wine vinegar
1 onion, cut in chunks	1 cup peeled, chopped tomatoes
1/2 cup green pepper chunks	1/2 cup finely chopped onion
1/2 cup cucumber chunks	1/2 cup finely chopped green pepper
2 cups tomato juice	
1 clove garlic, minced	1/2 cup finely chopped cucumber
1/2 teaspoon ground cumin	
1 tablespoon salt	Garlic croutons (recipe below)
Freshly ground black pepper	
1/4 cup olive oil	

Combine tomato, onion, green pepper and cucumber chunks. Purée them in a blender or food mill until smooth.

Then transfer the mixture to a large bowl or tureen and stir until well mixed and smooth. Add tomato juice, garlic, cumin, salt and pepper. Cover and chill. Before serving, stir in the oil and vinegar. Pass the finely chopped vegetable garnishes and garlic croutons separately so that each guest can add some of each to his soup bowl.

GARLIC CROUTONS

6 slices white bread	2 cloves garlic, minced
1/2 cup clarified butter	

Croutons made of dry bread keep their shape best, so spread the slices out to dry or toast them lightly. Remove crusts and cut the bread into one-half-inch squares. Clarify the butter by melting it in a saucepan, then separating the clear butter from the milky residue. Discard the residue. Transfer the clarified butter to a skillet, and put it over medium heat. Stir in garlic. Add the cubes of bread and sauté, stirring, until crisp and golden. Drain on a paper towel.

VEAL PICCATA

The secret of this dish is to sauté the scallops gently. Overdoing may dry them out and make them tough. When shopping, look for veal that is pale pink and fine textured.

Names for the cut vary in different markets: cutlets, *scaloppine*, collops, and even schnitzels.

If your butcher hasn't time to pound the scallops, you can do the job yourself with a kitchen mallet or the flat side of a cleaver. Some cooks suggest the edge of a heavy plate, but it takes courage to whack hard with a piece of china. Put a few scallops at a time between two sheets of waxed paper and pound them about one-eight inch thick.

3 pounds veal scallops, pounded thin	1/2 cup chopped fresh parsley
2/3 cup butter	2 teaspoons salt
1/2 cup chicken broth	Freshly ground black pepper
1/3 cup fresh lemon juice	1 lemon, sliced paper thin

Cut the veal into pieces about two inches wide and three long. Sprinkle with salt and pepper. Sauté the scallops over medium heat for 10 minutes or until they are brown and tender, turning once. Do as many pieces at a time as fit your largest skillet; use butter as needed. Pour off the fat from the skillet, add the chicken broth, stirring to deglaze the pan, then put all the pieces of veal back in. Before serving, add lemon juice and parsley. Cook over medium heat, stirring, until hot. Transfer to a platter and garnish with lemon slices.

RISOTTO ALLA MILANESE

This recipe, which comes from the famous Biffi Scala restaurant in Milan, is bright yellow and virtually oozes cheese and butter. Saffron, which colors the dish, is the most expensive spice in the world. Each thread must be hand-picked from a special kind of crocus. It takes 225,000 threads to make a pound, which can cost as much as $250. But you need only about 25 cents worth.

2 cups uncooked long-grain rice	4 cups cold beef broth
1 teaspoon saffron threads	1 teaspoon bottled beef extract

2 cups freshly grated Parmesan cheese	1/2 cup butter, melted

Put rice in a saucepan and crumble in saffron. Add the beef broth and meat extract. Bring to a boil, stirring occasionally. Reduce heat, cover and simmer for 15 to 20 minutes or until liquid is absorbed and rice is tender. Remove from heat and stir in one cup of cheese and the melted butter. Serve the rice immediately and pass the remaining cheese separately.

STRAWBERRY SHORTCAKE

Genuine shortcake, like grandmother's, is a sort of super baking-powder biscuit with extra butter to make it flakier. One warning: be sure to roll the dough thick enough. You may be tempted out of habit to roll it thin.

4 cups strawberries	1 teaspoon salt
Sugar	8 tablespoons butter
2 cups sifted flour	1/2 cup milk
2 teaspoons double-acting baking powder	2 cups heavy cream, whipped

Wash and hull the strawberries. Leave three cups of them whole and slice the remaining cup. Put them into separate bowls and sweeten to taste.

Preheat oven to 450°. Sift flour, baking powder and salt into a mixing bowl. With a pastry blender, cut in five tablespoons of butter until the mixture is coarse and grainy. Stir in milk. Form dough into a ball and roll it out one-half inch thick on a lightly floured board. Cut into six 3-inch rounds and place on a baking sheet. Bake for 15 minutes. Biscuits must be served warm. Split and butter them. Put whole berries on the bottom half of each biscuit, spoon on a generous amount of whipped cream, set the other halves of the biscuits in place and top with berries and more whipped cream. Garnish with sliced berries and berry juice.

Chicken in a Pot

If, to anyone over a certain age, a chicken in every pot is synonymous with prosperity, then surely a potted chicken like this one must seem like inflation. The bird—seen here in a double-exposure "X-ray"—is plump and brown, cooking in stock and wine and heaped around with early hints of spring—red new potatoes and baby carrots, the first of the season's new crop of vegetables.

Americans are fond of cooking chicken in many ways—we roast it for Sunday dinner, broil it, bake it, and we invented the very idea of deep frying it. But we have overlooked the classic French method of braising it—browning it and then simmering it in a very small amount of liquid so that the bird soaks up the savory steam and emerges juicy and succulent. Chicken in a pot is known by many different names in France, from *poularde à la bonne femme* to *poularde à la financière* to *poularde en cocotte*—which sounds as if it should come on the table doing a can-can.

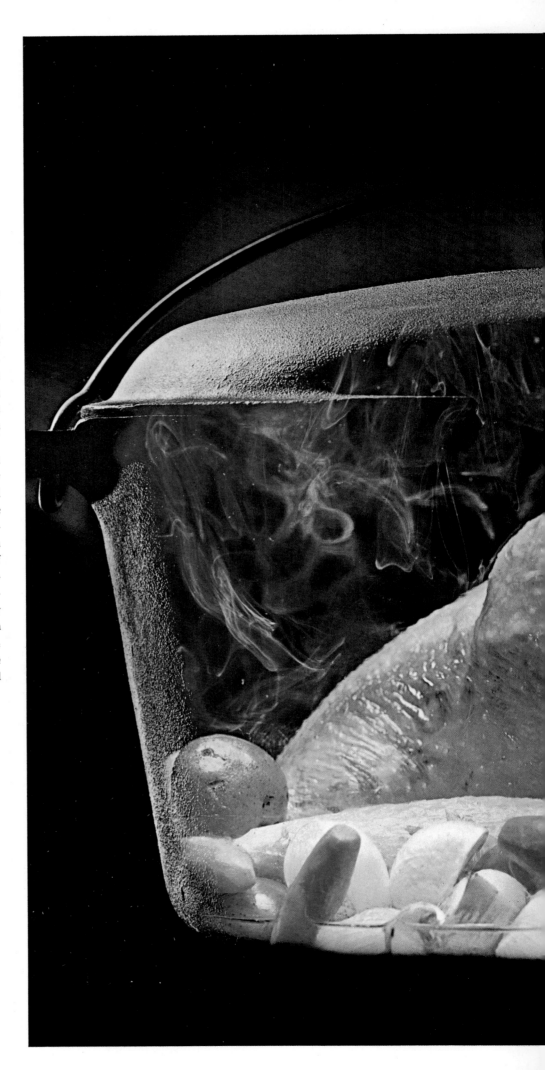

There isn't a single trick to making this meal—you don't need a light hand, a sure touch or a knowing eye. It is an easy, mostly cook-ahead dinner that doesn't lose a thing in the way of good eating by being so straightforward.

This is an international dinner with a slight Southern accent. The shrimp are given a French Provençal touch by the black olives and onions. The braised chicken with vegetables also has a French heritage whereas the pecan pie is from the Southern U.S. The combination is a very cordial entente.

Shop ahead for two items on the menu: try to get raw shrimp in the shell, good-sized if possible. But you can substitute frozen shrimp, or even a white-meated fish. Be sure you have a plump roasting chicken or a capon, not a stewing fowl, which will need much longer cooking. On the morning of the dinner make the pecan pie. You can also prepare the shrimp then if it is convenient. If you do, take it out of the refrigerator a half hour before serving. The oil in the appetizer will congeal if it is in the refrigerator more than a couple of hours. But by taking

---

MENU FOR SIX

COLD DEVILED SHRIMP

CHICKEN IN A POT WITH VEGETABLES
Parmesan popovers
Dry white wine

PECAN PIE WITH RUM WHIPPED CREAM

---

it out ahead and stirring it a few times it will come back to normal. The chicken will take a total of two hours to cook. Allow half an hour to brown it and while you are doing that, prepare the vegetables. The chicken can safely sit in its casserole on top of the stove for a while until you are ready to start braising it. If you allow an hour for cocktails, turn the chicken on 15 minutes before your guests arrive. Preheat the oven for the popovers—a crucial, but easily forgotten move. Half an hour before you sit down to the shrimp, add the vegetables to the casserole. Then make the popovers. If you line up all the measured ingredients beforehand it won't take you much more than five minutes to put them together. Chicken and popovers will be done as you finish the shrimp. Check the popovers when you start to clear away the first course. If they are done, take them out of the oven and out of their cups and keep them warm while you finish clearing the table and serving the chicken. Whip the cream for dessert before announcing dinner—or just before you serve dessert.

RECIPES

COLD DEVILED SHRIMP

This spicy dish is a pleasant change from the ubiquitous shrimp with cocktail sauce or shrimp salad. A delicious and inexpensive substitute would be a white-meated fish steak, such as halibut. Buy a two-pound fish steak, poach it for 10 minutes, then cut it into bite-size pieces and put them in the marinade.

2 pounds shrimp	1 tablespoon wine vinegar
1 lemon, thinly sliced	1 clove garlic, crushed
1 red onion, thinly sliced	1/2 bay leaf, broken up
1/2 cup pitted black olives	1 tablespoon dry mustard
2 tablespoons chopped pimiento	1/4 teaspoon cayenne pepper
1/2 cup fresh lemon juice	Freshly ground black pepper
1/4 cup oil	1 teaspoon salt

Shrimp are easiest to shell and devein when they are raw. Do this under cold running water. Bring a quart of water to a boil in a saucepan. Add the cleaned shrimp and cook them a scant three minutes. Drain at once and put them in the bowl you intend to serve them in. Add the lemon and onion slices, the black olives, well drained, and the pimiento. Toss together. In another bowl combine the lemon juice, oil, vinegar, spices and herbs and mix them together well. Stir this marinade into the shrimp mixture. Cover the dish and let it sit in the refrigerator at least two hours, giving it a stir once or twice. At the table, spoon it from the serving dish onto small plates.

CHICKEN IN A POT

Be particularly careful in selecting the ingredients for this dish since they are undisguised by sauces or heavy seasoning. The chicken must be a roaster or a capon. Use the small red new potatoes and small white onions. Baby carrots are ideal but if you can't get them, cut regular carrots into two-inch lengths. When you add the vegetables to the casserole, do it in layers, putting the ones that cook the slowest on the bottom. This saves having to add the vegetables at intervals. Since the finished platter is going to be heaped around with vegetables, the carver will surely appreciate a separate large plate to which he can transfer the chicken to cut it into serving pieces.

5 pound roasting chicken	18 small white onions, peeled
1/4 cup butter	
1/2 cup dry white wine	12 medium mushrooms, cut in half
1/2 cup chicken broth	
2 teaspoons salt	1/4 teaspoon rosemary
12 small new potatoes, unpeeled	1/2 cup chopped celery leaves
18 baby carrots, scraped	

The final effect of this dish will be much more attractive if you take time to truss and sew the chicken neatly. It will also be a good deal easier to brown. Tie the legs together, then tie the wings under the bird and sew up the cavity. Melt the butter in a large skillet and brown the chicken slowly. This will take about 30 minutes to do properly, as you must keep turning the chicken to brown it on all sides. Then transfer the chicken to a large casserole. Put wine, broth and salt into the skillet and bring them to a boil. Keep stirring to deglaze the pan, which means to loosen all the good brown bits that may have stuck to the bottom. Pour this over the chicken. Cover the casserole and cook over medium heat for 45 minutes. Then add the vegetables in layers—potatoes on the bottom, then carrots, then onions, and finally mushrooms. Sprinkle the rosemary and celery leaves on top. Cover the casserole again and cook for another 45 minutes or until the chicken is tender and the vegetables are done. Bring the chicken to the table on an extra large platter, surrounded by vegetables. Fill a sauceboat with juices from the casserole, and serve it separately, moistening each serving with a ladleful.

PARMESAN POPOVERS

A good popover should be a crisp crust surrounding next to nothing. They have an undeserved reputation for being hard to make. They aren't, as long as you're not tempted to open the oven door to see how they are coming along. Left alone, which they will be since the cook will be in the living room during most of their cooking, they will rise spectacularly. Two other tips will help: have all the ingredients at room temperature (which they will be if they've been measured earlier) and don't feel that you're being virtuous by beating the mixture an extra long time. Beat it only until well mixed and smooth. The cayenne and cheese give them an added flavor fillip. You may use popover or muffin pans if you don't have glazed custard cups—however, you will end up with more, but quite a lot smaller popovers.

9 tablespoons grated Parmesan cheese	1 cup sifted flour
3 eggs	1/2 teaspoon salt
1 cup milk	1/8 teaspoon cayenne pepper

Preheat oven to 425°. Very generously butter the bottom and sides of nine five-ounce custard cups. Put one tablespoon of cheese in the bottom of each. Set custard cups on a baking sheet. Beat eggs until well mixed with a rotary beater. Add the milk and the flour, salt and cayenne pepper. Beat just until smooth. Fill cups about half full. Bake, without peeking, for 40 minutes by which time the popovers should be brown and crisp to the touch. If they aren't, give them another five minutes.

PECAN PIE

The pecan is a native nut that both George Washington and Thomas Jefferson cultivated in a small way on their estates. The name, in Indian dialect, means "Hard to crack" but hybridizing has produced a "paper shell" that you can split with your fingers.

The pie is unconscionably easy to make considering that it is so good. It is merely a matter of putting all the in-gredients, thoroughly mixed together, into a pie shell. Use your favorite pie crust recipe, a mix, or, if you like, a frozen shell. They are perfectly acceptable substitutes, and anyway, everyone's attention is going to be happily riveted on what's inside.

9-inch unbaked pie shell	6 tablespoons rum
3 eggs	1/4 cup butter, melted
1 cup brown sugar, firmly packed	1 cup shelled pecans, broken in pieces
1/2 cup dark corn syrup	1/2 cup heavy cream
1/4 teaspoon salt	1 tablespoon sugar

Preheat oven to 375°. Beat eggs in a medium-size bowl until they are light-colored and fluffy. Add brown sugar, corn syrup, salt and four tablespoons of the rum and stir until the sugar is dissolved and the ingredients are thoroughly mixed. Stir in butter and pecans. Pour into pie shell and bake for 40 minutes or until a knife inserted in the filling comes out clean. Cool. Serve with whipped cream, to which you have added the remaining two tablespoons of rum and the tablespoon of sugar.

The Delicate Snail

To many food lovers the prime attraction of snails is their usual accompaniment —the garlic-and-butter sauce that lends such pungency to the dish. The way they are generally cooked, one authority admits, would give flavor to chewing gum. But overseasoning is the cook's fault, not the snail's. These slow-moving mollusks, which serve so splendidly as a base for sauces, do have a delicate but distinctive flavor of their own.

The preparation of fresh snails, or *escargots*, which are a gourmet's staple in France, is an arduous process many hours long. Few American cooks would be willing to go through it for the equivalent of six mouthfuls per person—no matter how delicious. But fortunately this is unnecessary in the U.S., for snails are generally available here frozen or canned and can be prepared, sauce and all, in a matter of minutes. These are usually the choicest of their kind—bred and brought up in the Burgundy wine country where they feed on the leaves of vintage vines.

There are two spring specialties in this dinner which are treated rather unconventionally. Lamb, at its most plentiful, is boned, then butterflied and marinated in a mixture highly seasoned with onions. And there is a variation on spring's most delicious offering, strawberries—one recommended even to traditionalists who think sugar and cream can't be improved on.

Buy your snails and the shells, which are usually sold with them, ahead of time. They may require some hunting. Look for them in gourmet shops or department stores. They are about as expensive to serve as a jumbo shrimp cocktail. On the day before the dinner, marinate the lamb. On the morning of the dinner prepare the snails completely, short of cooking them, and store them in the refrigerator. Sugar the strawberries, prepare the raspberries for the sauce, and keep them separately in the refrigerator. Shortly before the guests arrive, make the potato casserole and slice the zucchini and tomatoes. Take the lamb and snails from the refrigerator. If you have two ovens or the kind of stove in which the broiler

MENU FOR SIX
ESCARGOTS À LA BOURGUIGNONNE
BUTTERFLIED LEG OF LAMB
Potatoes savoyard
Zucchini with cherry tomatoes
Red wine

STRAWBERRIES CARDINAL

and oven are separate, you will have no timing problems at all with the final cooking of this dinner. If you have to work with one oven-broiler, follow this procedure: One hour and 10 minutes before serving time put the potato casserole in the oven. Bake it 40 minutes; it will not be completely cooked by then. Take the potatoes from the oven, cover them with foil to keep warm. Turn on the broiler, and broil the lamb on both sides, 10 minutes for each side. Remove lamb, turn the oven down to 425°, and bake the snails 10 minutes. When you take the snails out, put the potatoes and the lamb back in the 425° oven. They will both be done in 15 minutes, the time it takes to eat the snails. Just before you serve them, pour a little boiling water over the zucchini and cook over low heat. After the snails have been eaten, drain the zucchini, add the tomatoes and seasonings to them, put the vegetables back on low heat. By the time you have brought the lamb and potatoes to the table the vegetables will be heated through. Coat the strawberries with the sauce just before serving.

RECIPES

ESCARGOTS À LA BOURGUIGNONNE

You can be as fancy as you want about serving snails. You can go all out and buy individual small platters which have small indentations to keep the snails from rolling around, snail grabbers and snail forks. But you don't have to; the snails can be cooked in any baking dish, and you can arm your guests with cocktail napkins with which to pick up the very hot shells. You will need some small fork or pick to get the snail out of its shell. Try the snails without the gear once to be sure you really like them and are going to repeat the occasion. Dishes and holders will add up to quite an investment.

3 dozen canned snails	2 tablespoons finely
3 dozen snail shells	chopped shallots
½ pound butter	1 clove garlic, crushed
3 tablespoons finely	¼ teaspoon salt
chopped fresh	Freshly ground black pepper
parsley	French bread

Wash the snails and drain them. Wash the shells, dry them. In a small bowl cream the butter until soft. Add the parsley, shallots, garlic, salt, pepper, and mix the ingredients well. Insert a snail into each shell, pushing it in as far as it will go with your finger or a demitasse spoon. Fill the shell with some of the butter mixture, using as much as you can in each one. Place the snails in special snail dishes, or in a flat baking dish, with the open ends up. Place any left over butter mixture around the snails.

Bake in an oven preheated to 425° for 10 minutes until piping hot and bubbly. Serve at once with slices of French bread to dip freely in the garlic butter sauce, which will have overflowed the snail shells. Even though you may not usually serve the wine until the main course, the snails are so highly seasoned that wine would be welcome to drink along with them.

BUTTERFLIED LEG OF LAMB

If your butcher will not butterfly your lamb, you can do it yourself, once it has been boned. First cut the lamb so you can spread it out. Then make a series of small incisions, rather like letting out seams, so that the meat will lie as flat as possible. It will be very easy to carve, and because none of it will be wasted by being inaccessible, it is quite an economical way to serve lamb. The marinade which gives it a pungent flavor also tenderizes it, so there is no justification for overcooking it. Like all lamb, it should be served pink.

1 6-to-7 pound leg of	style mustard
lamb, boned and	2 teaspoons salt
butterflied	½ teaspoon oregano
1 clove garlic, crushed	½ teaspoon basil
¾ cup oil	⅛ teaspoon freshly ground
¼ cup red wine vinegar	black pepper
½ cup chopped onion	1 bay leaf, crushed
2 teaspoons prepared Dijon-	

Put the lamb fat side down in a shallow pan. In a small bowl mix the garlic, oil, vinegar, onion, mustard, herbs and seasonings together. Pour this marinade over the lamb. Cover pan tightly and refrigerate overnight, turning the meat at least once. Take the lamb from the refrigerator about one hour before you plan to cook it. Preheat the broiler. Place the meat along with the marinade in broiler pan, fat side up. Broil about four inches from the heat for 10 minutes. Turn, baste and broil 10 minutes on the other side. Lower temperature to 425°, transfer the meat to the oven and roast it about 15 minutes. Test with a sharp knife: the meat should be pink and juicy. Remove the lamb from the marinade and transfer it to a hot platter. There will be bits of browned onion on the surface of the lamb, which add to the flavor, but which you may scrape off if you wish. Carve the lamb into thin slices.

POTATOES SAVOYARD

2½ pounds potatoes	⅛ teaspoon freshly ground
6 tablespoons butter	black pepper
2 tablespoons chopped	1 cup grated Swiss cheese
fresh parsley	(¼ pound)
1 teaspoon salt	1¼ cups boiling beef broth

Peel potatoes and slice thinly. Keep covered in cold water until ready to use. Preheat oven to 425°. Rub the inside of a shallow two-quart baking dish generously with butter, using about two tablespoons. Drain potatoes and dry thoroughly between paper towels. Put a layer of potatoes in the baking dish, using half of the slices and overlapping them. Dot with two tablespoons of the butter, sprinkle on half the parsley, salt, pepper and cheese. Add a second layer of potatoes, again overlapping them. Sprinkle on the remaining parsley, salt, pepper, cheese and dot with the last two tablespoons of butter. Pour on the boiling broth. Bake in a 425° oven 55 to 60 minutes until potatoes are fork-tender, the top is well browned, and the broth has been absorbed.

ZUCCHINI WITH CHERRY TOMATOES

1½ pounds small zucchini	juice
1 pint cherry tomatoes, cut	1 teaspoon salt
in halves	¼ teaspoon sugar
3 tablespoons butter	⅛ teaspoon freshly ground
2 teaspoons fresh lemon	black pepper

Make sure the zucchini are uniform in size. Wash but do not peel them. Slice them about ½-inch thick. Put in a skillet, add boiling water to cover. Cook, covered, until barely tender, about 10 minutes. Drain well. Return the zucchini to the skillet and add the tomatoes, butter, lemon juice, salt, sugar and pepper. Toss them gently together to mix. Taste, add more seasoning if necessary. Cover and simmer until the tomatoes are heated through, which should only take about three minutes.

STRAWBERRIES CARDINAL

To true strawberry lovers this may seem like gilding the lily, but the sauce—which is so scant as to be just a coating —sweetens the berries and adds a sharp touch. Its brilliant color also makes a bowlful of strawberries a more beautiful sight than ever.

1½ quarts fresh	2 tablespoons sugar
strawberries	1 tablespoon orange liqueur
¼ to ⅓ cup sugar	1 teaspoon fresh lemon
1 10-ounce package frozen	juice
raspberries, thawed	Fresh mint sprigs

Empty strawberries into a colander and wash them gently under cold running water. Remove the hulls. Place berries on paper towels and gently pat them dry. If they are small, leave them whole; if large, slice them in half. Place them in bowl and sprinkle with one-quarter to one-third cup sugar. The amount you need will depend on the tartness of the berries, so taste them before you add the full amount of sugar. Stir lightly with a rubber spatula to distribute the sugar. Cover and chill for several hours. In electric blender blend the thawed raspberries with their syrup and the 2 tablespoons of sugar, at high speed until thoroughly puréed and slightly frothy. Strain to remove the seeds. Stir in the orange liqueur and lemon juice. Cover and chill. Just before serving, transfer strawberries to a bowl, and ladle the sauce over them. Use just enough to coat them lightly. Garnish with sprigs of mint.

Summer has alluring ways to keep wilting appetites alive. Fresh corn appears, to be eaten drenched in butter, on the cob of course. The hills turn blue with berries, which will eventually find themselves in deep-dish pies. The catch comes home, some of it for chowder, while prized bluefish are reserved for the barbecue.

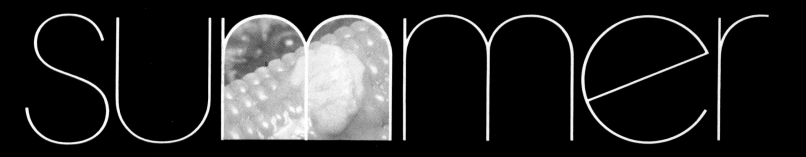

summer

Bluefish Barbecue

The recipe for this dinner is as follows: first, set the alarm for 5 in the morning. Then, take a 20-pound-test line (or eight-pound-test if you feel sporting), some jigs and plugs and weigh anchor. Six bluefish later you turn back with the ingredients of a great barbecue. However, if your luck is poor or early rising is not for you, you can produce approximately the same meal by relying on your fish store. Simply be sure the fish is fresh. Then breeze through the barbecue as though you had just reeled in the main course.

Many other fish besides the Atlantic bluefish shown here are ideal for barbecuing: walleyed pike from the Great Lakes area, rockfish from the Pacific Coast. If the fish are running small, either off the side of the boat or at the market, don't worry. One fish per person can make an attractive and manageable dinner. It will also provide a welcome switch from the red meat that is the rule at most summer barbecues.

The day you produce this barbecue, whether it be in the backyard or on the beach, you are also meant to have a good time with your guests. What work there is should be done the day before the party. Almost all the rest of the preparation is last-minute, over-the-coals cookery. This will leave you free to enjoy yourself just as though you were a guest at your own party.

This menu takes full advantage of the summertime. Fish and fishing are in season. Tender, young corn, grown right down the road, can be picked and eaten the same afternoon. There is a profusion of fruits at their peak—so many, so good, that to enjoy them all, a summer seems too short.

The day before the barbecue check through the menu mentally and make a list of what you're going to need to take with you if you are going to the beach. Imagine yourself, or your husband, cooking the dinner as well as eating it so that you don't forget utensils. You will need an ice chest big enough for the beer, the stuffed bread, the fish and the butter. If you want to serve the potato salad chilled, be sure the chest will hold it, or that you borrow an extra chest. You will need charcoal, unless you have a beach that is unusually rich in driftwood and willing scavengers. Don't forget newspapers and matches. Take the grill, tongs, a long cooking fork, a serving spoon, a sharp knife, the sturdiest paper plates available, forks and knives and a large supply of paper napkins.

Make the shortbread the day before. Leave it in the pan and cover it with foil. It is much less apt to break in transit that way. Make the stuffed bread and refrigerate it. It must chill at least four hours for the stuffing to be firm and it's even better if it stays in the refrigerator overnight. On the morning of the barbecue make the potato salad. It need not be kept cold and its flavor will be rich-

MENU FOR SIX
STUFFED BREAD

BARBECUED FISH
Roasted corn on the cob

FRENCH POTATO SALAD
Beer

WALNUT SHORTBREAD

Fresh fruit

er if it is kept covered at room temperature. If you are buying, not catching, the fish, pick them up the day of the barbecue, even though you may have ordered them ahead. Buy the corn as late as possible.

Temperament, prevailing winds and whether his tools are neatly at hand can all affect a husband's disposition and the general success of the barbecue ritual. There are ways to avoid laggard fires that won't start, and furious spouses. First, allow enough time. It will take at least half an hour from the time you start the fire until it's ready to cook on—when the briquets are gray, not red. And in addition allow a little extra time for fussing. Don't use too many briquets, 30 or 35 are plenty for most occasions. A quick way to start the fire is to soak the briquets in charcoal lighter fluid beforehand. (Never squirt the fluid into a fire that is already going—the results can be catastrophic.) Stack the briquets in a pyramid to start with—you can put most of them in a giant juice can with ends removed and holes punched in the sides to get the fire going fast. Then pull the can away with tongs and spread the briquets around. When cooking on a spit, push the coals to the back of the barbecue so that the spit turns in front of rather than over the coals. This prevents smoking and flaming up when fat from the spitted meat drips onto the grill. Unless your grill has openings at the sides or bottom use an inch of gravel as a fire bed. It lets the fire draw more easily and absorbs drippings. You will need to add charcoal during the cooking, so warm a few extra briquets on the edge of the barbecue. If you add them cold it will lower the cooking temperature considerably. Just before you start to cook, knock the gray ash off the coals—it holds back the heat—and try to keep the coals free of ash during the time you are cooking.

RECIPES

STUFFED BREAD

This is an easily managed version of canapés. It is also a good deal less tedious to make than dozens of little toast rounds. Get as crusty a bread as possible; it will not get soggy. Pull out as much of the bread's insides as you can —otherwise you will be serving more bread than stuffing, and it should be the other way around.

1 large loaf French or Italian bread	1/4 cup beer
1/2 pound liverwurst	1 tablespoon dry mustard
2 8-ounce packages cream cheese, softened	1/4 cup chopped watercress
	1/4 cup chopped onion
	1/4 cup chopped radish

Preheat oven to 350°. Cut the loaf of bread into three long pieces. Slice off the ends and discard them. Scoop or cut out the doughy center of the bread, leaving about one-fourth-inch-thick shell of crust. Crumble the bread you cut out of the shells into small pieces and toast on a cookie sheet for about 15 minutes or until lightly browned. During the toasting cut the liverwurst into small cubes. Stir the cream cheese until it is smooth and soft. Mix the beer and mustard thoroughly and stir them into the cream cheese. Add the watercress, onion and radish and mix well. Add the liverwurst and mix lightly. When the crumbs are browned, cool them to room temperature, then stir them into the cream cheese mixture. Pack the stuffing into the bread shells. This is easiest to do if you stand the shell on end and press the cream cheese stuffing in with a spoon or spatula. Wrap each chunk well in foil and refrigerate for at least four hours or until the stuffing is firm. To serve, unwrap and cut each chunk into the thinnest possible slices.

BARBECUED FISH

6 1-pound bluefish, cleaned and scaled	Salt
Cooking oil	Freshly ground pepper
	Lemon wedges

Cook the fish on a hinged grill so that it can be turned easily. Oil the grill thoroughly before you put the fish in it: the fish skin tends to stick to the grill, and generous oiling of both fish and grill will help prevent this. Don't flip the grill over and back as the fish cooks. Cook first one side, then the other. Too frequent turning of the grill is apt to damage the delicate skin and make it hard to keep track of the time necessary for cooking. The timing is crucial, as overcooking will easily dry out fish. They should be cooked about four inches from the fire for seven to 10 minutes per side or until they flake easily when tested with a fork. (Obviously, if you catch a big one, you will have to cook it longer and farther from the fire.)

When they are cooked, lift the side of the grill cautiously, loosening any skin that might be stuck to it with a sharp knife. Sprinkle with salt and pepper and serve with lemon wedges.

ROASTED CORN

18 ears of corn	1 tablespoon salt
2 cups of butter, softened	Freshly ground pepper

It's essential to know your guests when purchasing the corn. Some people will confine themselves happily to an ear or two, whereas a true corn addict, making the most of a short season, will eat as many ears as you offer him.

The best way to roast corn is also the simplest—in the husks. Cooking them that way gives the corn a delicious, smoky taste. First pull the husks down, remove the silk and rinse the corn in cold water, which helps keep it moist while it cooks. Then pull the husks back up again. You can cook the ears by putting them on a grill, turning them once or twice during a 15-20-minute period. But the better, tastier way is to put them directly in the coals. They are more apt to burn this way so it is necessary to watch and keep turning them.

Mix the salt and pepper into the butter ahead—one less step when everyone steps up to slather his own.

FRENCH POTATO SALAD

This potato salad is traditional in France. It uses oil and vinegar, not mayonnaise, and has a lively flavor.

3 pounds potatoes	with tops
1/2 cup olive oil	2 tablespoons chopped
1/4 cup tarragon vinegar	fresh parsley
1/4 cup beef consommé	1 teaspoon salt
1/4 cup chopped scallions	Freshly ground pepper

Peel and slice the potatoes. Put them into a pan with boiling salted water. Bring to a second boil, cover, reduce heat and cook for 12 to 15 minutes or until the potatoes are tender but still firm. Meanwhile, combine all the remaining ingredients and mix them well. When the potatoes are cooked, drain any water remaining in pan and immediately put the potatoes into a large bowl. Pour the oil and vinegar mixture over the warm potato slices and mix them gently but thoroughly together. All of the liquid should be absorbed by the potatoes. Cover and store at room temperature until ready to serve—or chill if you like cold potato salad.

WALNUT SHORTBREAD

2 cups soft butter	2 teaspoons vanilla
1 cup sugar	1/4 teaspoon salt
1 cup walnut pieces	4 cups sifted flour

Preheat oven to 325°. Cream the butter and sugar together until they are light and fluffy. Grind the walnuts into a coarse meal in a blender or food grinder. Beat the nuts, vanilla and salt into the butter-sugar mixture. Add the flour and mix well. Spoon the dough into a lightly greased jelly roll pan (15½ x 10½ x 1) and smooth it out to fill the pan evenly. The dough won't change shape as it cooks so level the top with a spatula if you want it perfectly even. Bake for 40 to 45 minutes or until lightly browned. Cool in pan. Cut into bars; it makes about 75 one-by-two-inch bars, which will keep well for several days in an airtight container.

FRESH FRUIT

When you select the fruit for the barbecue, keep in mind that it should be easy to eat and leave a minimum of mess behind. Peaches, plums, cherries and grapes are all in great supply and easy eating.

Melon Mosaic

Nature's best antidotes to summer heat come from the hottest places. The sweet honeydew and cantaloupe have slaked man's thirst throughout history in the Near East: the juicy watermelon has long been a substitute water source in torrid Africa. Now, in midsummer, melons are stacked in tempting display for careful choosing. Nearly every housewife has her way of testing their ripeness. Some popular, if not infallible, methods: sniff cantaloupes and honeydews for a sweet, musky aroma or press their blossom ends for an encouraging sign of springiness: thump a watermelon as a farmer does, for the telltale metallic sound of unripeness. A ripe chilled melon is refreshing if it is simply sliced and eaten by hand, small-boy style; or if it is part of an elegant mosaic of bite-size melon balls, as in the dessert at left, complemented with blueberries and a daiquiri sauce.

This dinner can be prepared completely indoors, or you can do it partially outdoors if you want to grill the ribs over charcoal for the outdoor flavor.

Only the ribs need last-minute cooking; everything else can be done in advance. First decide whether you will cook the ribs indoors or out and then organize your equipment and time accordingly. You will be preparing lots of spareribs so if you are cooking outdoors you will need a good-sized grill. You may want to borrow one so that you can have two in operation.

The night before, soak the barley for the soup. In the morning make the soup, refrigerate it, the barbecue sauce and the melon balls. Refrigerate the melon balls in their serving bowl. Prepare the rum-lime sauce and when chilled, add to the fruit. Wash the salad greens and refrigerate them wrapped in a towel. Make the salad dressing. At least three hours before serving dinner, prepare the batter for the onion rings and refrigerate it for an hour. If the ribs are cooked indoors, they should be baked in the oven for two hours before dinner is served. During the first hour the ribs are baking, cook the onion rings. When the onions are done—unfortunately they will take a full hour of your attention—place them in a bak-

---

MENU FOR EIGHT

YOGURT SOUP WITH FRESH MINT

BARBECUED SPARERIBS
French fried onion rings
Tossed green salad
Beer

MELON AND BLUEBERRIES IN RUM-LIME SAUCE

---

ing pan and set them aside so they can be reheated in the oven at the last minute. After the ribs have baked for an hour, been drained of fat and basted, continue roasting them for another hour.

Ten minutes before the ribs are done, serve the soup. It is eaten cold and should be served directly from the refrigerator. When you take the ribs from the oven put the onion rings in to reheat. They will be ready by the time you have tossed the salad and placed the ribs on a serving platter. Eating spareribs can, of course, be messy so be sure to offer moist towels or extra napkins.

If the ribs are to be cooked over an outdoor grill, you need to allow only an hour and a half in all for the job. First put the ribs in the oven to bake for an hour. Allow 45 minutes for the charcoal fire to reach the right heat level. One simple way to make sure the coals are not too hot is to place your palm over them at the height you prefer to cook the ribs; count "Mississippi one, Mississippi two," etc., until you reach seven. If you don't flinch before seven, the coals should be right for the ribs. Because the ribs have been precooked and the heat from the charcoal is more intense than oven heat, the ribs will need only 20 to 30 minutes of outdoor cooking time.

RECIPES

YOGURT SOUP WITH MINT

Yogurt is a form of fermented milk that is as old as the Old Testament. The consistency of heavy cream, it has an extremely refreshing sharp-sour taste.

1/4 cup pearl barley	mint
6 cups chicken broth	3 cups unflavored yogurt
2 tablespoons minced onion	3/4 teaspoon salt
1/2 cup finely chopped fresh	Freshly ground black pepper

Place the pearl barley in a small bowl; add water to cover and soak overnight. The next day, drain the barley in a strainer, and rinse well. Then put it into a medium-sized saucepan with the chicken broth and the minced onion. Bring it to a boil, lower heat and simmer for 15 minutes—or until the barley is tender. While the barley is cooking, chop the mint, using only the tender leaves. Dried mint is not a satisfactory substitute. When the barley is tender, remove it from the heat. Add the mint leaves. Let the mixture cool to room temperature. Add the yogurt, and stir until the soup is smooth. Add the salt and pepper to taste. Serve the soup icy cold.

BARBECUED SPARERIBS

8-9 lbs. spareribs (3 sides)

BARBECUE SAUCE

3 8-oz. cans tomato sauce	3 tablespoons brown sugar
1/2 cup water	2 tablespoons honey
1/2 cup minced onion	2 teaspoons dry mustard
1 clove garlic, minced	1 1/2 teaspoons chili powder
1/4 cup red wine vinegar	1 teaspoon salt
3 tablespoons Worcestershire sauce	2 slices lemon

Preheat the oven to 325°. Place the spareribs on racks in foil-lined roasting pans. You may have to cut the sides in half to fit into the pans. Cover with foil and bake for an hour. Prepare the sauce by mixing together all of its ingredients in a saucepan. Bring to a boil, lower the heat and simmer for half an hour. Remove the foil from the ribs, pour off the fat that has collected and increase the oven temperature to 425°. Brush the ribs with the sauce and roast for about another hour, basting and turning them frequently until they are fork-tender and thoroughly glazed. Cut each side into pieces of two or three ribs each. Serve on a large platter.

To barbecue outdoors, coat the ribs with sauce and place on the grill when the coals are ready. Keep the sauce at hand in a small saucepan. Baste and turn the ribs frequently, using a long-handled basting brush and fork.

FRENCH FRIED ONIONS

These are light and crunchy; they can be fun to cook, too —if it is not a hot day.

BATTER

1 cup sifted flour	½ cup plus 3 tablespoons
1 teaspoon baking powder	beer
½ teaspoon salt	2 tablespoons melted butter
2 eggs	

Sift together the flour, baking powder and salt. Beat the eggs slightly, and add the beer and the melted butter. Measure the actual beer, and pour it carefully to avoid lots of foam. Stir the dry ingredients into the liquids and mix together just until smooth. Cover and refrigerate the batter for an hour.

3 Bermuda onions (about	½ cup flour
2¼ pounds)	1 quart cooking oil

Peel the onions and slice about one-eighth-inch thick. Separate the onion slices into rings. Frying the very small rings can be tedious, so they may be discarded. Put the onions in a large bowl or paper bag and add the one-half cup of flour. Toss until the onions are coated lightly. An electric skillet is easiest, otherwise use a large, heavy skillet. Pour in cooking oil to a depth of one and a half to two inches. The oil should never be more than halfway up the side of the pan. The fat will bubble up when the onions are added. Set the electric skillet for 375°. To test the temperature of the oil in an ordinary skillet use a deep-fat thermometer. If you don't have one, drop in a small cube of bread and count to 60; if the bread turns a golden brown, the temperature of the oil is right. You will need tongs, a slotted spoon and paper towels to drain the onions. Using tongs, dip the onion slices, one by one, into the batter, letting all the excess drip back into the bowl. Then put the rings into the pan, but don't crowd them together. When they are golden on one side, turn them and brown the other; this will take only two or three minutes. Remove onions with slotted spoon and drain. Wait a minute before adding more onions to the pan to permit the oil to come back to the right temperature. You may need to adjust your heat occasionally as you cook the onion rings. If your batter becomes too thick while standing, add a little more beer. Continue cooking until the batter or the onions are used up. Transfer the onions to a foil-lined baking pan. Keep loosely covered, and at room temperature, if you are not planning to serve them at once. Reheat for just a few minutes in a hot oven before serving them.

MELON IN RUM-LIME SAUCE

1 cantaloupe	⅓ water
1 small honeydew melon	1 teaspoon grated lime rind
⅛ of a small watermelon	6 tablespoons lime juice
1 cup fresh blueberries	½ cup light rum
⅔ cup sugar	

Cut the cantaloupe and honeydew melons in half and remove the seeds. With a melon scoop, form the fruit into small balls. Do the same with the watermelon, working around the seeds. Pile the melon balls and the blueberries into a serving bowl and chill. In a small saucepan, mix the sugar with the water; bring to a boil, reduce heat and simmer for five minutes. Add the lime rind and let cool at room temperature. Stir in the lime juice and rum. Pour the sauce over the melon balls and berries and chill, covered, for several hours. Decorate with sprigs of mint and add additional rum, if desired.

Icy Lemon Soup

A famous chef named Louis Diat came along half a century ago and made cold soup a gourmet dish by transforming hot potato soup into Vichyssoise. Then the refrigerator came along and made cold soup an easy-to-do dish for almost every cook. The soup at right, at any temperature, is a new experience for most Americans. It is avgolemono which, when served hot, is a mainstay of Greek cookery. Chilled, it is a surprising start for a summer dinner. A frothy blend of eggs and lemons (the name literally means egg-lemon), chicken stock and a sprinkling of rice, it has a refreshing tartness, a sunny appearance and a texture that is as smooth as a breeze.

This is a dinner full of unexpected flavors and textures. The soup is tart and the roast duck is gingery, the peas are crunchy and the grape pie is smooth.

Despite the disparate ancestry of the dishes on this menu, they combine well and add up to a light, highly seasoned dinner, ideal for warm weather.

The meal is a blessed rarity; from start to finish it is truly easy to do. Almost everything can be prepared hours ahead. What is left to do after the guests arrive will take about 10 minutes. On the day before the dinner make the pie shell and the custard filling since it takes overnight to set. It is not runny and will not make the pie shell soggy. On the morning of the dinner make the soup, and put the grapes and glaze into the pie shell. You will have to squeeze a fair number of lemons. After

═══════════════

MENU FOR SIX

AVGOLEMONO SOUP

ROAST DUCK CHINESE-STYLE
Snow peas and water chestnuts
Hot rolls
Red wine

GRAPE PIE

═══════════════

the soup and the dessert are in the refrigerator, you don't have to do another thing until just two hours before your guests arrive. Then coat the ducks with the seasoned soy sauce. While they wait for half an hour, slice the scallions and water chestnuts and defrost the snow peas. Put the ducks in the oven and baste them just before the first guests arrive. You will have to baste them again during the cocktail hour but it will only take you a second. Before you serve the soup, check the ducks—they should be done. Remove them from the oven, keep them warm and heat the rolls, following directions for the kind you have bought. After the soup course, while your husband carves the ducks, cook the vegetables. They take three minutes and need only a few quick stirs. Dessert should be kept refrigerated until serving time.

RECIPES

AVGOLEMONO SOUP

If you make the soup the Greek way, you will, of course, use homemade stock. But you can do quite well by using canned broth, diluting three cans of the condensed kind with two cans of water. You must use fresh lemons.

When you combine the broth with the beaten eggs, don't expect the mixture to thicken very much. It should have the consistency of heavy cream. Remember it will thicken further in the refrigerator.

In a slightly thicker form, which is achieved by simply cutting the chicken broth way down, this soup becomes a classic Greek sauce. It is used often on meats, fish and vegetables, so when you make this soup you will be learning two dishes for the trouble of one.

6 cups chicken broth	3 eggs
1/4 cup long-grain rice	1/4 cup fresh lemon juice
1 teaspoon salt	1 lemon, sliced thin

Combine chicken broth, rice and salt in a large saucepan. Bring to a boil then reduce the heat, cover and simmer until the rice is just tender. Long-grain rice should cook in 15 minutes, converted rice may need up to five minutes more. Remove pan from heat. In a bowl, beat eggs until fluffy and pale yellow, then beat in lemon juice. Slowly stir about two cups of the hot broth into the egg-lemon mixture and whisk vigorously. Pour this mixture back into the rest of the soup. Whisk it until slightly thickened. Cool to room temperature, then refrigerate until icy cold. The soup will thicken and settle somewhat as it chills. Before serving, stir it. Garnish with lemon slices.

ROAST DUCK CHINESE-STYLE

China was the first country to raise domestic ducks—and, not surprisingly, Chinese cookery has over 100 different ways for dealing with the birds. This version, although not an authentic regional Chinese dish, uses characteristic Chinese spices and seasonings and has the extra crisp skin common to many Chinese versions. When the duck is first basted it seems to turn alarmingly black. Don't be concerned. The skin will be darker than the usual roast duck, but will still be attractive.

2 four-to-five-pound ducklings	1/2 cup honey
1/2 cup soy sauce	1/2 cup dry sherry
2 tablespoons ginger	1 clove garlic, quartered

Wash ducklings and dry them thoroughly inside and out with paper towels. Mix three tablespoons of the soy sauce with one tablespoon of the ginger. Brush this mixture over the ducks' skin and inside the cavities. Set the ducks on the rack of a shallow roasting pan—two, if one will not hold both ducks—and let them stand at room temperature for 30 minutes to absorb the ginger-soy flavor. Meanwhile, preheat oven to 325°. While the ducks are roasting combine the remaining soy sauce and ginger, honey, sherry and garlic in a saucepan. Bring to a boil, stirring until honey and ginger are well mixed in. Reduce heat and simmer for 10 minutes, stirring occasionally. Remove and discard the pieces of garlic. The ducks will roast a total of two and a half hours. They should be basted well with the ginger mixture after one and a half hours, then basted again after another half hour. They are done when the drumsticks move up and down easily.

SNOW PEAS AND WATER CHESTNUTS

Snow peas don't taste any more like peas than water chestnuts taste like chestnuts. They are eaten pod and all and their flavor is quite different from standard peas —a slightly bitter taste like such salad greens as dandelions. Water chestnuts are not nuts at all but bulbs, which grow under water. They have a rather sweet flavor, and a distinctive crunchy texture. They are imported from Asia and are widely available canned.

3 10-ounce packages frozen snow peas or 1½ pounds fresh snow peas	1 5-ounce can water chestnuts, sliced
3 bunches scallions	2 teaspoons salt
4 tablespoons peanut oil	1 teaspoon monosodium glutamate

Thaw frozen snow peas, then put them on paper towels to dry. If you have fresh snow peas, wash and dry them, break off tips and pull off side strings. Fresh or frozen, keep the snow peas whole. Slice scallions diagonally into one-inch pieces, using white part and about two inches of the green. Heat the oil in a large skillet. Add scallions and cook over medium heat for one minute, stirring constantly. Add snow peas, water chestnuts, salt and monosodium glutamate. Continue cooking and stirring for two or three minutes or until the peas are very hot and faintly browned.

GRAPE PIE

1 10-inch piecrust (recipe below)	1½ teaspoons vanilla
½ cup cornstarch	3 cups halved seedless green grapes (about 1¾ pounds)
¾ cup sugar	
⅛ teaspoon salt	⅓ cup currant jelly
2½ cups milk	1 tablespoon water
5 egg yolks	

Combine the cornstarch, sugar and salt in a heavy sauce-

pan. Heat the milk to the boiling point and gradually add to the cornstarch mixture, whisking vigorously over very low heat until the mixture thickens and just begins to bubble. Beat the egg yolks until blended. Stir a little of the hot mixture into yolks, then pour the yolks back into cornstarch mixture and cook, stirring, for about seven minutes or until custard is as thick as a stiff mayonnaise. Use a rubber scraper if you think any may be sticking to the bottom. Remove custard from stove, let cool and stir in vanilla extract. Spoon custard into pie shell. Cover with plastic wrap and refrigerate overnight. The next day pave the top of the custard with the halved grapes, overlapping them to cover the custard completely. Make a glaze by melting the currant jelly with water in a heavy saucepan over low heat. Stir the jelly until it is smooth and syrupy. Ladle the syrup over the pie, coating the grapes evenly. Return to the refrigerator and chill thoroughly before serving.

PASTRY FOR PIECRUST

Use this recipe, which is excellent for slightly heavyhanded pastry cooks, or your own recipe.

1½ cups sifted flour	6 tablespoons salad oil
¾ teaspoon salt	1½ tablespoons ice water

In a small bowl, mix the flour with the salt. Add the oil and blend in well, using a fork. Sprinkle on the water and mix well. Press the mixture into a ball. If it is too dry and will not hold together, add up to 1 more tablespoon of oil. Wipe the top of your work surface with a damp cloth. Put down a 14-inch square of wax paper —the wet surface will hold the paper in place. Place the ball of pastry on the paper and flatten it slightly. Cover with another piece of wax paper. Roll out gently, working from the center out, until you have a 12-inch circle. Peel off top sheet of paper. Lift bottom sheet of paper and pastry by the corners. Place, paper side up, in the pie plate. Gently peel off the paper. If the pastry tears, just press it together with your fingers. Work the pastry into the plate, build up and crimp the edges. Prick pastry well. Chill for about 15 minutes. Bake in a preheated 450° oven 12-15 minutes until golden.

Elegant Cannelloni

Americans are almost as extravagant as Italians in their enthusiasm for pasta, but tend, when cooking at home, to stick to spaghetti. They miss a lot by

this oversight, for many pasta dishes are subtle, even elegant. Cannelloni, small rolls of stuffed pasta, demand virtuosity. The pasta is light, the meat stuffing airy as a mousse and the two sauces totally different. One is smooth and creamy, the other well-flavored with herbs and tomatoes. The result is stunningly subtle and rich. And the preparation, exacting but fascinating, gives the cook a chance to display a fine Italian hand—or develop one.

This dinner is Italian and subtly flavored—which may seem to be a contradiction in terms to people who feel that Italian cooking has to be overwhelmingly seasoned.

If you wish to be consistently Italian, choose an Italian wine, a Valpolicella or Bardolino. Serve after-dinner coffee in the living room so that your guests will not be eating a coffee dessert and drinking coffee at the same time.

Although it takes quite a while to prepare this dinner, there is almost no work to do once your guests arrive.

The amount of work you have to do depends very much on whether you plan to make your own pasta. That takes an hour and is finicky work but worth it. You can, however, make out perfectly well with store-bought manicotti if you feel noodlemaking is not your strong point.

It will help you a lot if you can do several things at once—really a necessity for anyone with ambitions of being a more than adequate cook. Start on the morning of the dinner with the meat filling. Once it is simmering, assemble the tomato sauce. When that is cooking cook the cauliflower, shape and refrigerate it. All three projects will

be finished at about the same time—approximately an hour and a half after you begin. Purée the meat in the blender while it is still warm and then refrigerate it until you are ready to finish the cannelloni. Make the granita, which takes almost no time, and put it in the freezer.

If you're going to do it—now's the time to make the pasta. After you cook it, keep it covered with damp paper towels until ready to use. If you are using store-bought manicotti, boil about two and a half hours before the guests are due. At this point make the mornay sauce, finish the meat filling and fill the noodles. Make the *salsa verde*. Set the table. Just before your guests arrive, put the final touches on the cannelloni. Twenty minutes before you are ready to sit down, put the cannelloni in a preheated oven. Ladle some *salsa verde* over the molded cauliflower just before serving. Pass the rest with it. After you have eaten the first course, move the granita from freezer to refrigerator, and put the cannelloni under the broiler for a minute. Just before serving the granita, chop it briskly with a wooden spoon and spoon it into sherbet glasses.

RECIPES

CAULIFLOWER IN SALSA VERDE
This dish is as beautiful to look as it is to eat.

1 large head cauliflower	2 tablespoons chopped watercress
½ pound spinach	
1 cup olive oil	2 tablespoons minced, pitted black olives
¼ cup lemon juice	
2 tablespoons capers, drained and chopped	2 tablespoons chopped pimiento
2 tablespoons chopped fresh parsley	1 teaspoon salt
	Few grains cayenne pepper

Wash and trim the cauliflower and break it into florets. Put them into an inch of boiling salted water and cook for 10 to 12 minutes or until just tender. Drain and rinse well with cold water. Take a medium-size round mixing bowl and arrange the florets snugly in it with the flowers pressed against the sides of the bowl and the stems pointing into the center. Pack the center full of the remaining cauliflower. Put a plate on top of the cauliflower and weight it down. Let stand for at least 15 minutes, then tip the bowl carefully without removing the plate and drain off any liquid. Place bowl, weight and all, in the refrigerator for at least two hours. Wash and dry the spinach leaves and refrigerate. Combine the remaining ingredients to make the *salsa verde*. Mix them well. Chill.

To serve, remove weight and plate from cauliflower. Place a serving plate over the bowl and turn over quickly. Remove the bowl carefully. Florets will turn out in a

dome shape and will hold together. Arrange the spinach around them. Spoon on some *salsa verde* and pass the rest at the table.

CANNELLONI
There are many versions of cannelloni—some filled with chicken or cheese, and others with a meat stuffing. In a traditional Italian dinner, cannelloni, like any pasta dish, is served in addition to a main course, but this recipe is more than adequate—at least for American tastes—as a main course in itself. It provides three cannelloni per person, but you may find two are enough for light eaters.

In making your own noodles, you will find the dough is a bit more difficult to work with than piecrust. It should be rolled as thin as possible since it thickens a little when cooked. There are noodlemakers, rather like a wringer on an old-fashioned washing machine, which make the job easier, but they are a substantial investment—worth buying only if you are going to be making a lot of pasta.

If you decide against homemade pasta, buy manicotti tubes—they are about four inches long and an inch in diameter. No matter what the directions on the box tell you, cook the tubes for 10 minutes, four at a time with one tablespoon of olive oil floating on top of the boiling water. Some manufacturers advise no cooking at all before filling the tubes, and others urge only two or three minutes. But the sauces they recommend are thinner than the ones for this dinner and the noodles cook more completely in them. For this recipe the tubes must be limp and no longer sticky before you fill them.

Cannelloni is a five-stage operation. First the noodles. Then a meat filling—a mixture of beef and veal, seasoned with wine and cheese. A tomato sauce, a cheese sauce, then the whole thing is put together, baked and finally slipped under the broiler until a crusty, golden brown.

PASTA

2¼ cups sifted flour	2 tablespoons salad oil
3 eggs	Flour
4 tablespoons water	

Place the two and one-quarter cups of flour in a large mixing bowl. Add eggs, water and oil and mix them together. Turn the dough out onto a floured surface and knead until smooth, about five minutes. It will be very stiff. Cover with a towel and let stand 30 minutes. Divide the dough in half and, with a floured rolling pin on a well-floured surface, roll the dough as thin as possible. Cut into four-inch squares. You may need as much as half a cup of flour to roll out the dough, and you will have enough dough to make 22 to 23 squares. This allows for a few discards, since you will only want to fill 18 squares.

Add one tablespoon of vegetable oil to six quarts of salted water and bring to a rolling boil. Drop in pasta squares nine at a time and let them cook eight to 10 minutes or until tender. Remove them with a slotted spoon and spread them on damp paper towels. Keep them covered with damp paper towels until you are ready to fill them.

MEAT STUFFING

2 tablespoons olive oil	3 egg yolks
1 medium onion, chopped	1½ teaspoons salt
1 carrot, chopped	Freshly ground black pepper
1 pound boneless veal, cubed	7 tablespoons grated Parmesan cheese
1 pound boneless beef, cubed	¼ cup chopped fresh parsley
1 cup dry white wine	½ cup mornay sauce (recipe below)

Heat olive oil in large skillet. Add onion and carrot and sauté until the onion is soft. Dry the veal and beef cubes, which should be small, on paper towels. Add them to the vegetables and brown on all sides over medium heat. Add the white wine, cover and simmer for one hour. Put meat and vegetables with their liquid into a blender and blend until smooth. Do only a little at a time. When all the meat is blended, add the egg yolks, salt, pepper, three tablespoons of the Parmesan, parsley and one-half cup of the mornay sauce. Mix ingredients together thoroughly.

MORNAY SAUCE

4 tablespoons butter	¾ teaspoon salt
4 tablespoons flour	¾ cup grated Swiss cheese
3 cups milk	

Melt butter, blend in flour and cook slowly for two minutes. Add milk and stir until the sauce comes to a boil. Remove it from the heat; add salt and cheese, stirring with a whisk until smooth.

TOMATO SAUCE

¼ cup olive oil	½ teaspoon basil
¾ cup finely chopped onion	¼ teaspoon thyme
2 8-ounce cans tomato sauce	1 teaspoon salt
2 tablespoons tomato paste	½ teaspoon freshly ground black pepper
¼ cup dry red wine	

Heat oil in a saucepan. Add onion and cook slowly for 15 minutes, stirring several times. Add remaining ingredients and bring to a boil. Reduce heat and simmer about 40 minutes, stirring several times, until the sauce has thickened slightly.

To assemble cannelloni: preheat oven to 350°. Place three tablespoons of meat stuffing on the center of each pasta square, spreading the mixture out to make a center strip down the length of the square. Roll the square up and place it, seam side down, in a large buttered baking dish. If you cannot fit all the cannelloni in one layer you will need two dishes. Pour the remaining mornay sauce over the cannelloni, spreading it evenly. Then spoon the tomato sauce over the top. Sprinkle with remaining four tablespoons of grated Parmesan cheese. Bake at 350° for 25 minutes or until the sauce is bubbly. Put the cannelloni under broiler for a minute or two to brown the top.

ESPRESSO GRANITA

This is a kind of water ice, or sherbet, named for its grainy texture. It may remind you of the cups of ice with syrup poured over them that are sold on the streets of Italian neighborhoods in the summertime. The flavor is just like a strong cup of espresso.

2 cups boiling water	2 teaspoons cocoa
2 tablespoons instant espresso coffee	¼ cup sugar
	½ teaspoon vanilla

Pour boiling water onto the instant espresso, cocoa and sugar and stir well. Let the mixture cool. Add the vanilla. Pour into ice cube tray without dividers. Put in the freezer until the mixture is frozen about half an inch in from the edge of the tray. How long this takes will depend on your freezer—probably an hour or two. Take it out of the freezer and chop the ice with a wooden spoon, breaking it up so that the mixture is mushy. Put it back in the freezer. When it is completely frozen—allow another hour—chop again. Twenty minutes before you plan to serve it, move it from the freezer to a refrigerator shelf. Just before serving, take it out and, leaving it in the tray, chop it again with a wooden spoon, breaking up any big clumps. It should be slightly soft but still icy.

Salade Niçoise

A basket of greens—with leaves as bright as grass or light as lemon, with curly tendrils or sturdy stalks—is pleasant food in weather that would wilt anything but lettuce. But the greens can also support a salad hearty enough to make a full dinner. The Salade Niçoise, which originated in the area around Nice, makes marvelous use of regional specialties—black olives from the groves which cover the hillsides, fresh vegetables like tomatoes, beans, artichokes and potatoes from Provence's fertile fields, tuna from the Mediterranean. They are all as easy to get in American supermarkets as in the stalls at Nice and, though other ingredients can be added, these are an ideal combination. In almost all Provençal cookery garlic is required—in this case it is added to the salad dressing.

Any variety of greenery makes a good background for Niçoise. Each kind has its own personality, and almost every combination of them is a happy one. Boston and Bibb lettuce are tender, Belgian endive is crisp. Chicory has a slightly bitter taste, dandelion greens are sharp, and watercress has a welcome tang.

This dinner is a monument to all the easy ways out. For the most part you open cans and get somebody else to do the cooking for you. The menu is intended for an outdoor party, and although the recipes given here serve six, they can quite easily be adapted or enlarged for a much bigger group.

It is very hard to find an excuse to cook Chinese-style ribs. They are too heavy to be a good appetizer before a usual main course and they aren't really suitable as a main course themselves. This menu provides the perfect occasion. A light, tart salad follows the ribs—the ideal accompaniment—and there is the additional virtue of cooking them outdoors. Sangría, a Spanish wine punch subtly flavored with lemon and peach, is

MENU FOR SIX

CHINESE BARBECUED SPARERIBS

SALADE NIÇOISE
Garlic dressing
French bread
Sangría

CREPES
WITH BLUEBERRY SAUCE

an antidote to summer thirsts and is pleasant to drink throughout dinner. The blueberry crepes finish things off with a sweet touch.

What little preparation there is should, and can, easily be done hours ahead of time. Early in the day of the dinner wash the salad greens, dry them, and keep them wrapped in the refrigerator. Make the garlic dressing, the blueberry sauce and the crepes—which will keep perfectly well for several hours. An hour or so before dinner precook the ribs, assemble the ingredients for the sangría and put the salad together. Then get the fire for the barbecue started—which might well be your husband's job—so that it will be ready for cooking by the time the guests have arrived.

RECIPES

CHINESE BARBECUED SPARERIBS

With this recipe the ribs are precooked in a soy sauce marinade in the oven. But they are finished on a barbecue grill which gives them an added flavor of charcoal, gets the cook out of the kitchen and provides a little entertainment for the guests. The ribs should be put on the grill when cocktails start—and these should be served out of doors so that the barbecue chef is not deserted and everyone can work up an appetite over the sizzle and smell of the cooking. The ribs must be cut apart for serving and they will cook best if separated just before they go on the grill. But since they must be turned and basted on the grill this may be a nuisance. If your husband does not have much patience, keep the racks of ribs intact and slice them apart after they are cooked.

Since eating ribs is always a messy operation, pass warm moist napkins around on a tray after this course (remove them as soon as they've been used). At the very least, offer your guests plenty of paper napkins and bring on the cloth ones with the main course.

If it should rain on the day of the dinner or if you don't want to get into the barbecue ritual, the ribs can be prepared very satisfactorily in the oven. Follow the recipe below to the point of putting the ribs on the grill. Then pour off the marinade, set it aside as a basting sauce and transfer the ribs to a shallow pan. Arrange them in a single layer and return them to the oven for another 40 to 45 minutes. Turn them occasionally and baste if necessary until they are tender and brown on all sides.

4 pounds spareribs	4 tablespoons dark brown
½ cup soy sauce	sugar
½ cup dry sherry	2 cloves garlic, crushed
½ cup water	

Preheat oven to 350°. Arrange the ribs in a large roasting pan. Combine all other ingredients, stir well and pour over them. Cover the pan with foil. Bake 45 minutes, turning the ribs once or twice. Take the ribs from the pan and save the marinade for basting. Set the barbecue grill as high above the bed of coals as possible. When the coals are gray, arrange the ribs on the grill. Cook them for 20 to 30 minutes or until the meat is browned and tender, turning and basting frequently with the soy marinade so they won't dry out.

SALADE NIÇOISE

This is so easy it's almost hard to believe that it's going to any good. Except for boiling up a few eggs, beans and potatoes, all the work has been done by the people who put the ingredients into their cans and jars. There are many arguments about what should go into Niçoise. Some people insist on croutons and others won't admit artichokes. This recipe has more ingredients than many, and is a very happy combination.

2 pounds potatoes, boiled and sliced	into chunks
	1 pint cherry tomatoes
2 cups cooked cut green beans	1 cup pitted black olives
1 cup cooked artichoke hearts	6 hard-cooked eggs, quartered
3 cups garlic dressing (recipe below)	1 large green pepper, cut in rings
Salad greens	½ cup canned or bottled red pepper strips
1 large onion, thinly sliced	2 2-ounce cans rolled anchovies with capers
3 7-ounce cans of tuna, drained and broken	¼ cup chopped parsley

Combine potatoes, beans, artichoke hearts and onion with the garlic dressing. Marinate the mixture in the refrigerator for a couple of hours, stirring gently two or three times. To serve, line a salad bowl with greens. Drain the marinated vegetables, keeping the dressing for use later, and spoon them onto the greens. Put the tuna in the middle of the bowl and arrange the tomatoes, olives, eggs, red and green peppers and anchovies around it. Sprinkle lightly with parsley. Pass the dressing at the table or sprinkle a little onto the salad just before you serve it.

GARLIC DRESSING

2 cups olive oil	1 tablespoon dry mustard
1/2 cup tarragon vinegar	1 teaspoon sugar
1/4 cup fresh lemon juice	1 tablespoon salt
2 cloves garlic, crushed	Freshly ground black pepper

Combine mustard, sugar, salt and a generous amount of pepper. Mix in garlic. Add vinegar and lemon juice and stir thoroughly. Add oil and mix well. Stir or shake vigorously just before using. Makes about three cups.

SANGRÍA

1 bottle dry red wine	2 tablespoons sugar
1 7-ounce bottle club soda	1 peach, sliced
Juice of a whole lemon	1 lemon, sliced thin

Put about a dozen ice cubes in a large pitcher. Add lemon juice, sugar and sliced fruit. When you are ready to serve, add the wine and club soda and stir vigorously. In pouring, be sure each wine glass gets an ice cube and a slice of fruit.

If peaches are unavailable, orange slices will do well instead, in fact many kinds of fruit are used in Spain. This drink goes down very easily, so have extra bottles of wine and soda on hand if the pitcher needs replenishing.

CREPES WITH BLUEBERRY SAUCE

Preparing this elegant dessert is surprisingly smooth going provided you do the crepes ahead of time. The perfectionist's way of making crepes is in a crepe pan, a shallow skillet about six inches in diameter with slanting sides. The correct technique involves tilting the pan as soon as you have ladled in the batter so that each crepe will fill the entire bottom of the pan. This makes them all of uniform size and shape but it can be tricky to turn the crepe over with no room at the sides to insert the spatula. Instead of the crepe pan, use a good-sized cast iron skillet. Pour in only enough batter to make a four-to-five-inch crepe in the middle of the pan, leaving yourself room to maneuver. This is not as professional a method, but you can keep two skillets going at once without feeling harassed. The results are indistinguishable from the crepes made in the traditional way. In making the batter don't overbeat. Let it rest 20 minutes or so before using. Use only enough butter to keep the crepe from sticking and don't turn it more than once. Crepes cook quickly and are ready to be turned in 60 to 80 seconds. Consider the

first one a test to check the consistency of the batter, the amount you need for each crepe and the heat of the pan. It is not as difficult as it sounds: if you can make pancakes for breakfast, you can make crepes for dinner.

CREPES

4 eggs	1/2 teaspoon salt
1/2 cup flour	2 cups milk
1 tablespoon sugar	Butter

Beat eggs well, add flour, sugar and salt and beat until smooth. Add milk gradually, beating constantly as you do it. Melt about one teaspoon of butter over moderately high heat in a skillet. When the butter sizzles, pour in two tablespoons of batter, enough to make a crepe about five inches in diameter. Cook until brown on each side, about two minutes in all. Remove from skillet and lay crepe flat on a linen towel. Add butter to the pan and cook the next crepe. This batter makes about 24 crepes.

To keep the crepes, spread a length of towel on a baking sheet. Arrange the crepes singly on the towel, then fold the extra length of toweling back over them and repeat with another layer. Don't stack the crepes one on another or they will get soggy. Just let them sit at room temperature until you are ready to serve. Then heat the crepes (while they are in the towel) in a 250° oven for five to eight minutes or until they are warm to the touch. Roll them up or fold them into quarters on the dessert plates. Ladle blueberry sauce on the crepes, having first warmed it over low heat on the stove.

BLUEBERRY SAUCE

1 quart fresh blueberries	2 tablespoons water
1/2 cup sugar	1 teaspoon grated lemon rind
2 tablespoons fresh lemon juice	2 tablespoons kirsch

Wash the berries and drain them thoroughly. Combine sugar, lemon juice and water in a saucepan. Add the berries and bring to a full boil, stirring constantly but gently. Remove from heat and stir in lemon rind. Let cool, then add the kirsch.

An alternate way of serving this dessert is to assemble it in a chafing dish at the table. This method eliminates heating the crepes and the sauce in the kitchen and is a dramatic flourish as well. Put as many folded or rolled crepes as you can comfortably fit in your chafing dish —eight will fit in one of average size—and ladle the blueberry sauce over them. Allow the combination to heat through before serving.

Cornish Game Hens

The skin is brown and crackly. Juice can be seen bubbling beneath its still-golden patches. The smell is heady—of hot charcoal and roasting meat and with the fragrance of thyme and tarragon.

These are Rock Cornish game hens roasted, medieval style, on a spit for a 20th Century barbecue. The hens are chubby creatures that weigh about a pound apiece and are served one to a person. A specially developed variety first marketed about 15 years ago, the Cornish hen has a great deal of meat on it, almost all of it white. Its flavor is delicate, well suited for herb butter and barbecuing. The birds actually seem designed to be eaten with the fingers which, like all eating and cooking outdoors, makes almost everything taste better.

This is a vacation dinner. It has a holiday air about it—outdoor cooking, a fresh salad and a favorite Italian dessert. In certain parts of the country it also gives the whole family an excuse for some food-hunting expeditions.

Although this is intended as a midsummer feast there are many things on the menu that are good any time of the year. Baked clams are a treat whenever you serve them, and as a hot appetizer would be very welcome in the winter. This Italian-style recipe has lots of seasoning and would make a fine beginning for any dinner that was not too highly seasoned itself. The Cornish game hens can be done in the oven, but they are not quite the same without the zest of the charcoal flavor. They are receptive to many sauces though, and very easy company fare. The buckwheat groats are a happy change from the usual round of potatoes, rice and pasta. They are a coarse, humble cereal, but even when prepared in the simplest way have a distinctive taste. Cooked this way, enriched with bouillon, tangy with onions, with delicate mushrooms and crunchy pine nuts, buckwheat groats become truly memorable—and they are just as good on a cold winter evening as in August.

If you are vacationing at the shore, on either the East

MENU FOR SIX

BAKED CLAMS OREGANO

BARBECUED GAME HENS WITH HERB BUTTER
Buckwheat groats with pine nuts
Cucumber and tomato slices
Sour cream dressing
Dry white wine

ZABAGLIONE

or West Coast, your children can easily produce the main ingredient for the first course. Clamming requires a pail to put them in, a rake to dig them with, bare toes to find them with, plus the knowledge that you are clamming in safe, unpolluted water. If you have any doubts, substitute a trip to the local fisherman's wharf, which is often pretty good fun anyway. So much for the children's part. The outdoor barbecue works off the hankering of most men to be a born chef and boy scout at the same time. The salad calls for tomatoes and can be an excuse for another expedition, this time to a farmer's market.

Everything about this dinner is short order, and the shorter the better. The clams should be procured, whatever your method, on the day of the dinner and left soaking, in their shells, until an hour or so before dinner. At that time open them and assemble the baked clam dish but don't risk drying it out by putting it in the oven before the guests arrive. The big problem of timing is the barbecue: husbands never start the fire early enough. An hour before dinner make the zabaglione. The groats and the salad are best prepared at the last minute. They can be done simultaneously and will probably keep you away from your guests only about 15 minutes.

RECIPES

BAKED CLAMS OREGANO
The hardest part of making this dish is opening the clams, unless you have a husband or fishman willing to do it for you. Select small hard-shell clams—cherrystone or littlenecks on the East Coast, rock clams on the West Coast. (Quahogs, which you use in chowder, are really too big to be eaten this way.)

Scrub the clams well and let them sit in cold water or brine (one-third cup of salt to a gallon of water). The trick is how to get at the clam. Hold the shell in the palm of your left hand with the hinge inward. Take a blunt-ended clam knife and very carefully insert it between the shells. Cut around the entire clam, twisting the knife a little as you go to pry the shell open. Cut the muscle at the hinge and remove the top shell. Several types of easy-to-use clam openers are available, but there is an even easier way out. Put the clams on a baking dish and pop them into a hot oven for a scant four or five minutes, just long enough for them to open, or steam them for an instant on top of the stove. This sacrifices a bit of the flavor and may make the clams a little tougher (and of course can only be done if the clams are going to be baked afterward), but it does cut down on the Band-Aids.

24 hard-shell clams on the half shell
2 tablespoons fresh lemon juice
1/4 cup freshly grated Parmesan cheese
1/4 cup seasoned bread crumbs
1/4 cup finely chopped fresh parsley
2 cloves garlic, crushed
1 teaspoon oregano
1/2 teaspoon salt
Freshly ground black pepper
Olive oil

Preheat oven to 425°. Open clams, discarding top shell and loosening the meat from the bottom shell. Drain them well. Arrange them in their shells, of course, in a shallow baking pan. Sprinkle each one with a little lemon juice. Combine the cheese, bread crumbs, parsley, garlic, oregano, salt and pepper and spoon the mixture over the clams. Put enough on each to cover the clam entirely, about one teaspoonful per shell. Put about an eyedropper's worth of oil on top of each one and bake for 15 minutes. Serve with additional slices of lemon.

BARBECUED GAME HENS
The only work that the indoor cook has to do on these birds is to arrange them properly on the spit. The hens are so small that you don't have to sew up the cavity,

and if you arrange them six on a spit, they will hold each other in place so you do not have to truss them elaborately. These small birds will hold best if they are skewered through the sides. Tie each bird's feet together and tie the wings beneath the hens. The string may burn away but the only alternative, light wire, is a nuisance and also a little unappetizing to remove. Whichever way you do it, be sure the birds are secure on the spit and tied into equal compactness so that they will all be the same distance from the fire.

6 game hens	1 teaspoon thyme
6 small onions	¼ cup fresh lemon juice
Celery leaves	1 teaspoon paprika
1½ cups butter	1 teaspoon salt
2 teaspoons tarragon	Freshly ground black pepper

An hour or so before dinner wash the game hens in cold water and pat them dry with paper towels. Stuff the cavity of each one with an onion and a few celery leaves and tie wings and feet. Impale the hens on the spit. Put the butter into a small skillet or saucepan and sprinkle the herbs over it, rubbing the leaves between your fingers to release their flavor. Melt the butter over low heat, stirring it to blend the herb flavors through. Remove from the stove and stir in the lemon juice, paprika, salt and pepper. When the coals for the barbecue are gray, brush the hens liberally with butter and start them roasting. Using a pastry brush, baste frequently with the butter. Roast for 45 minutes to an hour or until the skin is well browned and the drumsticks can be moved easily.

BUCKWHEAT GROATS WITH PINE NUTS

If you have never eaten this before, the mere sound of it may make you feel it should be relegated to the breakfast table. It *is* a cereal, but a coarse-grained one that is not mushy and has a very definite and nutty flavor. This method of preparing groats *(kasha,* it is called in Russia where it is eaten a lot) breaks up the cereal texture with nuts and mushrooms and adds seasonings which enhance the flavor. The dish is pungent and quite rich.

2 cups buckwheat groats	1 cup chopped onions
8 ounces pignolia nuts or pine nuts	6 cups beef broth
1½ cups butter	2 teaspoons nutmeg
2 cups sliced mushrooms	2 teaspoons salt
	Freshly ground black pepper

Sauté nuts in one cup butter until they are golden brown, which will take about five minutes. Remove nuts with a slotted spoon, drain and reserve. In the butter left in the saucepan, sauté mushrooms and onions until the onions are golden, probably another five minutes. Add beef broth, nutmeg, salt and pepper and bring to a full boil. Slowly pour in the groats, stirring constantly. Reduce heat and boil gently for five minutes. Cover and continue cooking five minutes more. Stir in the remaining one half cup butter and the pine nuts. Serve immediately.

TOMATOES AND CUCUMBERS IN SOUR CREAM

6 tomatoes	1 teaspoon sugar
3 cucumbers	2 teaspoons salt
1 pint sour cream	Freshly ground black pepper
4 tablespoons wine vinegar	

Slice the tomatoes and cucumbers, arrange them on a platter and chill. Combine sour cream, vinegar, sugar, salt and pepper and stir them well. Spoon the sour cream mixture over the vegetables and let them marinate in the refrigerator until ready to serve. But do not let mixture stand more than 30 minutes or the vegetables will "bleed" and dilute the sauce.

ZABAGLIONE

This Italian wine custard can be served hot or cold and can even be made in a chafing dish at the table on a more formal occasion if you feel up to it. If you do, use half an eggshell as a measurer for the wine. For each yolk use a half-shell full of Marsala. The proportions of wine to egg will come out the same as in the recipe but it's a fine showman's touch. Marsala is the classic wine to use, but Madeira or sweet sherry can be used instead.

8 egg yolks	1 cup Marsala
½ cup sugar	

Combine egg yolks and sugar in the top of a double boiler, over hot but not boiling water. Do not permit the water to touch the top pan. Whisk the egg yolks until they are pale and foamy. Add Marsala gradually, beating constantly, until the custard has doubled in bulk and begun to thicken. Remove from heat. Serve hot or cold.

Herring
Salad

Herring, one of the most plentiful fish in the sea, usually winds up in a jar, and appears on the table as an appetizer. But in countries that ring the North Sea and the Baltic it is often the mainstay of a hearty main course, herring salad. The standard ingredients are shown here in a bed of greens: clockwise from herring *(at top)* are egg white, beets, pickle, veal, anchovies, potatoes, egg yolk, onion and parsley. For best effect the ingredients are served this way, then mixed with a sour cream dressing. The briny bite of herring still stands out, unblunted by the cream and the competition.

The pungent flavor of the herring salad determines the balance of this menu—a subtle soup to start with, plenty of dark bread and beer to eat and drink with the salad itself, and a light, cooling dessert.

The most important ingredient in this salad is, of course, the herring, and you may find a bewildering assortment to choose from —salted, smoked and pickled. This recipe calls for pickled herring—and even at that the choice can still be confusing. Use Bismarck herring—whole fillets pickled in vinegar and spices. Rollmops are Bismarck herring rolled around spears of dill pickle or onion rings, and they can be substituted.

The entire dinner can be prepared on the morning of

MENU FOR SIX

CUCUMBER SOUP

HERRING SALAD
Beer
FROZEN PEACH MOUSSE
BRANDIED PEACH SAUCE

the day you are going to serve it. Make the dessert first so it will have plenty of time to freeze. Then start the veal cooking for the herring salad, then the potatoes and eggs. Make the soup. While the cooked salad ingredients cool off, chop the rest of the ingredients for the salad. Refrigerate all the salad ingredients separately, and chill the soup too.

Prepare the sour-cream dressing, the dessert sauce and stock the refrigerator with beer. You will find that the herring salad raises quite a thirst, and that the beer will be very popular. Lightly butter thin pumpernickle bread to serve with the salad. Assemble the salad just before serving the soup.

RECIPES

CUCUMBER SOUP

2 cucumbers	1 pint sour cream
1 quart buttermilk	1 teaspoon salt
1/4 cup chopped parsley	2 tablespoons lemon juice
2 scallions, white part only	2 tablespoons fresh dill

Cut six thin unpeeled slices from one cucumber and set them aside. Peel, seed and chop the remainder of that cucumber, plus the other one. Place half the chopped cucumber in an electric blender. Moisten each batch of cucumber to be blended with a cup of buttermilk. Blend, adding half of the parsley and scallions. Repeat with remaining cucumber. Pour the puréed cucumbers into a large bowl and with a wire whisk beat in the remaining buttermilk, sour cream, salt and lemon juice. Cover the soup and refrigerate it until dinner time. Serve the soup from a large tureen and float the six cucumber slices and sprigs of dill on top. If there is no tureen, serve the soup in individual bowls and garnish each with a slice of cucumber and dill.

HERRING SALAD

Although this recipe calls for arranging the salad ingredients separately in a bowl, then mixing them together with the dressing at the table, you may, if you prefer, mix them with one cup of dressing ahead of time. What this sacrifices in appearance it may make up for in flavor, since the tastes blend together and are enriched by a couple of hours in the refrigerator.

1 pound veal stew meat	herring
2 tablespoons butter	2 tablespoons capers,
1 tablespoon water	drained
2 medium potatoes	1 1/2 cups chopped red onion
3 eggs	1 1/2 cups chopped dill pickle
3 5-ounce jars of Bismarck	1/2 cup chopped parsley

1 2-ounce can flat anchovy fillets, drained	Romaine
	1 lemon, in small wedges
1 8-ounce can whole beets, drained	Sour-cream dressing (recipe below)

Lightly brown the veal chunks in the butter, then add one tablespoon of water, cover the pan and braise the veal for one hour. Let it cool, then trim the pieces and cut them into cubes about the size of dice. Meanwhile peel and dice the potatoes; cook them in boiling salted water for 15 minutes or until tender. Drain and cool. Put the eggs in a saucepan, cover them with cold water, bring to a boil, cover pan and turn off heat. Let the eggs stand for 20 minutes, by which time they will be hard cooked. Cool them at once by putting them into cold water for a few minutes, which keeps the yolks from discoloring and makes the eggs easier to peel. Rice the whites and yolks separately by putting them through a sieve. While the veal, potatoes and eggs are cooking, drain and trim the herring. Cut the fillets into one-half-inch squares. Mix the capers with the herring pieces. Finely chop the onion, pickle and parsley. Cut the anchovies into small pieces, julienne the beets.

When everything is cooked and chopped, sliced and diced, refrigerate all ingredients covered, in separate bowls, until you are ready to arrange the salad. Then set out the ingredients as attractively as you can. If you are using a round bowl arrange them as shown on the preceding page. If you are using a platter arrange them in strips. Garnish the serving dish with leaves of romaine and with lemon wedges.

At the table mix the ingredients together with about half the amount of the sour cream dressing. Do this carefully as it can become a messy job if you work with abandon. Pass the rest of the dressing in a sauceboat or small bowl for guests to help themselves.

SOUR CREAM DRESSING

¼ cup butter	1 teaspoon paprika
2 cups sour cream	1 teaspoon salt
⅓ cup vinegar	Freshly ground black pepper

Melt the butter in a medium-sized saucepan. Remove it from the heat and stir in the sour cream. Mix in the vinegar, paprika, salt and pepper. Put the dressing into a serving bowl and refrigerate until ready to use.

FROZEN PEACH MOUSSE

3 egg yolks	1½ cups heavy cream,
¾ cup sugar	whipped
⅛ teaspoon salt	1½ cups cubed peaches
¾ cup milk	Brandied peach sauce
¾ cup light cream	(recipe below)
½ teaspoon vanilla extract	

Beat the yolks for a minute or two, gradually add sugar and salt and continue beating until the mixture is thick and creamy. In a saucepan scald the milk and light cream and slowly pour a stream of the hot liquid into the egg yolks and sugar, stirring vigorously. Return this custard mixture to the saucepan and put it back on the stove. Heat slowly, stirring, until the liquid thickens enough to coat the back of a spoon. Do not boil or the mixture will curdle. Cool it to room temperature and chill it, stir in the vanilla and fold in the whipped cream. Pour into two ice-cube trays and freeze until the outside rim is frozen solid but the center is still mushy—about two hours.

Peel and cube enough peaches (about two medium-size ones) to make 1½ cups of chunks. If the peaches do not peel easily, drop them into boiling water, let them stand for a minute or two and then douse with cold water. Cover cubed peaches tightly with plastic wrap so that they will not discolor and set them aside. When the mousse that is freezing has reached proper consistency, pour it into a bowl and beat with an electric beater until smooth. Fold in peach chunks. Have ready a one-quart soufflé dish with a wax-paper collar tied around the outside and extending two or three inches above the top. Pour in the mousse mixture and place plastic wrap across the top of the collar. Then return the mousse to the freezer until it is frozen—about four to six hours. At serving time, remove the plastic wrap, untie the wax-paper collar and gently peel it off. The mousse will stand an inch or so above the rim of the dish. Top each serving with a ladleful of brandied peach sauce.

BRANDIED PEACH SAUCE

3 cups peach slices	⅓ cup brandy
1 tablespoon lemon juice	

Put two cups of peach slices (four medium peaches) into a blender, about a cup at a time, and purée at low speed. Cube the additional one cup, stir into purée with lemon juice and brandy. Cover and chill. Spoon over each serving of mousse at the table.

Fruit in Sauternes

Pale juicy honeydews, crunchy crimson watermelon, delicate seedless grapes, strawberries at their sweetest, peaches at their most melting, blueberries with a tang of northern air about them—this delicious profusion offers one of summer's great pleasures. The cook who has had to be miserly with fresh fruit all year can now be lavish. Chilled, drenched with sauternes, the fruit becomes a magnificent dessert that pleases the senses—a refreshing taste, a joyful mixture of colors and, as you lift it to your mouth, a sweet perfume that evokes the fragrance of a midsummer garden.

This dinner will require some rather odd chores. You will have to soak wheat in a giant pot, squeeze spinach to dry it out, open 32 clams, and do a fairly lengthy, but not arduous, job of chopping, slicing, dicing and mincing. But your dinner will be prepared and you will be out of the kitchen long before your guests arrive—an ideal situation for a summer dinner.

It is virtually impossible to prepare a properly varied fruit in wine for fewer than eight people. Therefore plan the whole meal for eight.

If you have a friend, or a daughter who is handy, enlist her help. For although the cook gets off lightly by having almost everything prepared ahead of time, she has a very full morning of work. The *vitello,* the *tabbouli* and the fruit all require a good deal of chopping and cutting. First, put the wheat for the *tabbouli*—which is a salad—in to soak. It should sit in water for about three hours. Meanwhile cook the veal for the *vitello tonnato.* This will take about three hours too. While it cooks, cut up the fruit, add the wine, put it in a serving bowl and refrigerate it. Leave out the banana; it must be added just before serving. Prepare the topping for the clams and put it in the refrigerator. Mince the herbs for the salad.

When you drain the wheat, add the herbs and dressing right away and put the *tabbouli* in the icebox until ready to serve. When the veal is done, take it from the pot and let it cool. Cook down the stock and prepare the sauce from it. Chill it, along with the wine you are going to drink. You will have had a full morning, but you don't have to do any more cooking until the very last minute. You must decide ahead of time on your clam-opening strategy. You can have the fish store do it and pick the clams up a couple of hours before dinner and keep them in the refrigerator. Since they are going to be cooked this will not hurt them. However if this is not convenient you will have to open them at home. If your husband knows how, fine—give him a big apron, a clam-opening gadget, and half an hour at the sink. But if not, and you don't want to struggle with them yourself, put them into a hot oven for three minutes or so, until they can be pried open easily. About 15 minutes before dinner turn the oven on to broil, spread the topping over the clams. Slice the veal, arrange it on a platter, and spoon the sauce over it. Then put the clams under the broiler for eight minutes. Add sliced banana to the fruit just before serving.

RECIPES

CLAMS ROCKEFELLER

This is a first course that is more often prepared with oysters but is equally good with clams. It supposedly originated at the turn of the century at Antoine's restaurant in New Orleans, where the first thunderstruck guest who tasted it cried out that it was "as rich as Rockefeller."

In view of that, allow four clams per person. Use cherrystone clams if you like large mouthfuls; if you don't, switch to littlenecks. There is no difference except size. If you own a blender this is not a difficult dish to prepare, but there are a couple of tricks involved. The main one is to be sure that the ingredients are properly drained. Squeeze the spinach until your hands ache; it must be absolutely dry. Drain the clams after they are opened. String the celery; otherwise a topping that should be creamy will be stringy. This recipe calls for Pernod, a licorice-flavored cordial. But you can substitute a pinch of dried fennel seed. It will give approximately the same flavor.

Thaw the spinach and squeeze all of the moisture out of it. Pick it up by the fistful and squeeze until the spinach feels dry. When finished, you should have only about one-half cup of spinach. Put spinach, parsley, celery, onion, garlic, butter, Pernod and Tabasco into the blender and blend at low speed, stopping the blender and stirring whenever it clogs. When the mixture is puréed and absolutely smooth, spoon it into a mixing bowl. Stir in the bread crumbs. (There will be about one cup.) Refrigerate until ready to use. To make the clams Rockefeller, preheat the broiler. Rinse the clams, open them, and drain off all the water and juice. Cut clam muscle to free it from shell, but leave clam in the shell. Spread one teaspoon of the spinach topping over each clam. Arrange the clams in shallow baking pans. It is useful to line the pans with coarse salt—which will steady the clams and retain the heat—but not essential. Broil about six inches away from the heat for eight minutes, or until lightly browned.

VITELLO TONNATO

This dish—braised veal with a tuna-mayonnaise sauce —is surely one of the world's most unlikely combinations and one wonders how it ever happened. The story is that Caterina, cook to the Marchese Casati of Milan, 200 years ago had the perennial problem of unexpected guests. Ingeniously she used the only things left in the kitchen—a

32 clams on the half shell	1 small clove garlic,
1 package frozen chopped	quartered
spinach	1/2 cup butter, melted and
1/2 cup chopped fresh	cooled
parsley	1 tablespoon Pernod
1/4 cup chopped celery	1/4 teaspoon Tabasco
1/4 cup chopped onion	1/4 cup dry bread crumbs

cold veal roast, some tuna fish. The dish she created is still one of Milan's prides. The sauce has a sharp but not overpowering flavor which ideally suits the bland veal.

1 5-pound boned and rolled leg of veal	2 tablespoons salt
2 7-ounce cans tuna	Freshly ground pepper
3 tablespoons oil	2 cups chicken stock
2 garlic cloves	1 2-ounce can flat anchovy fillets
2 onions, coarsely chopped	6 tablespoons lemon juice
2 carrots, coarsely chopped	2 cups mayonnaise (recipe below)
2 celery stalks, cut up	
¼ cup chopped parsley	4 tablespoons capers
2 bay leaves	1 lemon, thinly sliced
½ teaspoon thyme	

Drain the oil from the cans of tuna into a Dutch oven or large pot with a tight-fitting cover. Add the extra oil and garlic and brown the veal lightly. Remove meat and set it aside. Add onions, carrots and celery to the oil and garlic and cook, stirring frequently, for five minutes or until the onion is translucent. Add parsley, bay leaves, thyme, salt and pepper, chicken stock, tuna, the drained anchovies and two tablespoons of lemon juice. Stir the mixture well to dissolve any particles that may stick to the bottom of the pot. Bring to a boil, then add the veal. Reduce heat, cover and simmer three hours. Remove the veal from the pot and cool it to room temperature. Then chill in the refrigerator. Meanwhile put the pot back on the stove and reduce the vegetable-tuna mixture—you should have between five and six cups—to about four cups, stirring from time to time to prevent burning. Purée the vegetable-tuna mixture in a blender, or put it through a food mill. Add two cups of the purée to two cups of mayonnaise along with four tablespoons of lemon juice and two tablespoons of capers. Refrigerate. Before serving, slice the veal thinly and arrange the slices on a large platter. Spoon half the tuna-mayonnaise over them, garnish with lemon slices and the rest of the capers. Pass the remaining sauce at the table.

BLENDER MAYONNAISE

2 eggs	½ teaspoon dry mustard
2 tablespoons lemon juice	1 teaspoon salt
1 tablespoon vinegar	1½ cups oil

Combine eggs, lemon juice, vinegar and seasonings in the blender; cover and blend at high speed for 30 seconds until well mixed. With the blender running at medium speed, take off the cover and slowly drip in the oil. The secret of making mayonnaise in the blender is to add the oil very slowly. Blend until thick and smooth.

TABBOULI

This unusual dish comes from the Middle East. Its basis is cracked, or bulgur, wheat, a cereal—and it may strike some of your guests as odd when you tell them it's their salad. Actually it is light, fluffy and piquant when tossed with herbs and an oil-and-lemon dressing. It should be served on the same plate as the *vitello tonnato*. The wheat is sold by the box in most groceries; if yours doesn't have it try a health-food store. In this recipe the wheat is cooked by being steeped in hot water, the ancient Levantine technique. Mince the parsley, mint and scallions fine, so they thoroughly blend into the wheat.

2 cups bulgur wheat	(about 2 medium tomatoes)
8 cups boiling water	
1 cup minced parsley	½ cup lemon juice
½ cup minced mint	½ cup olive oil
½ cup minced scallion with 2 inches of the tops	2 teaspoons salt
	Freshly ground pepper
1½ cups chopped tomato	

Put the wheat into a large pot or mixing bowl and pour the water over it. Cover and let stand for two to three hours, or until the wheat is light and fluffy. Drain off excess water and shake the wheat in a strainer until it is very dry. Add all the rest of the ingredients to the wheat and stir until thoroughly mixed. Chill for at least one hour before serving.

FRESH FRUIT IN SAUTERNES

Use whatever fruit is at its best—the dessert will not change appreciably if you add some choices of your own, like fresh pineapple, or leave out some that might be hard to get, like the apples or grapefruit which are less widely available in summer than at other times of the year. Be sure to use sweet sauternes, since the fruit is not sugared. All French sauternes is sweet, but if you use American sauternes you must specify, otherwise you may get the dry version.

½ large honeydew melon	2 oranges
5 pounds watermelon	1 grapefruit
1 pint strawberries	1 peach
1 pint blueberries	1 apple
½ pound assorted grapes, red and seedless	1 cup sauternes
	1 banana

Make balls of the honeydew and watermelon. Rinse the strawberries and drain them well. Hull them but do not cut them or they will lose their color. Rinse and pick over the blueberries. Rinse grapes and remove the stems. Peel the oranges and grapefruit, divide them into sections. Peel and slice the peach. Rinse and core the apple and slice it thinly but leave the peel on. Combine all these fruits in a large serving bowl—there will be at least 12 cups of fruit—and pour the sauternes over them. The amount of fruit may vary, but be sure to use enough sauternes to coat all the fruit, especially the peach and apple which will darken otherwise. Stir gently. Refrigerate for at least two hours. Just before serving, slice the banana and gently stir it into the bowl.

New England Fish Chowder

No self-respecting Yankee may admit it but New England fish chowder is just one more example of French cooking. It was invented, not by thrifty Puritan housewives, but by the women of Brittany who waited at the water's edge for seafaring husbands, brewing hearty fish stews to greet them with as they stepped ashore. The caldron they cooked in was a *chaudière,* hence chowder.

But New Englanders have given their fish (and their clam) chowder a style which distinguishes it from the Breton soup, which was made with water and whatever fish or vegetables came easily to hand. In New England milk is the base; potatoes and salt pork are included along with any white-meat fish, like whiting, haddock or halibut. But whatever the local variations, there is no question that the chowder owes some of its greatness to the French side of the family.

This is a substantial dinner with two hot courses that won't heat up the house on a summer night. You have only a few minutes of top-of-the-stove cooking to do once your guests have arrived.

You may need to order the meat ahead of time, for veal is not as commonplace in the United States as it is in Europe. Scallops of veal are "scaloppine" in Italy, where they are the most popular meat, and "escalopes" in France. In France, where this dish originated, it is known as Veal Chasseur (the word is cacciatore in Italian —usually associated with chicken) which literally means "hunter style" and gastronomically means that it is cooked with white wine, mushrooms, shallots, and sometimes tomatoes.

MENU FOR SIX

FISH CHOWDER

VEAL SCALLOPS WITH MUSHROOMS
Romaine with watercress dressing
Rolls
Dry white wine

FRESH PEACH CAKE

Make the chowder the day before the dinner. Its flavor will improve considerably overnight. Make the peach cake in the morning on the day of the dinner. During the afternoon wash the salad greens and prepare the dressing. Cook the veal an hour before your guests arrive —it can sit in the pan, covered, to be reheated just before serving. Heat the chowder just before you plan to sit down. While it is being eaten, simmer the veal very gently. It will be heated through by the time you finish the soup. Put the dressing on the salad just before bringing it to the table. If you have baked the peach cake in an attractive pan you can slice it from the pan at the table. Otherwise cut the cake in the kitchen and put the slices on a dessert platter.

RECIPES

FISH CHOWDER

1½ pounds halibut, haddock, whiting or any firm-fleshed white fish	1 teaspoon salt
	¼ teaspoon curry powder
	3 tablespoons flour
6 cups water	2 cups raw potatoes, peeled, diced
2 ounces salt pork, diced	
½ cup butter	1 cup light cream
½ cup chopped onion	½ cup milk
½ cup chopped celery	2 tablespoons chopped fresh parsley
1 small leek, finely chopped (use some of the top)	

Remove the skin and any bones you can from the fish; cut the fish into half-inch chunks. In a large pot, or soup kettle, combine the fish and the water. Include any large bones from the fish. If possible, try to get some extra ones from your fish store; they add a lot of flavor. Bring to a boil, lower heat and simmer for 15 minutes. Drain the fish and reserve one quart of the stock. Remove the large bones and very carefully pick over the fish for any smaller ones. If you use a small whole fish, or a piece that looks bony, cook it as above, but leave it in one piece. Then skin it, remove the bones, and cut it into pieces. The pieces themselves need not be uniform. Put the fish in a small covered bowl and set aside. Rinse out the pot you have been using, and dry it. Put the diced salt pork in the pot, cook over moderate heat until it is crisp and golden brown. Drain on paper towels and set aside. Add the butter to the pork drippings, along with the onion, celery and leek. If you cannot get the leek, use three scallions, or spring onions, instead. Sauté a few minutes until the vegetables are wilted, but do not let them brown. Add the salt and the curry powder. Stir the flour in until smooth. Stir in the reserved fish stock and the potatoes. Cook over moderate heat until the potatoes are tender, stirring occasionally, about 15 minutes. Remove from the heat and add cream, milk, fish, and salt pork. Cover and refrigerate several hours, or overnight, to blend the flavors. To serve reheat it gently; it must not boil. If you are not able to watch it carefully, reheat the soup in the top of a large double boiler. Pour into a tureen, add a large dot of butter, sprinkle with parsley, and pass a pepper mill at the table.

VEAL SCALLOPS WITH MUSHROOMS

Veal scallops, which come from the leg, are very tender meat, need relatively short cooking over no higher than moderate heat. The paler the meat, the younger, and therefore the tenderer, it will be.

2 pounds veal scallops, ¼-inch thick	chopped shallots or onion
1½ teaspoons salt	¾ cup beef broth
¼ teaspoon freshly ground black pepper	¾ cup dry white wine
½ cup flour	1 large tomato, peeled, seeded and diced
6 tablespoons butter	1 teaspoon tarragon
2 tablespoons olive oil	½ teaspoon savory
1½ pounds mushrooms, sliced	½ teaspoon dry mustard
2 tablespoons finely	2 tablespoons chopped fresh parsley

Have your butcher prepare the veal for you, pounded until it is one-quarter-inch thick. Mix the salt and pepper with the flour, and spread on a sheet of wax paper. Dip each piece of veal into the flour, coating it lightly on both sides. Shake the pieces well to remove any excess. The purpose is to allow the veal to brown nicely; too much flour will make it gummy. This all has to be done at the very last minute; but it is not involved at all. Using the largest skillet you own that has a cover, melt three tablespoons of the butter with the olive oil. When it begins to bubble and sputter, start adding the veal. Do not let the pieces touch. The veal will start to shrink almost at once; add a few more pieces. Cook the veal over moderate heat, until golden brown on both sides. It will take about three minutes on each side. As the veal slices brown, remove them to a bowl; keep adding pieces until all are cooked. Since the scallops have virtually no fat, if overcooked or cooked at too high a heat, they will dry out and toughen. Add an additional one tablespoon of butter toward the end, when the skillet is getting dry. When all the veal has been browned, add the remaining two tablespoons of butter to the skillet. Add the mushrooms and sauté them until barely golden, stirring them often so they brown evenly. They will still be firm. Remove the mushrooms and add them to the veal in the bowl. Put the shallots or onion, broth and wine in the skillet. Bring to a boil, lower heat and, with a whisk, stir rapidly to loosen the "bits" at the bottom of the pan. Add the tomato, tarragon, savory and mustard. Add the veal and mushrooms, along with the juices that have collected in the bottom of the bowl. Spoon sauce over the meat. Cook, covered, over low heat, for 30 minutes, basting and turning occasionally. To serve, arrange the veal with the mushrooms on a warm platter and sprinkle it with the chopped parsley.

ROMAINE WITH WATERCRESS DRESSING

2 heads of romaine lettuce (if they are large, use one head)	Juice of one lemon
	1 tablespoon tarragon vinegar
1 bunch watercress	1 teaspoon salt
1 bunch small radishes	1/8 teaspoon dry mustard
9 tablespoons olive oil	1/8 teaspoon sugar

Wash the romaine, watercress and the radishes. Shake the greens well to remove as much moisture as possible. Roll them up in several thicknesses of paper towels and put in the refrigerator to crisp. Do this several hours ahead of time. Greens must be absolutely dry or the dressing will not cling to the leaves. Remove the blossom and stem ends of the radishes, and slice them paper thin. Keep them in ice water in the refrigerator until you are ready for them. Remove the coarse stems from the watercress, keeping only the very thin, delicate stems and the leaves. Gather watercress together and, using a chopping board and a large, sharp, heavy knife, chop the watercress as you would parsley, holding the tip of the knife on the board with your left hand.

In a small bowl mix the oil, lemon juice, vinegar, one-half teaspoon of the salt, mustard and sugar. Add the chopped watercress, stir well. Chill. Before serving tear or break the romaine leaves into bite-size pieces. Sprinkle the greens with the remaining one-half teaspoon salt; add the drained, sliced radishes. Pour the dressing over all and toss.

FRESH PEACH CAKE

The point of this dessert is to have more peaches than cake. When you put it together the batter will appear alarmingly thick and will make only a shallow layer on the bottom of the pan—but it will puff in the cooking. Buy 10 peaches, so you will have plenty. Be sure the fruit is ripe. When you buy peaches—consider the background color, not the blush—it should be creamy. And never be optimistic about buying peaches: Don't buy green ones thinking they will ripen. They never will.

1 cup sifted flour	1/4 cup shortening
1 1/2 teaspoons baking powder	1 egg
	1/4 cup milk
1/2 teaspoon salt	1/2 teaspoon grated lemon rind
1/4 cup sugar	

TOPPING

8-10 large ripe peaches, peeled, pitted and quartered	3 tablespoons soft butter
	1/4 cup flour
	1/4 cup light brown sugar
3 tablespoons sugar	1/4 cup apricot preserves
3/4 cup slivered almonds	1 tablespoon water

Preheat the oven to 400°. Grease and flour a 12x9x2-inch cake pan or baking dish. Sift the flour, baking powder, salt and sugar into a small bowl. With a pastry blender, or your fingers, work in the shortening until it resembles coarse meal. Beat the egg with the milk and stir into the flour mixture along with the lemon rind. Stir just enough to blend it. Spread the batter evenly in the prepared pan. It will make a very thin layer, but don't worry; it will bake up and around the peaches. Arrange the peaches on top of the batter, round side up. Sprinkle the fruit with the three tablespoons of sugar. Bake for 35 minutes. While cake is baking, whirl the almonds in a blender until they are the consistency of fine powder, or put them through the finest blade of a food chopper. Mix the almonds well with the soft butter, flour and the brown sugar. When the cake has baked the 35 minutes, take it from the oven, but do not turn the heat off. Border the top of the cake with the almond mixture. Put the cake back in the oven for an additional 10 minutes. Meanwhile press the apricot preserves through a sieve into a small saucepan. Add the tablespoon of water and cook a minute or two just until the preserves melt. When you take the cake from the oven brush the tops of the peaches with the preserves.

Deep-Dish Blueberry Pie

The early settlers quickly discovered the delicacy of the blueberry, particularly those that grew on the coastal barrens of Maine. They transformed the fruit into deep-dish blueberry pie—unpretentious, as American as the flag and about the juiciest, tangiest eating there is.

But Yankees are not ones to rest on their laurels. Down Easters also produced slump (stewed berries with dumplings) and grunt (baked berries with dumplings). They are named for the way Pa was apt to come to the table. Then came duff (steamed blueberry pudding), flummery (slices of buttered bread and cooked berries) and fool (puréed berries served cold). These runny, eat-it-with-a-spoon desserts can be made anywhere in the United States now, since we think enough of the blueberry to cultivate it widely, the only country which does.

This dinner has a homey air about it. All the courses, even the main one, despite its long French name, are unpretentious. But they are far from plain—the clams are jauntily seasoned with garlic, the cold beef is set off with a shimmering wine jelly, and the pie is an abundance of berries and juice.

The main course is served cold, but everything else is served hot—or at least warm. The appetizer is hot and the pie should still be warm. This combination of hot and cold makes the dinner equally suitable for the warmest evening and for a summer night with an unexpected chill.

Considering how little work there is to this dinner, it takes a lot of time to get it done. This is entirely because the *boeuf à la mode* has to sit at various stages, which requires the sporadic attention of the cook but practically no effort. On Dinner-day minus one and a half—that is, the night before the day before the party—put the beef in

MENU FOR SIX
SCALLOPED CLAMS
BOEUF À LA MODE EN GELÉE
Tossed green salad with
oil and lemon dressing
Red wine

DEEP-DISH BLUEBERRY PIE

the marinade. Let it sit overnight in the refrigerator. The next day braise the meat (a process that again requires a minimum of attention). Then cool it and its broth separately. On the morning of the day of the dinner, cook the carrots and clarify the broth. Arrange the beef and carrots on a platter, glaze them with the broth which has been chilled to the consistency of honey—this is the most time-consuming part of the operation. Put the beef platter and remaining broth back into the refrigerator to set.

About two hours before the guests are due, make the blueberry pie. You will want to serve it warm, so after you take it out of the oven don't put it in a cool place. It will be just right when you serve it. While the pie is baking, assemble the clam scallop and put it in the refrigerator, covered, until you are ready to cook it. Make the salad and the dressing. Twenty minutes before you sit down, put the clams in the preheated oven.

RECIPES

SCALLOPED CLAMS

This dish is most often made with oysters, but it is every bit as good made with clams. If you can get fresh clams, ask for cherrystones—each is a perfect mouthful—and freeze the clam juice for a future fish stock. If you can't get fresh ones, buy canned, which will be shucked. Authentic New England recipes call for "common cracker crumbs"—but these are virtually unavailable outside Boston's city limits, so use any unsalted milk cracker. You probably won't have eaten this kind of cracker since you left the first grade. Make crumbs by crushing the crackers with a rolling pin between sheets of wax paper.

1½ cups milk cracker crumbs	2 tablespoons chopped fresh parsley
6 tablespoons butter, melted	½ teaspoon salt
	Freshly ground black pepper
3 dozen clams, shucked and drained	½ cup heavy cream
	¼ cup sherry
1 small clove garlic, minced	1 tablespoon butter

Preheat oven to 400°F. Mix the crumbs with the melted butter, being sure to coat the crumbs well. Line the bottom of a shallow nine-inch baking dish with half of the crumb mixture. Arrange the shucked, well-drained clams on top of the crumbs. Sprinkle with garlic, taking care to distribute the tiny pieces evenly, and with parsley, salt and pepper. Pour the cream and sherry over the top. Then add the remaining crumbs, covering the clams completely so they will not dry out. Dot with one tablespoon butter and bake in oven for 20 minutes, until the juice is bubbly and the crumbs are lightly browned.

BOEUF À LA MODE EN GELÉE

This is essentially a cold pot roast, served with aspic. But it is a very special version of that familiar dish. In the first place the meat is marinated for hours in wine and brandy. It is then braised with calves' feet or veal knuckles, whichever you can get, to make the broth jell, and with an assortment of herbs and diced salt pork for flavoring. Madeira is added, so that the amber jelly, which will finally be diced and heaped around the platter, has a rich baronial flavor.

This dish, which can be provincial eating in France, can be quite formal fare as well. Marcel Proust, dwelling on its elegance, writes of the family cook Françoise, who has "gone herself to Les Halles to procure the best cuts of rump steak, shin of beef and calves' feet, as Michelangelo passed eight months in the mountains of Carrara choosing the most perfect blocks of marble for the monument of Julius II." And finally, the platter: "the cold beef, spiced with carrots, made its appearance, couched by the Michelangelo of our kitchen upon enormous crystals of jelly, like transparent blocks of quartz."

3 pounds bottom round	1½ cups red wine
1 large onion, sliced	¼ cup brandy
1 carrot, sliced	⅓ cup olive oil
2 cloves garlic, halved	2 tablespoons butter
Few sprigs parsley	⅛ pound salt pork, diced
1 bay leaf, broken	2 calves' feet, cut crosswise or 2 veal knuckles, cut in pieces
½ teaspoon thyme	
1 teaspoon salt	
Freshly ground black pepper	1 10½-ounce can consommé

½ cup Madeira 12 carrots, cut in ovals
2 egg whites, beaten

Wipe the meat with a damp cloth and place it in a deep bowl. Place the sliced onion, carrot, garlic, parsley and bay leaf over and around the meat. Sprinkle with thyme, salt and pepper. Pour the wine, brandy and olive oil over the meat. Cover and refrigerate for at least six hours or overnight, turning once. Remove the meat from the marinade, and put the liquid and vegetables aside. Carefully pat the meat dry with paper towels. This is important, as the roast must be completely dry in order to brown properly.

Melt the butter in a heavy flameproof casserole and in it brown the meat and the diced salt pork, turning the meat so that it browns on all sides. Add the calves' feet, consommé and the reserved marinade and vegetables. Bring to a boil, cover, reduce the heat and simmer for three hours. Remove the meat from the broth and set it aside. Strain the broth, discarding the salt pork, calves' feet and vegetables. Place the broth in a bowl and the meat on a platter and let them cool separately. Wrap the beef in foil and place it and the cooled broth, covered, in the refrigerator.

When the broth has thoroughly chilled, which will take several hours, remove the layer of fat from it and place it in a saucepan over a very low flame. When the broth is melted, stir in the Madeira and the beaten egg whites and continue stirring as the broth comes to a boil. Let it boil two or three minutes, turn the flame down very low and let it stand for 10 minutes. Line a strainer with several layers of wet cheesecloth, a filter paper or a linen towel and pour the broth through it. This operation, which turns the murky broth into a clear amber liquid, may take as long as an hour. While it is going on, cut the meat into slices one-quarter-inch thick and cook the carrots.

Drop the carrot ovals into boiling water. Return to a boil and cook for 15 minutes. Drain and shake the cooked carrots over a very low flame to dry them out. Set the carrots aside to cool. Place the slices of beef on a platter, overlapping them slightly. Trim the slices, if necessary, to make them look neat. Arrange the cooled carrots in neat bunches flanking the meat. By this time the broth should be completely clarified and cool enough to go into the refrigerator.

Let the broth chill in the refrigerator until it begins to thicken. It should take about one-half hour to reach the proper consistency. When the broth runs off a spoon like molasses, spread a coating over the slices of meat and the mounds of carrots. When you have a glaze of jelly on the meat, place the platter in the refrigerator to set. Let the remaining jelly set in a shallow pan in the refrigerator. When it is completely firm, which may take two hours, dice it with a well-chilled knife and arrange it in mounds to alternate with the carrots on the beef platter.

DEEP-DISH BLUEBERRY PIE

This is a delicious dessert just as it is, but if you don't object to calories, you can go all out and serve it with whipped cream or vanilla ice cream.

1 quart blueberries 2 tablespoons lemon juice
1 tablespoon flour Pastry for one-crust pie
¼ cup sugar (recipe below)

Preheat oven to 400°F. Wash and drain the blueberries. Mix flour and sugar together, then lightly toss the mixture with the blueberries until they are coated. Pour them into a one-and-a-half-quart casserole. Sprinkle the lemon juice over the berries.

Meanwhile, make the pastry and roll it out so that it is about one inch larger all around than the top of the casserole. Place the pastry over the berries, trim edges and press the pastry to the sides of the casserole. Flute the edges and cut several slits in the pastry to let the steam escape. Bake 30 to 35 minutes, until the crust is browned.

PASTRY FOR ONE-CRUST PIE

1 cup flour ⅓ cup shortening
½ teaspoon salt 2 tablespoons ice water

Sift flour and salt together; cut in shortening until the mixture resembles tiny peas. Stir the ice water in with a fork until the mixture begins to hold together. Shape it into a ball and roll it out on lightly floured board.

*Fall brings encouragement to
return to the kitchen, to give a party,
to make a pot-au-feu, a chocolate
cheesecake. Most food for fall—the
squash, the apples, the chestnuts—is
available through the winter, and the
menus that follow will be suitable
as long as the evening air
has that edge that gives an appetite.*

autumn

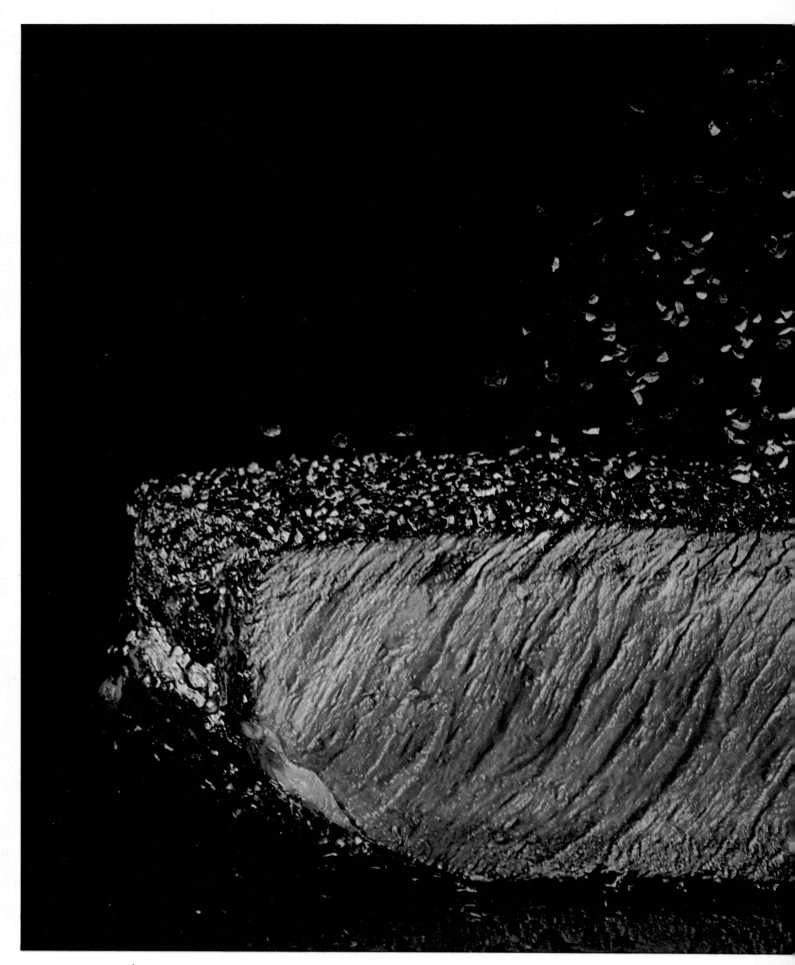

Steak au Poivre

No other country in the world dotes as we do on the perfect steak. Americans believe, in much the same way that they believe in the flag, that they know better

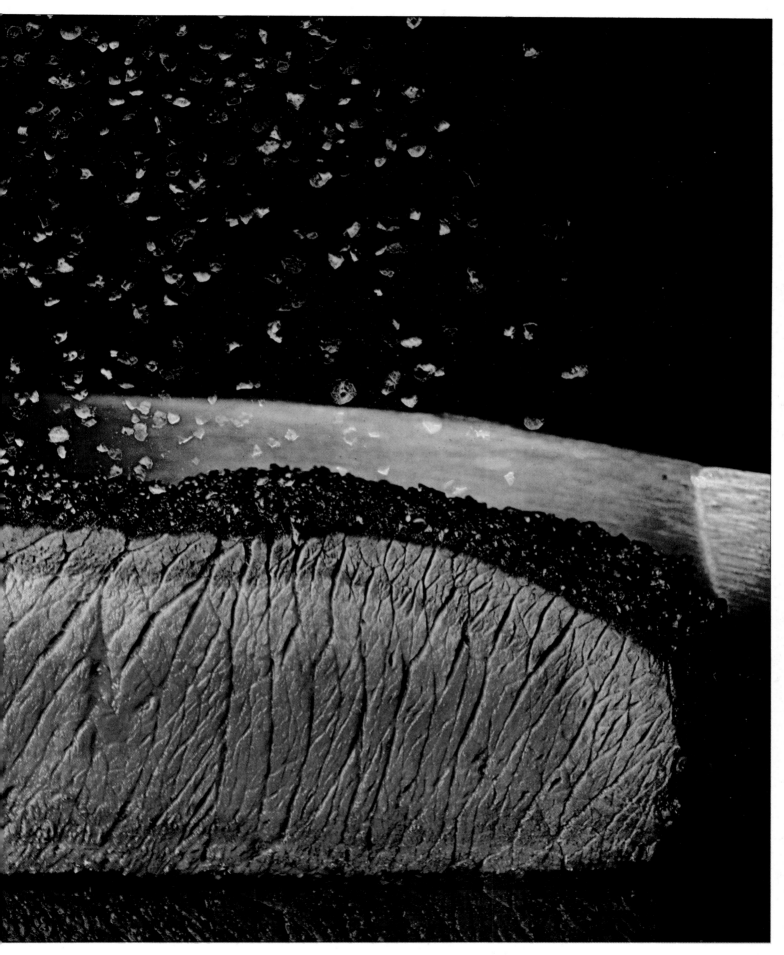

than anybody else how to cook a steak. The French technique proposed here may seem a sacrilege—encrusting the meat with pepper and cooking it on top of the stove. But the result is juicy and aromatic and the cooking is easy to control. In pan-broiling, the timing is more certain than in conventional broiling and the job a good deal less messy. The thin layer of cracked pepper, which you might expect to make the meat fiery hot, instead gives it a pungent head-clearing flavor.

This is a meat-and-potatoes dinner, robust, unfussy. All the elements of the menu are simple but each one has a special touch—there is a surprise in every dish.

Vegetables are the first course, but here two different marinades liven them up. The steak is spicy and the baked potatoes are salted with caviar. Cheesecake and chocolate join in making a sensational and unexpected dessert.

It's a snap to get this dinner to the table. Prepare the dilled carrots and the mushrooms à la Grecque the day before the dinner and marinate them in the refrigerator until you are ready to serve them. The longer they sit in their marinades the better they will taste. The chocolate cheesecake must also be made ahead of time—the day before or first thing on the morning of the dinner. It will take you about

MENU FOR SIX

DILLED CARROTS

MUSHROOMS À LA GRECQUE

STEAK AU POIVRE
Baked potatoes with caviar
Tossed green salad
Red wine

CHOCOLATE CHEESECAKE

two hours to put it together and it should chill five hours more.

You will have virtually nothing to do on the day of the dinner (if you have made dessert beforehand) until an hour before your guests are due. Wash the salad greens and make a vinaigrette dressing. Set the table, decork the wine and preheat the oven for the potatoes. Take the steak out of the refrigerator and pepper it. As your guests walk in the door, put the potatoes in the oven—they will take an hour to bake. Prepare the frying pan for the steak as you are dishing up the first course. As you sit down to eat the appetizer put the steak in the pan. Timing is everything: use a timer and be prepared to get up from the dinner table to turn the steak over. When serving the cheesecake, remember to cut very thin wedges.

RECIPES

DILLED CARROTS

Use baby carrots if you can get them. If not, pare large carrots down into small ovals by using a vegetable scraper. Try to get fresh dill. If you can't, substitute dried dill weed in the marinade, and dust the finished carrots once over lightly with chopped parsley.

2 bunches carrots	fresh dill
1 cup white vinegar	or one teaspoon dried dill
2 tablespoons sugar	weed and one
2 teaspoons salt	tablespoon chopped
Freshly ground black pepper	fresh parsley
2 tablespoons chopped	

Drop the carrots into boiling water and cook them just until they are tender, about 10 to 15 minutes. Drain them and place them in a small mixing bowl. Combine the vinegar, sugar, salt, pepper and one tablespoon chopped fresh dill or one teaspoon of dill weed and pour over the carrots. Cover and refrigerate overnight. Drain and serve sprinkled with the remaining tablespoon of chopped fresh dill or with the chopped parsley.

MUSHROOMS À LA GRECQUE

As for the mushrooms, buy the smallest ones you can. Look for ones that are tightly furled—on which you can see very little of the dark pleating between the cap and the stem; this is a sign of freshness.

1 pound small mushrooms	1 teaspoon salt
1 3/4 cups water	1 stalk celery with leaves,
1/2 cup olive oil	quartered
Juice of one lemon	4 sprigs parsley
2 tablespoons white vinegar	8 peppercorns

6 coriander seeds	1 tablespoon chopped fresh
1/2 teaspoon thyme	parsley
1/4 teaspoon fennel seeds	

Wipe the mushrooms—don't ever wash them—with a damp cloth and set them aside. In a saucepan combine the water, oil, lemon juice, vinegar and salt. Tie the celery, parsley, peppercorns, coriander seeds, thyme and fennel seeds in a square of cheesecloth and add this *bouquet garni* to the liquid. Bring the mixture to a boil, reduce the heat and let it simmer, covered, for five minutes. Add the mushrooms and simmer seven minutes longer. Remove the saucepan from the heat and let the mixture cool. Cover and refrigerate overnight. To serve, drain the mushrooms and sprinkle with the parsley.

STEAK AU POIVRE

The result in pan-broiling is the same as in conventional broiling—but the process is simpler. It is easier to control the cooking because the steak is in full sight, and you can touch it occasionally—the best test for doneness there is—without getting on your hands and knees as you must with most broilers. Raw meat feels mushy to the touch. Well-done meat feels firm; rare meat is soft and springy. If you can teach yourself to recognize these distinctions, it will save you worry, but in the meantime a slight incision will do the trick and won't do any harm. Pan broiling produces a fair amount of smoke. You will have to open a window or turn on an exhaust fan.

If you have a pepper mill that grinds coarsely, use it; otherwise be sure to crack your pepper by hand. Pepper cracked before it was packaged is bound to have lost a lot of its flavor.

4 pounds boneless sirloin steak, cut 1½ inches thick	1½ tablespoons freshly cracked peppercorns Salt

Your steak should weigh four pounds after the butcher has boned it, so count on buying one weighing four and three quarters to five pounds. (The only reason for boning it, incidentally, is to be able to fit a steak of this weight into a frying pan.) When you take the steak from the refrigerator (an hour before you plan to serve it), try it for size in the skillet you intend to cook it in —preferably a 12-inch cast-iron one. You may have to tie or skewer the meat. With a rolling pin or with a mortar and pestle, crack enough peppercorns to make one and a half tablespoons of pepper. Sprinkle both sides of the steak with the pepper, then press the pepper into the meat with the heel of your hand and let stand at room temperature. Twenty-five minutes before you plan to eat the steak, rub the inside of the skillet lightly with a piece of suet cut from the steak, sprinkle with a thin layer of salt and place over high heat until the salt begins to brown and the pan is almost but not quite smoking. Add the steak and cook for 10 minutes. Turn, with two wooden spoons so as not to puncture the meat, and cook for 10 minutes on the other side. This will give you a rare but not bloody steak.

BAKED POTATOES WITH CAVIAR

6 baking potatoes	½ pint sour cream
1 4-ounce jar red caviar	

Preheat the oven to 375°. Scrub the potatoes and rub the skins with butter to prevent them from splitting or drying out. Prick the potatoes once or twice with a fork so they will not explode in the oven. Bake for about an hour or until they can be easily pierced with a fork. To serve, cut a cross in the top of each potato, push the sides together slightly, forcing the meat of the potato upward. Place a generous tablespoon of sour cream in each, stirring it in slightly, and then top each one with a tablespoon of red caviar.

CHOCOLATE CHEESECAKE

This is a very unlikely-sounding combination that is totally different from conventional cheesecake or any chocolate dessert you've ever eaten before. You must have a spring-form pan to make it in and it will be simpler to do if you have an electric mixer, or an electric beater. The preparation is really foolproof.

18 chocolate wafers	1 cup sugar
¼ cup butter	3 eggs
¼ teaspoon cinnamon	2 teaspoons cocoa
1 package (8 ounces) semisweet chocolate	1 teaspoon vanilla
1½ pounds cream cheese	2 cups sour cream

Preheat oven to 350°. Take the cream cheese out of the refrigerator and let it stand at room temperature to soften. Crush enough wafers with a rolling pin or in a blender to make one cup of crumbs. Melt butter in saucepan. Mix in crumbs and cinnamon. Press the crumb mixture on bottom of an eight-inch spring-form pan, then buckle sides on. Chill. Melt the chocolate in the top of a double boiler, stirring occasionally. In a large bowl beat the now-softened cream cheese until fluffy and smooth, using an electric mixer. Beat in the sugar. Add the eggs, one at a time, beating after each addition. Beat in the melted chocolate, cocoa and vanilla, blending them thoroughly together. Beat in the sour cream. Pour the mixture into a spring-form pan. Bake one hour and 10 minutes. The cake will still be runny but will become firm as it chills. Cool at room temperature, then chill in the refrigerator for at least five hours before serving. If any cracks develop, decorate the top with chocolate shavings, which will make it look attractive and hide all sins.

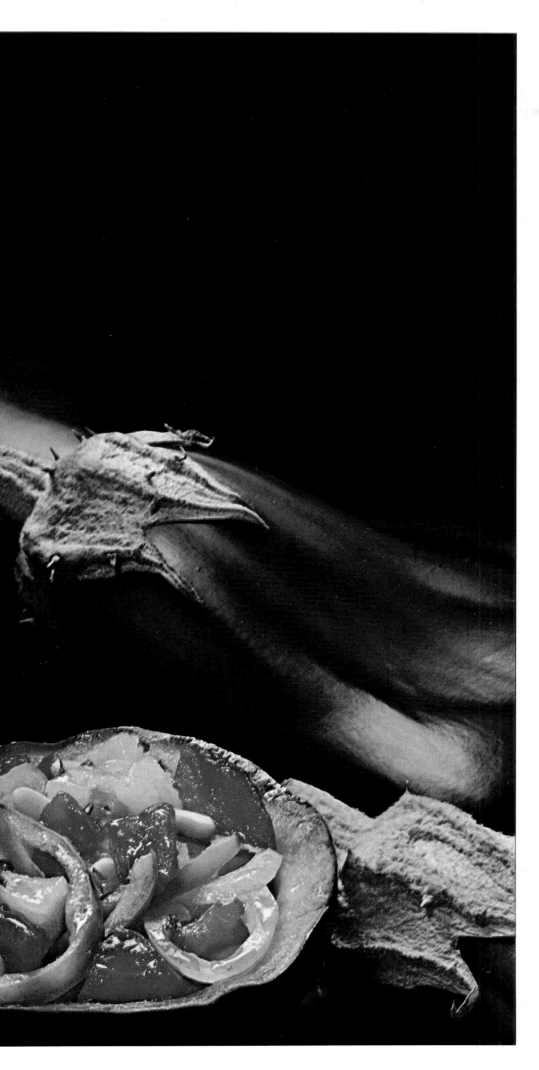

Stuffed Eggplant

It is told of this delectable eggplant dish that a certain holy man once swooned after simply inhaling its fragrance, and it has ever since been known as *Imam Bayildi* or The Priest Fainted.

A vegetable that could be cooked a different way on each of a thousand and one nights, the eggplant is widely used in the Near East and is also virtually a staple in Italy, Britain and France. Actually the eggplant grows better here than in Europe, yet relatively few Americans appreciate its unique "meaty" flavor or chameleonlike adaptability; perhaps this is because, like breadfruit, it suffers from a spectacularly drab name.

What gives this whole dinner an exotic cast is the way the ingredients are paired. The favorite meat of the Arab countries, lamb, is cooked with dill, an herb powerful enough to ward off the Evil Eye when carried in a packet over the heart. Rice is prepared with fine egg noodles to become rice pilaf; and the torte, essentially an Austrian dessert, is Turkified by a dousing of sweet-honey syrup.

Although this dinner is Middle Eastern, in inspiration at least, it does not require that your guests have a natural liking for the bizarre. The dishes may be unfamiliar but they are not outlandish. The Imam Bayildi is quite a little like ratatouille, the lamb is a creamy stew, and the honey nut cake a sweet but very simple dessert.

Shop for small eggplants. Keep in mind that each guest is going to receive half of one and that if you buy ones weighing over a pound they will be too much—both to eat and to look at. The day before the dinner make the lamb stew up to the point of adding the mushrooms. If you feel like it, you can make the cake while the stew is cooking. It will take about the same amount of time—an hour—from start to finish, and will keep perfectly well until the next day. On

MENU FOR SIX

IMAM BAYILDI

LAMB WITH DILL
Rice pilaf
Garden lettuce salad,
oil and lemon dressing
Red wine

HONEY NUT CAKE

Turkish coffee

the morning of the party prepare the eggplants and the stuffing, but do not assemble the dish until the last minute. In the late afternoon wash the lettuce for the salad, make the salad dressing and cut up the mushrooms. Half an hour before you plan to sit down put the stew on to heat. Whip the cream and refrigerate it. Fill the eggplant shells. Ten minutes before sitting down add the mushrooms to the stew, sauté the rice and noodles for the pilaf (which takes only a few minutes), add the broth to them and cook. After you have finished eating the first course, stir the sour cream into the stew and let it heat while you bring the pilaf, which will be finished by now, to the table. Serve the salad. The cake should be cut in very small portions and served with a dollop of whipped cream on each piece.

RECIPES

IMAM BAYILDI

Don't try to do this dish in a hurry—at least not the first time. It is not difficult, but dicing and removing the eggplant meat without damaging the shell is tedious and requires care. Drain the tomatoes thoroughly before adding them to the stuffing or else the stuffing will be too wet. The separate elements are discouragingly unattractive-looking until they are put together. Then, astonishingly, they combine to make an unusually pretty dish.

3 small eggplants	¼ teaspoon oregano
2 onions	⅛ teaspoon freshly ground
1 green pepper	black pepper
4 medium tomatoes	2 tablespoons fresh lemon
6 tablespoons olive oil	juice
1 clove garlic, minced	2 tablespoons chopped
1½ teaspoons salt	parsley
½ teaspoon sugar	¼ cup pine nuts

Place the eggplants in a large pot and cover them with boiling water. You may have to do them one at a time, as they take up a lot of space and must not be crowded. If you jam them in, you may bruise them when you turn them. Cook them, uncovered, in rapidly boiling water for five minutes. Turn them often, using a wooden spoon so you don't puncture the skin. Transfer them to a pan of cold water to cool quickly. While they are cooling, peel the onions and slice them thinly. Cut the green pepper into thin julienne strips. Keep the vegetables separate as they are to be added to the pot at different times. To peel the tomatoes easily, dip them, on the end of a kitchen fork, into boiling water for about 30 seconds. The skins will slip off with the help of a sharp knife. Remove the core and scrape out the seeds and drain them. Cut

them into small chunks. Split the cooled eggplants in half lengthwise. You are now going to remove the eggplant pulp without piercing the eggplant shell—if possible. Cut around the inside of each half, about one-half inch from the edge. Next cut the pulp into squares, but do not cut too deeply; leave a half inch of uncut pulp on the bottom of each shell. Scoop out the now-diced pulp —a serrated grapefruit spoon is ideal for this. Try not to pierce the skin as you do this—but if you dig too deeply once or twice it will not be a disaster. Measure one quart of the diced pulp, discard the extra, if any. Place the eggplant shells on a paper-towel-lined tray, skin side up, and chill until ready to use. They will be limp now but they will look fine when filled.

Put three tablespoons of the olive oil in a large skillet, sauté the sliced onions and the pepper strips until they are just wilted—about five minutes. Add the garlic and the diced eggplant; cover and cook, stirring occasionally, until the eggplant is done—about seven minutes. Add the seasonings, stir, then cook about two minutes. Remove from the stove, then gently stir in the cut-up tomatoes. Transfer the mixture to a large bowl. Mix in the remaining three tablespoons olive oil and the lemon juice. Chill well—at least four hours. Just before serving, pat the inside of the eggplant shells with paper towels and, using a slotted spoon, divide the vegetable mixture among the shells, heaping it up as much as necessary. Sprinkle each eggplant half with parsley and pine nuts.

LAMB WITH DILL

Dill seeds are best known for their association with pickles, but they can be used to add spirit to everything from sauerkraut to apple pie. Native to the area around the

174

Black Sea, they turn up often in Middle Eastern cooking and add a distinctive flavor to this stew. The final result will be creamy, smooth and tender.

3½ pounds lean lamb, cut from the leg, in 1½-inch cubes	⅓ cup red wine
	1½ teaspoons dill seed
3 tablespoons butter	1 pound mushrooms
½ cup chopped onion	½ cup sour cream
5 tablespoons flour	Salt
1¾ cups beef broth	Freshly ground black pepper

Wipe the lamb with paper towels as moist pieces are difficult to brown. Melt the butter in a large, heavy Dutch oven or casserole. Add some of the lamb—just enough to cover the bottom of the pot. Cook over moderately high heat, turning often, until lightly browned on all sides. It should not be allowed to get crusty. When the meat is browned, transfer it to a bowl. Continue until all the lamb is browned. Add the onions to the pan and cook a minute or two. Return the lamb and any juices to the pot. Sprinkle the flour over the lamb and, using a wooden spoon, mix well to coat the pieces. Add the broth, wine and dill seed. Bring the stew to a boil, stirring occasionally, lower the heat, cover and simmer for an hour, until the meat is tender. Cool, then chill, covered, several hours, or overnight. Remove any fat that has settled on top. Before serving, place the stew over low heat and let it simmer until heated through. Meanwhile, wipe the mushrooms with a damp cloth, cut off the coarse stems, and cut the mushrooms into quarters. If they are small, just cut them in half. Add the mushrooms to the stew, cover and cook gently for 20 minutes, stirring occasionally. Taste the stew and add salt and pepper if necessary. Stir in sour cream and heat through; do not let it boil. At the table serve the lamb and its sauce over the pilaf.

RICE PILAF

Pilaf can also be spelled pilaff, pilaw, pilau, and there are even more ways to cook it. This version couldn't be simpler to make, but the stock gives it flavor and the noodles add a satisfying crunch.

4 tablespoons butter	2 teaspoons salt
½ cup fine egg noodles	3 cups chicken broth
1½ cups long-grain rice	

Melt the butter over moderately low heat, using a heavy, good-sized pot. Add the egg noodles and cook them, stirring constantly, until they are just lightly browned, which will take about four minutes. Watch carefully so they do not burn. Stir in the rice and cook for a few minutes until the grains lose their translucent quality. Add the salt and the chicken broth—be careful here, as there will be some sputtering when you add the cold liquid to the hot rice. Mix well and bring to a boil. Turn the heat as low as possible, cover with a tight-fitting lid and cook for 20 minutes. Uncover and fluff up the rice with a fork.

HONEY NUT CAKE

Like all Middle Eastern desserts, this cake is very sweet. If you know in advance some of your guests are not sweet fanciers, serve a bowl of mixed fruit along with the cake so they can suit themselves. In any case, be sure to cut the cake into very small portions.

1½ cups zwieback crumbs	⅛ teaspoon salt
1½ cups finely chopped walnuts	5 eggs, separated
	¾ cup sugar
1½ teaspoons baking powder	1 teaspoon vanilla
	½ cup cream, whipped
½ teaspoon cinnamon	

SYRUP

2 cups water	⅔ cup honey
1½ cups sugar	2 tablespoons light rum

Preheat oven to 325°. About two dozen zwieback make one and a half cups of crumbs. The best way is to use a blender. Break up cookies and do a few at a time. If you don't have a blender, crush the cookies between waxed paper with a rolling pin. The nuts should be chopped until they are fine but not powdery. Mix crumbs and nuts in a large mixing bowl. Stir in baking powder, cinnamon and salt. In a smaller bowl, using an electric beater, beat egg yolks until thick and pale; then gradually beat in sugar. The mixture will be very thick. Using a wooden spoon, work the egg mixture into the crumb mixture; both are very thick, so this takes a little effort. Beat egg whites until stiff and fold them into the mixture also. Turn the batter into a greased 9x9x2 baking pan. Even it out with a spatula. Bake for 30 minutes. While cake is baking, prepare syrup. In a medium-sized saucepan combine water, sugar and honey. Bring to a boil, stirring occasionally, lower heat and simmer for 25 minutes. Remove from heat and stir in rum. Slowly pour as much syrup over cake as it will absorb. After a few minutes, add any remaining syrup. Cover and let stand at room temperature for six hours. Serve with whipped cream.

TURKISH COFFEE

If you want to go all out, serve Turkish coffee after dinner. You will have to get the coffee itself, which has a bittersweet taste, at a specialty shop. You can make it in a saucepan if you don't have a *cezve* handy—which is a Turkish coffeepot. A *cezve* is very much like a butter melter, which will also do nicely if it's a big enough one.

To make coffee for six demitasses put two cups of cold water, six heaping teapoons of coffee and, depending on how sweet you like your coffee, four or five teaspoons of sugar into a saucepan. Bring the water to a boil and turn off the heat at once. Pour the coffee quickly into the cups while it is still frothy and bubbling. This froth is really grounds, which will settle in the bottom of each cup. Obviously, Turkish coffee drinkers never drink more than half a demitasse cupful at a time.

A Spicy Rolled Beef

In Europe it would be called a *paupiette* or a *roulade*. But the Argentinians have a more vivid way of putting it—*matambre*, from *mata hambre*, which literally means it kills hunger. They also have a more vivid way of preparing it, transforming a rolled beef into a multicolored fiesta dish. Wrapped inside the flank steak, jelly-roll style, and seen at right in cross section are corn, carrots, peas, pimiento and chili pepper. This dish dates from the days of the stagecoach when travelers across the endless pampas carried a roll of beef to see them through the journey. Many recipes for *matambre* exist in Argentina where, until the last few years, beef was so plentiful that steak was automatically served as a side dish with every meal. But none is peppier than this vegetable-studded version, enlivened with garlic and chilies.

Other Latin American specialties accompany this dinner. The chicken soup garnished with slices of avocado was invented on the streets of Mexico City. Black beans, a Brazilian staple, accompany the main course, as does a chili sauce. Although it may come as a surprise to many North American cooks, not every Latin chili sauce need be a searing experience. This one is provocative without being incendiary.

Almost everything on this dinner turns up in the wrong place. The salad is in the soup and the soup is in the vegetable. Much of this topsy-turvy condition is brought about by Latin touches, but the dessert is entirely north of the border.

The main course of this dinner is hearty and moderately hot. It is therefore served with plenty of beer and is set off by a delicately flavored soup and a light dessert.

Depending on where you live, you may have to do your shopping in advance. Black beans are available in Mexican or Spanish neighborhoods and in many delicacy stores. Chili peppers may also take searching out. They come in several colors (red, green, yellow), many names (*jalapeño, pequin, serrano*) and in varying degrees of hotness. They are usually available in cans at specialty stores, but if you can't find any, use a dash of cayenne pepper instead. Since avocados are often picked and shipped while still hard, select one ahead and keep it at room temperature until it is as soft as a ripe peach, then refrigerate it until ready to use.

The beans should be soaked overnight, but if you forget to do this all is not lost. You can boil up the beans

MENU FOR SIX

CHICKEN AND AVOCADO SOUP

MATAMBRE WITH CHILI SAUCE
Baked black beans
Beer

PUMPKIN CHIFFON PIE

for two or three minutes, and then soak them for only one hour. Make the dessert the morning of the dinner. Chill it, covered, in the refrigerator until dinner. In the afternoon start on the soup, *matambre* and beans. First precook the beans, which will take about 45 minutes. While the beans are simmering make the soup. When the chicken breast has poached in the broth, put it in the refrigerator to chill. This makes it easier to cut it into thin julienne strips. Stuff and roll the steaks. Make the chili sauce. An hour before the guests are expected, put the beans and the beef in the oven. They cook in the same-temperature oven for the same time—two hours. Julienne the chicken breast. Put the chicken into the soup pot. Before you serve the first course take the *matambre* out of the oven and let it rest to make carving it neater. Take the beans out of the oven but keep them covered and warm. Turn the heat on very low under the chili sauce. Just before you bring it on, slice the avocado into the steaming soup—if you do this any earlier the avocado will discolor, and, instead of a dramatic first course, you will have a drab-looking one.

RECIPES

CHICKEN AND AVOCADO SOUP

This soup is to Mexico City what onion soup is to Paris. It originated outside the streetcar barns in the Indianilla section of the city. It was popular with workers and with all-night partygoers who were served "Caldos de Indianilla" in stalls along the street, and has been appropriated by many restaurants. It is sometimes served with rice and slices of hot pepper along with the avocado.

If you have enough homemade chicken stock on hand, or want to make it, by all means do so; it can only make your soup richer. But you can successfully use canned chicken broth in this recipe, since poaching the chicken in the broth, adding onion and spices, should dispel any suspicion that the stock is not your own.

6 cups chicken broth	1/2 teaspoon oregano
1 whole chicken breast	1/2 teaspoon salt
2 onions, sliced	1/4 teaspoon freshly ground
1/2 teaspoon ground	black pepper
coriander	1 ripe avocado

Pour the chicken broth into a large saucepan. Add chicken breast, onions and seasonings. Bring to a boil, reduce heat, cover and poach in the simmering broth for 20 minutes. Remove the chicken breast and let it cool. Strain the stock into a saucepan and set it aside. Discard the cooked onions. When the chicken is cold and firm to the touch, peel off the skin. Then, using the sharpest knife

you own, cut it into small julienne strips. Just before serving, stir the strips into the soup and heat. Peel the avocado, cut it into thin slices and add to the soup. The slices will float on top.

MATAMBRE

This dish uses flank steak, a cut which usually gets to the table as London broil. It is ideal for this dish—when braised, it emerges from the pot both tender and juicy. If your butcher will do it, have him butterfly the steaks. However, it is perfectly simple to do yourself: take a long sharp knife and slit the steak, starting at one of the long sides and cutting through almost to the other side. But be careful that you don't cut all the way through and end up with two separate pieces. Open the steak and pound it. This is more attractive when the meat is rolled.

2 flank steaks (about two	chili pepper
pounds each), butterflied	1 clove garlic, crushed
1 cup frozen mixed	1 teaspoon salt
vegetables, thawed	1 cup beef broth
1/2 cup finely chopped onion	1 celery stalk, sliced
1/4 cup finely chopped green	1 carrot, sliced
pepper	1 onion, sliced
1/4 cup finely chopped	1 clove garlic, chopped
pimiento	Chili sauce (recipe below)
2 teaspoons finely minced	

Preheat oven to 350°. Pound the butterflied steaks as thin as possible. Trim off any excess fat and cut the edges straight so that the finished steaks are roughly square, about 12 by 12. Lay the steaks side by side, overlapping the edges an inch or two, so that when you roll them they hold together as if they were one piece of meat. Combine the mixed vegetables, chopped onion, green pepper, pimiento, chili pepper, crushed garlic and salt; mix thoroughly. Spread this mixture evenly over the steaks, covering the entire surface. Roll the two steaks up, jelly-roll fashion, as tight as possible. Tie the roll securely every two inches, using five lengths of string. Put the roll in a shallow casserole and add the beef broth, sliced celery, carrot and onions and chopped garlic. Cover and braise for two hours, basting the meat several times. Move the *matambre* to a platter about 15 minutes before serving. This will make the meat firmer and the carving easier. Serve with chili sauce.

CHILI SAUCE

4 tablespoons butter	1 tablespoon chili powder
1 onion, finely chopped	1 teaspoon salt
1 green pepper, finely chopped	Freshly ground black pepper
1 clove garlic, minced	1 cup tomato juice
2 tablespoons flour	1 cup beef broth

Melt butter in a medium-size skillet. Add onion, green pepper and garlic and sauté for five minutes or so, stirring frequently, until the vegetables are translucent but not browned. Blend in the flour, chili powder, salt and pepper. Stir over low heat for two minutes. Stir in the tomato juice and beef broth. Cook, stirring, over medium heat until slightly thickened. Serve hot.

BAKED BLACK BEANS

The Indians of the Southwest and of South America raised beans in nearly every color of the rainbow: yellow, red, white, black and multicolored. In most of our cookery we rely on the pale ones, but in Latin America colored beans, particularly black ones, are a cooking staple. If you can't locate any black ones, substitute kidney beans —but it won't be quite the same. When you are pre-cooking them, simmer and stir gently. Otherwise the skins will break and the beans will get mushy.

1 pound dried black beans	1 bay leaf
1/4 pound salt pork, cut in four pieces	1 cup white wine
2 celery stalks with leaves, cut up	1 teaspoon thyme
1 carrot, cut up	1 teaspoon salt
1 onion stuck with two whole cloves	1/4 teaspoon freshly ground black pepper
2 cloves garlic	2 tablespoons chopped fresh parsley
1 dried chili pepper	1/2 pint sour cream

Wash the beans, cover them with cold water and soak overnight. Drain them and put them with the salt pork into a large pot. Add enough water to reach one inch above the beans. Tie the celery, carrot, onion, garlic, chili pepper and bay leaf in cheesecloth and put them into the pot. This may seem a nuisance, but it makes it easier to take them out of the pot later. Bring to a boil, reduce the heat, cover and simmer for 45 minutes. Remove and discard the salt pork and cheesecloth bag. Drain the beans, but save the liquid. Put the beans in a two-quart casserole. Add the wine, one cup of bean liquid, thyme, salt and pepper. (Save the remaining liquid for later use.) Cover and bake at 350° for two hours or until beans are tender but not mushy. Stir the beans during the cooking, and add more bean liquid if they seem dry. Just before serving, add the parsley. Pass the sour cream to spoon over them at the table.

PUMPKIN CHIFFON PIE

This variation on the autumn standby is made light and fluffy by the addition of extra eggs, and it has a healthy dollop of rum. The toasted coconut topping adds crunchy texture and a nutty flavor.

1/2 cup brown sugar	4 eggs, separated
2 envelopes gelatin	1 1/4 cups canned pumpkin
1/2 teaspoon salt	1/3 cup rum
1/2 teaspoon cinnamon	1/2 cup sugar
1/4 teaspoon nutmeg	9-inch gingersnap pie crust
1/4 teaspoon ginger	(recipe below)
1 cup milk	1/2 cup coconut flakes

Thoroughly mix brown sugar, gelatin, salt and spices in a saucepan. Stir in milk, egg yolks and pumpkin. Cook, stirring frequently, over low heat for 10 minutes or until the gelatin is completely dissolved. Let it cool, then stir in the rum. Chill in the refrigerator until the mixture thickens enough to mound slightly when dropped from a spoon. It must be about the consistency of mayonnaise. Beat egg whites until stiff. Beat in the sugar, a little at a time, then continue beating until smooth. Fold the egg whites into the pumpkin mixture. Ladle into the prepared crust and chill until firm—at least two hours. Meanwhile, toast the coconut flakes. Spread them on a baking sheet and brown them in a 350° oven for five to 10 minutes. To serve, sprinkle toasted coconut over the pie.

GINGERSNAP CRUST

1/2 pound gingersnaps	1/4 cup butter, melted

Make crumbs of the gingersnaps by whirling them in a blender a few at a time, or by crushing them with a rolling pin. Measure out the crumbs—there may be some left over. Mix the crumbs with the butter in a nine-inch pie plate, using your fingers to blend thoroughly. Press and pat the mixture firmly to make a smooth coating on the bottom and around the sides of the pie plate.

Lamb Chop Shish Kebab

Americans call it shish kebab. The Russians call it shashlik. In the Middle East it's just kabob, and in France it's a brochette. Whatever you call it, it's meat cooked on a skewer with vegetable fixings which are both tasty and pleasing to the eye. It is suitable for a distinguished dinner menu at any time of the year, and its preparation requires little fuss.

The hearty and rather elegant kebab shown here has rib lamb chops threaded on skewers along with tart slices of lemon, crisp chunks of green pepper, tiny juicy tomatoes, crunchy onions, the surprise of zucchini and fat mushroom caps. The dish can be cooked almost anywhere —over a beach campfire, on a patio grill or in the kitchen oven. However there is a knack to doing it right. When the skewer is removed from the fire, each ingredient must be at its proper degree of doneness. Precooking and marinating some of the vegetables is the simplest and best solution to this problem. But this is virtually the only work the cook will have to do since a well-filled skewer comes close to being a meal in itself.

In making this dinner the refrigerator will be your best friend. There is very little cooking to it. Virtually everything can be assembled beforehand and then left to get tastier in the refrigerator until ready to serve.

This dinner is convenient. There is no need to worry about the soup getting cold. The main course is a one-plate operation. Dessert is gooey, but it is not fussy to serve.

With an hour or so of work in the morning behind you, you can breeze into the house in the evening just ahead of all your guests, and still present them with a fine dinner. The only chores for the day before the party are to do the marketing—and to be sure you have enough skewers. Allowing for second helpings, you need a dozen. If you have to buy new ones, be sure they're long—about 18 inches. On the morning of the dinner cook the soup. While it is on the stove assemble the

MENU FOR SIX

CHILLED PEA SOUP

LAMB CHOP SHISH KEBAB
Barley with mushrooms
Shandygaff

CASSATA ALLA SICILIANA

cake, except for the whipped cream. Wrap the cake in wax paper and refrigerate it. All this shouldn't take more than 20 minutes. Purée the soup and refrigerate it too. Prepare the marinade, add the chops and vegetables to it. Put them in the refrigerator. Finally, put the wine for the soup, the beer and ginger beer for shandygaff in the refrigerator. An hour before dinner light the barbecue fire—if it's still warm enough to cook outdoors—and make sure the fire is big enough to spread across the grill. Add the wine and light cream to the soup. Whip the heavy cream and apply it generously to the cake. Put both soup and cake back in the refrigerator. Remove the meat and vegetables from the marinade and arrange them on the skewers. Start the barley, which takes about half an hour to cook and can sit awhile without causing any problems.

RECIPES

CHILLED PEA SOUP

3 10-ounce packages frozen peas or 5 pounds fresh peas, shelled	1 teaspoon chervil
	1½ teaspoons salt
	Freshly ground pepper
½ cup chopped onion	Fresh mint
1 tablespoon butter	½ cup chilled white wine
1¼ cups beef broth	2 cups light cream
4 cups water	

Sauté onion in butter in a large saucepan until onion is soft. Add peas, broth, water, chervil, salt and pepper and bring to a boil. Reduce heat and simmer uncovered until peas are very soft—about 30 minutes. Purée the soup in a blender or a food mill. Strain it, cut up six mint leaves and stir them in. Chill at least three hours. Before serving, stir in wine and cream, and correct the seasoning. Garnish with more mint.

LAMB CHOP SHISH KEBAB

The only knack to this dish is to get everything to come out properly done at the same time. The chops of course will determine the overall cooking time, but you will have to be sure that the tomatoes don't turn to mush and that the onions do not come out hard as golf balls. The way to avoid such disaster is to keep the tomatoes icy cold until the last minute and to parboil the onions. Spread a little softened butter around the mushrooms just before you cook them to keep them from drying out. The other vegetables will take care of themselves.

18 single-rib lamb chops cut about one inch thick	18 small onions
	18 medium mushrooms
Marinade (recipe below)	2 medium zucchini
3 large green peppers	3 tablespoons butter
18 cherry tomatoes	2 lemons

Ask the butcher to shorten the rib chops by cutting off the long rib ends. Or cleave them off yourself. Arrange the chops in the bottom of a large roasting pan and pour the marinade over them. Then prepare the vegetables.

Trim ends off the onions and drop them unpeeled into boiling water; parboil one-inch onions for five minutes, one-and-one-half-inch onions for eight minutes. Drain the onions and rinse in cold water, then slip off the skins. Wash the mushrooms and cut off the caps. Set the stems aside to use in the barley dish. Wash the zucchini but do not peel it. Trim off the ends, cut the zucchini into 18 slices about a half inch thick. Wash the peppers, cut them in sixths lengthwise and remove seeds. Put the onions, mushroom caps, zucchini and peppers in with the marinating chops. Cover and chill for at least three hours, spooning the marinade over the vegetables from time to time. Wash and stem the tomatoes and chill them separately. About half an hour before dinner, assemble the skewers. String two chops and two each of the vegetables on each of six skewers, arranging them attractively. Be sure to run the skewers lengthwise through the chops. Spread mushrooms with butter. Cut each lemon into six slices, and put one on each skewer. For second helpings put one chop and one each of the vegetables and lemon slices on another set of six skewers. Lay all the skewers on a tray lined with foil so excess marinade can drip off, then put them back into the refrigerator.

If you are cooking outdoors, arrange the first set of skewers on your outdoor grill about four inches above low-burning charcoal. If you are going to cook this in the stove, set the broiler pan four inches under the heat. Grill for 10 or more minutes outdoors, depending on how hot the fire is and how well done you want the chops to be. In the broiler, the chops should be ready in 10 minutes. Either way, turn the skewers at least once while they cook. When your husband de-skewers each serving he should not make a grand gesture and push all the food off from the hilt of the skewer. Take a few pieces off at a time, or you will have tomato juice rather than tomatoes.

MARINADE

1½ cups oil	1 clove garlic, minced
1 cup fresh lemon juice	1 tablespoon oregano
2 teaspoons salt	½ teaspoon thyme
Freshly ground pepper	¼ teaspoon rosemary
1 tablespoon chopped onion	

Combine all ingredients and stir well.

BARLEY WITH MUSHROOMS

2 cups pearl barley	¼ cup butter
½ cup chopped mushrooms	4 cups chicken broth
½ cup chopped onion	

Sauté mushrooms (you can use the stems saved from the shish kebab) and onion in butter over medium heat until soft, but not brown. Stir in barley and chicken broth. Bring to a boil, reduce heat to a low simmer, cover and cook for 25 to 30 minutes or until all the liquid is absorbed. Barley will stay hot for about 15 minutes if kept covered, but it may also be prepared ahead and reheated by sautéing it in additional butter. The added cooking does not change its texture.

SHANDYGAFF

This is a British drink familiarly known as shandy, half beer and half ginger beer (or substitute bitter lemon). It is a light, slightly spicy drink, which your guests—unless they're on the British pub circuit—may not have run into before. The beer and the ginger beer must both be thoroughly chilled.

CASSATA ALLA SICILIANA

This dessert is frankly an extravaganza, although it is much lighter than you might think from reading the ingredients. Be generous with the measurements here —anything Sicilian should be done with flourishes, and desserts are no exception.

1½ pounds ricotta or cream-style cottage cheese (about 3 cups)	½ cup almonds, chopped
	6 tablespoons diced, mixed candied fruit
½ cup sugar	1 8-inch sponge cake
2 teaspoons vanilla extract	6 tablespoons rum
1 ounce unsweetened chocolate, grated	1½ cups heavy cream

Combine ricotta, sugar and vanilla in a large bowl and beat a minute or two until light and fluffy. (If you substitute cottage cheese, it will be easier to get it smooth if you put it through a sieve.) Mix in the chocolate and almonds and four tablespoons of the fruit. Cut the sponge cake into three thin layers. Place the bottom layer on a serving plate and sprinkle it with two tablespoons of rum. Spread with half the ricotta mixture. Cover with the second cake layer, sprinkle that with two tablespoons rum and spread it with the rest of the ricotta. Add the third cake layer and sprinkle it with the rest of the rum. Wrap it in paper and chill at least three hours. About one hour before serving, whip the cream and spread it over the top and sides of the cake. Sprinkle top with remaining two tablespoons of fruit. Chill again until ready to serve.

Grilled Scampi

Shrimp, those delicate 10-legged crustaceans, are the world's favorite seafood. They are avidly eaten from Japan to Sweden, and Americans consume over 330 million pounds a year, more than we eat of any other shellfish. Most Americans prefer the jumbo sizes, like the ones shown here, which come from the Gulf of Mexico. The jumbos will even make an admirable substitute for the miniature lobsters used in Italy's prized *scampi* recipes. Grilled in the shells, jumbo shrimp are a scrumptious dish for friends who don't object to messy fingers.

Starting with the first whiff of garlic from the kitchen, this dinner is clearly a rich mixture of heady aromas and flavors. Since some of the dishes are likely to be strangers to your guests, it's best to invite brave as well as hearty eaters.

From first course to dessert, these foods are handsome and appetizing. The *spiedini* are skewers of brown toast and creamy cheese, sauced with anchovies. The shrimp stand proudly as juicy and buttery morsels in their crackling red shells. Lemon bleaches the rice to brilliant whiteness. Dark and light greens make an attractive salad which should be served as a separate course so its refreshing crispness won't be overlooked. The biscuit tortoni adds an elegant final touch.

This dinner is far from formal, but nonetheless it should be served in four courses, so it will require a lot of tableware—including two dozen plates. The *spiedini* are easier to deal with if they're baked on individual skewers (the big pins for trussing turkeys work well). Serve them on salad-size plates. Six jumbo shrimp willl just about fill a dinner plate, so you may like to set out low bowls for the rice. As the shrimp cook their shells tighten, and oyster forks will help get the meat out. Even so, they're messy to eat. After your guests have finished, pass big linen napkins, moistened with warm water.

In some ways, this is an easy dinner to make. The dessert is done hours ahead, and the chopping and mincing chores can be cleaned up early in the day. The *spiedini*, shrimp and rice, however, must be cooked at the last minute. Make the tortoni early in the morning and place in the freezer, covered with plastic wrap.

Both the *spiedini* and the shrimp can be got ready for the oven when you have an hour free. Assemble and skewer the bread and cheese, wrap them in foil, arrange them on a baking sheet and put them in the refrigerator. Make the anchovy sauce and chill it, tightly lidded. Get the shrimp ready to broil, sauce and all; marinating gives them added flavor. Cover and refrigerate them. Wash and dry the greens, make the salad dressing, and chill the wine.

Take the *spiedini* and sauce and the shrimp out of the refrigerator and let them warm up to room temperature before cooking. Fifteen minutes or so before dinner, start preheating the oven to 375°. About five minutes before dinner, open the foil covers of the *spiedini* and put them in the oven. Set the sauce over low heat until it comes to a bubble again. Put the rice in a pan and bring it to a boil over high heat. Don't plan to leave the kitchen now—the cheese melts fast and needs watching. When you take the *spiedini* out of the oven, put the shrimp in. Lower the heat under the rice and cover it. By the time you will have finished eating the first course, the shrimp and rice should be ready for the table. Serve the tortoni directly from the freezer.

MENU FOR SIX

SPIEDINI ALLA ROMANO

GRILLED SHRIMP
SCAMPI-STYLE
Lemon rice
Dry white wine
Chicory and romaine salad with
vinaigrette dressing

BISCUIT TORTONI

RECIPES

SPIEDINI ALLA ROMANO

This tasty combination was invented by Roman shepherds centuries ago. The bread and cheese are threaded on small skewers (in Italian, *spiedini*) like shish kebabs, then baked. If you're not familiar with mozzarella, you may be surprised at how fast it melts. Uncooked, it is a white, rubbery cheese with a mild flavor and is firm enough to slice easily. In the oven, it seems to become a puddle *presto*. The secret of getting the bread toasted without overdoing the cheese is to bake the *spiedini* until the cheese melts, and run them under the broiler for half a minute or so just to brown the bread. Here are the ingredients:

3 3-ounce or 2 4-ounce hero loaves of Italian bread
1 8-ounce ball of mozzarella cheese
¼ cup butter, melted
Anchovy sauce *(recipe on next page)*

Preheat oven to 375°. Trim crusts and ends from bread; cut small loaves in half crosswise, larger ones into thirds.

You should have six pieces that look like stubby sticks of butter—about one and a half inches high and wide and about two and a half inches long. Starting at one end of each piece, cut four slits one-half inch apart; cut just to about one-quarter inch of the bottom so that the slices will stay together and form a kind of fan. Cut the ball of mozzarella into thirds, then cut each third in half. Cut each piece of cheese into four slices one-quarter inch thick and about an inch square. Fit cheese slices into the slits in each stick of bread as neatly as possible. Gently thread bread and cheese on skewers. Holding the skewers upright, brush the bread with butter. (If you're making the *spiedini* ahead of time, wrap them up now and refrigerate them.) Arrange the skewers on a foil-covered baking sheet. Bake for five minutes, or until the cheese melts. The bread will be a light gold color. To toast it to a deeper brown, run the skewers under the broiler for 30 or 40 seconds, watching them carefully. To serve, slide the toast and cheese off the skewers onto small plates and pour anchovy sauce over them.

ANCHOVY SAUCE

8 flat anchovy filets (one-half can)

1 clove garlic

½ cup butter

Mash the anchovy filets with a fork to make a paste. Put the garlic through a press and mix it into the anchovies. Melt the butter in a small skillet over low heat. Add the anchovy and garlic mixture and stir until smooth, well blended and hot.

GRILLED SHRIMP SCAMPI-STYLE

In Venice, the true *scampi* are traditionally grilled in their shells, and purists add only a little sunflower-seed oil and butter, and scorn any other seasoning. In the U.S. when jumbo shrimp take the place of scampi, the sauce is a heady one flavored with parsley, lemon juice and a lot of garlic.

You will need big shrimp for grilling, so look for the "under fifteens" (less than 15 shrimp to a pound), even "under tens." In some parts of the country, big shrimp are known as "prawns," other places they are sold as "jumbos." Buy them fresh or frozen if you can find them, but be sure they are raw, or green. Above all, they must still have their shells on or you will have an entirely different dish.

36 jumbo shrimp

6 cloves garlic

2 teaspoons salt

¾ cup butter

¾ cup olive oil

¼ cup minced parsley

2 tablespoons lemon juice

Freshly ground black pepper

Parsley sprigs

Preheat broiler. Use a sharp knife or scissors to split the raw unshelled shrimp through lengthwise almost to the tail, leaving all the feet on and the shell intact. Remove the sand veins and pat the shrimp dry. Crush the garlic with a press or cut it up and crush it, with the salt, in a mortar and pestle. Melt the butter and stir in the garlic and salt, oil, minced parsley, lemon juice and pepper.

Holding the shrimp by the tips of the tails, dip them one by one into the butter sauce. Arrange them in a single layer in one or two flat baking dishes—flesh side up. Don't crowd them. They may look floppy while raw, but they will curl and "stand" better as they cook. Stir the remaining butter sauce and spoon it over the shrimp. Broil for 15 minutes six inches from the heat. Serve with plenty of sauce. Garnish with parsley sprigs.

LEMON RICE

1 large lemon

1½ cups uncooked long-grain rice

3 cups water

2 teaspoons salt

Grate the lemon rind and set it aside. Squeeze the lemon and combine three tablespoons of juice with the rice, water and salt in a saucepan. Bring to a boil, stir, cover and reduce heat. Simmer for 15 minutes or until the rice is tender and the liquid absorbed. Cooking times vary, so check directions on the rice package. Serve the rice garnished with grated lemon rind.

BISCUIT TORTONI

3 eggs, separated

¾ cup confectioners' sugar

½ cup crushed macaroons

¼ cup finely chopped toasted almonds

¼ cup finely diced candied red cherries

2 tablespoons brandy

1¼ cups heavy cream, whipped

Buy the macaroons the day before you plan to make this. Open them and let them dry out—they will be easier to crush—or put through a blender. Beat the egg yolks with the sugar until smooth and thick. Stir in the macaroon crumbs, almonds, cherries and the brandy. Beat the egg whites until stiff; fold in. Fold in the whipped cream, mixing well, but gently. Spoon into freezing trays, cover with foil, and freeze three to four hours until firm.

A Lavish Antipasto

The tidbit has been flagrantly neglected in U.S. cookery, where the very word conjures up nothing more than a potato chip or a watercress sandwich. Almost every other cuisine has some delectable assemblage that starts a dinner off with verve —hors d'oeuvre in France, *zensai* in Japan, *zakuski* in Russia. None is better eating than Italian antipasto—not the too-familiar salami-with-celery of spaghetti joints, but stylish antipasto full of surprises like the one at right. The mushrooms are filled with a homemade blend of ham and cheese, and the big home-roasted peppers are pungent. But the cook still gets off lightly: mild Provolone, fiery peperoncini, sausage and sardines, can all be procured at a good delicatessen.

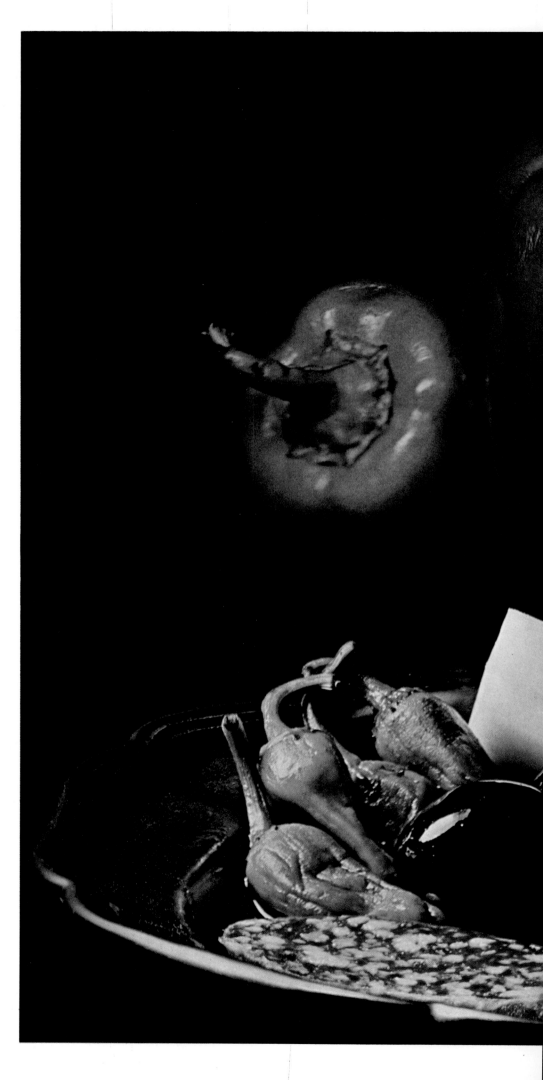

Off to an Italian start with antipasto, this dinner carries on in the same style. The main course, *osso buco*, is a masterwork of northern Italian cooking. The *gnocchi* served with it are a light Latin version of potato dumplings, and the meal is finished off with a combination of two products bountiful in Italy—oranges and red wine.

In any Italian dinner there is no such thing as just a little garlic. One bite of the roasted pepper in the antipasto will make this clear—and it gets clearer as the meal goes on.

Plan this dinner when you are going to have a little extra time for cooking. Most of the preparation must be done on the day of the dinner and some of the steps are tedious and under pressure can turn out to be exasperating. In advance, find a delicatessen that has Provolone and an outstanding salami. Ask your butcher to order the veal shanks if he doesn't have them on hand. You will only have to prepare three antipasto items at home,

MENU FOR SIX

ANTIPASTO
with thin breadsticks

OSSO BUCO
POTATO GNOCCHI
Mixed green salad,
oil and lemon dressing
Red wine

ORANGES IN WINE

and one of them, the roasted peppers, can be made as far ahead as you wish. On the morning of the dinner, assemble, but do not bake, the mushrooms for the antipasto. Cut up the radishes and keep them in cold water. Put the can of olives in the refrigerator. Prepare the *gnocchi,* the most time-consuming item on the menu, except for the last half hour of baking. Prepare and refrigerate dessert. Wash the salad greens, make an oil and lemon dressing, set the table. About three hours before the guests arrive start the *osso buco.* Do all the top-of-the-stove cooking before you change. Just before your guests arrive open the wine and put the *osso buco* in the oven. Half an hour before you announce dinner, bake the mushrooms. Fifteen minutes later put the *gnocchi* in the oven, which will heat through while you are eating the antipasto. As you clear away the antipasto, put the *gnocchi* under the broiler. This only takes an instant, so keep an eye on it.

RECIPES

ANTIPASTO

Remember that this dish is meant to provoke, not satiate the appetite, so be stingy with everything. The mushrooms are best served warm, the sardines and cheese at room temperature, and everything else chilled.

½ pound Genoa salami, thinly sliced	Ham-filled mushroom caps
½ pound Provolone cheese, sliced	Radishes with mustard butter
1 8-ounce can ripe olives	Roasted pepper rings
2 4-ounce cans sardines	2-ounce can rolled anchovies with capers
1 12-ounce jar *peperoncini*	

Arrange salami, cheese, olives, sardines, *peperoncini* (which are pickled peppers), mushroom caps and radishes in a circle on six salad plates. In the center put a ring of green pepper and place an anchovy in the middle of each loop. Limit seconds to the homemade items—you'll find they are in greatest demand anyhow.

HAM-FILLED MUSHROOM CAPS

1 pound mushrooms	2 tablespoons grated Parmesan cheese
Olive oil	
¼ cup minced onion	1 egg
1 clove garlic, minced	1 tablespoon chopped fresh parsley
½ cup finely chopped ham (about 4 ounces)	½ teaspoon oregano
½ cup fine dry bread crumbs	½ teaspoon salt
	Freshly ground black pepper

Wash but do not peel mushrooms, which should be about as big around as a half dollar. Remove stems and spoon out a little of the inside of the cap to make a pocket for stuffing. Chop enough mushroom stems to make one half cup. Heat one quarter cup oil in a skillet. Add the mushroom caps and toss them in the oil just long enough to coat them. Remove caps from pan and set aside. Add chopped mushroom, onion and garlic to pan. If the mixture seems dry add another tablespoon of oil. Cook over low heat for 10 minutes, until mixture has cooked almost to a pulp. Remove pan from heat and stir in ham, bread crumbs, cheese, egg, parsley, oregano, salt and pepper. Spoon the mixture into the mushroom caps. To bake, preheat oven to 325°. Arrange caps in a baking dish and pour a little oil over them. Bake for 30 minutes.

RADISHES WITH MUSTARD BUTTER

18 radishes	1 tablespoon prepared mustard
¼ cup softened butter	

Clean radishes, leaving stem ends on and cut back strips of peel into "petals." Combine butter and mustard and spread on radishes. Chill.

ROASTED PEPPER RINGS

3 large green peppers	1 clove garlic, minced
½ cup olive oil	½ teaspoon salt
2 tablespoons red wine vinegar	Freshly ground black pepper

Preheat the broiler. Wash and dry peppers. Place peppers in the broiler pan, about three inches from the heat. Broil for about 10 minutes, turning several times until the skin is blackened all around. Watch carefully to prevent the peppers from burning. When the peppers are cool enough to handle, peel off skin. Cut off the stem ends, remove seeds, and cut peppers into rings. Combine oil, vinegar, garlic, salt and pepper and pour over pepper rings. Cover and marinate for at least two hours.

OSSO BUCO

This dish, which originated in Milan, is literally translated as "hollow bone"—a misnomer, since the best part of the whole dish is the marrow inside the bone. It is helpful to serve an oyster fork to get at the marrow, but even if you prefer not to, warn your guests not to overlook it. The veal shanks should be young ones—weighing about a pound and a half apiece, otherwise they require much longer cooking. Whatever its age, the meat must be cooked until it begins to fall off the bone.

6 pounds veal shanks	2 cloves garlic, minced
1/4 cup flour	1 cup dry white wine
1/2 teaspoon salt	1 cup beef broth
1/4 teaspoon pepper	2 1-pound, 13-ounce cans
1/2 cup olive oil	tomatoes, drained
1 medium onion, minced	1/2 teaspoon basil
1 medium carrot, minced	1/2 teaspoon rosemary
1 rib celery, minced	*Gremolata* (recipe below)

Ask the butcher to saw veal shanks into two-inch pieces. Preheat the oven to 325°. Coat the chunks with flour seasoned with salt and pepper. Heat one-quarter cup oil in a heavy skillet. Add a few pieces of veal at a time and brown them to a dark, crusty color. While the veal is browning, sauté onion, carrot, celery and garlic in one-quarter cup oil in a large casserole or Dutch oven. Cook, stirring occasionally, until the vegetables are tender. When all the veal is browned, arrange it on top of the vegetables. Stand the pieces up to preserve the marrow inside the bones. Put the wine, beef broth, tomatoes and herbs into the pan used for browning the veal. Cook, stirring, until the mixture boils. Pour over the veal. Cover the casserole and bake for one and a half hours or until the veal is very tender. Spoon off any visible fat. Remove veal to a platter. Test sauce for seasoning. Ladle it over the shanks. Pass the *gremolata* at the table.

GREMOLATA

This garnish is not quite as lethal as it sounds—parsley is the traditional Italian antidote for garlic. Passing it separately allows the sissies to skip it.

6 cloves garlic, minced	1/2 cup chopped fresh
2 tablespoons grated lemon	parsley
rind	

Combine the ingredients and mix well.

GNOCCHI

This recipe is finicky work but the results are worth it and unlike any other potato dish you've ever eaten.

3 pounds potatoes, peeled	3 egg yolks, slightly beaten
1 1/4 cups grated Parmesan	2 teaspoons salt
cheese	Freshly ground black pepper
1 1/2 cups flour	Melted butter

Boil potatoes in plenty of boiling salted water for 20 minutes or until tender. Drain, then put pan back over low heat, shaking vigorously, for about two minutes or until potatoes are dry. Mash potatoes or put them through a food mill. Stir in three-quarters cup of the cheese, the flour, egg yolks, salt and pepper and one and a half tablespoons melted butter. On a lightly floured board, with the palms of your hands, roll out a small amount of the potato dough to form a rope about one half inch thick. Using a sharp knife, cut rope into one-inch lengths. Line up pieces on baking sheets or wax paper until all the dough has been rolled out and cut. Then cook the pieces, small batches at a time, in a skillet in two inches of simmering water, until they rise to the surface. It takes only about five minutes. Remove the cooked pieces with a slotted spoon, draining them carefully, and stack them in a shallow baking dish two or three deep. Preheat oven to 325°. Sprinkle *gnocchi* with the remaining half cup cheese and pour one half cup melted butter over all. Bake for 30 minutes. Brown quickly under the broiler.

ORANGES IN WINE

This dessert is icy cold, clear and refreshing.

3/4 cup sugar	1-inch stick cinnamon
1 cup water	1-inch vanilla bean
1 cup red wine	4 lemon slices
2 cloves	6 large seedless oranges

Combine sugar and water in a saucepan and cook, stirring until sugar dissolves. Add wine, cloves, cinnamon, vanilla bean and lemon slices. Bring the mixture to a boil and cook for 15 minutes, then strain it. Meanwhile peel the oranges and cut off all the white membrane. Slice thinly. Pour the hot wine syrup over the orange slices and refrigerate for at least four hours or until thoroughly chilled.

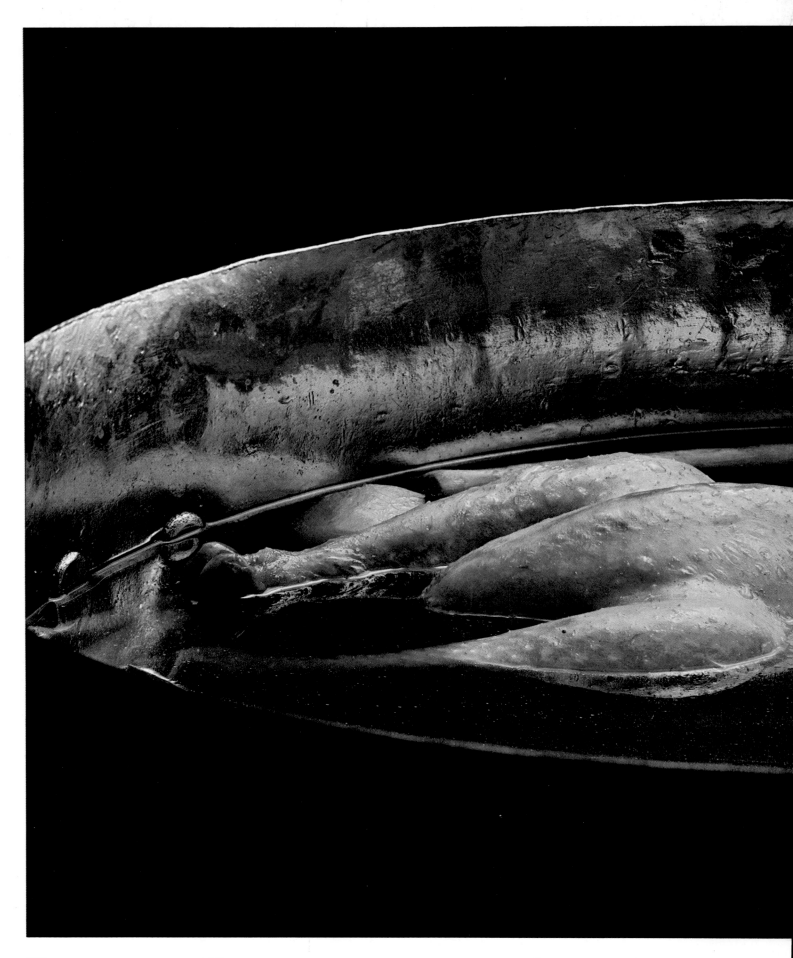

Pot-au-Feu

There is an autumn edge to the air, and appetites that languished through the summer are once again craving hot and rib-sticking meals. What better way to satisfy this craving than with that French

basic of simmer-on-the-back-of-the-stove gastronomy, *pot-au-feu?*

This dish has been a French institution for centuries. When King Henri IV said every good Frenchman was entitled to a chicken in his Sunday pot—before a similar pronouncement was erroneously attributed to Herbert Hoover—he was talking about *pot-au-feu*. Tasty, hearty and inexpensive, it has always been a special favorite of the peasant. But it is also a joy to the Parisian *haut monde* who consider its simplicity a needed weekly respite from the sauce-laden, liver-assaulting French cuisine.

For this dinner you literally put all you have into one pot. Everything basically important in the meal comes from the *pot-au-feu*—the soup, the meat, the vegetables. All else is trimmings, although they are very nice and necessary ones. Since it takes almost all day to cook *pot-au-feu,* pick a cool one.

The cook has many options when preparing this dinner. In the first place there are hundreds of versions of *pot-au-feu,* and you can vary them to suit your taste. As for the way to serve it—all in one, or soup first, meats and vegetables later —put the soup on first, giving it the stage alone for some well-merited attention. As for making bread, baking it at home is admittedly not for everyone, so you may want to substitute a store-bought or brown-and-serve version. But since you're going to have to spend a lot of time in the kitchen anyway, why not arrange things so that the bread goes into the oven as the guests come in the door? They will be bowled over by the smell of freshly baking bread during the cocktail hour.

This *pot-au-feu* calls for beef, chicken and sausage. Several cuts of beef are quite acceptable. Rump roast or brisket is the best. The brisket has more fat, which will keep it from drying out during the long cooking time. However it does mean that you'll have to do more skimming off as the cooking progresses. The rump is less tender, though it is also less fatty and holds together better. Or you can use a bottom round, sirloin tip, or a

MENU FOR SIX

BOUILLON

HOMEMADE BREAD
POT-AU-FEU
Mustard, horseradish
and sour pickles
Chicory salad,
vinaigrette dressing
Red wine

GINGERBREAD
WITH HOT LEMON SAUCE

chuck roast. A stewing chicken is the best kind of bird for this dish. If you can't get one, then use a roaster, which is much younger, lighter and more tender. With a roaster, cut the cooking time down to about an hour and a half. Polish sausage, or *kielbasa,* a lightly smoked, garlic-flavored pork sausage, works well with the other meats. If that is unobtainable, any country sausage that is not too spicy will serve. The vegetables are storable staples that you can buy well ahead of time. The only one that may cause difficulty is leeks. A standard item in French cooking, they are becoming increasingly available here. If you can't get them, just do without and don't worry. You will need a 12-quart pot to accommodate the *pot-au-feu.*

When doing this dinner, plan more than the menu ahead of time. On the day of the dinner, plan also to pay the bills or write letters. The *pot-au-feu* is not difficult to make, but it does require the cook's presence for five or six hours, adding this or removing that from time to time. The bread takes three or four hours to do and during most of that time will occupy you only briefly. While the *pot-au-feu* is cooking you should have plenty of time to give the bread the attention it needs, set the table, wash the salad greens and make the gingerbread. If the last-minute timing on the bread is too much of a cliff-hanger, make it in the morning, wrap it in foil and heat it up quickly at serving time.

RECIPES

POT-AU-FEU

There is nothing tricky to making a good *pot-au-feu.* No fussing is required, and although timing is everything on this dish, it is not of the split-second variety. For the dinner to be at its best each ingredient should be cooked to just the right degree. In this recipe, or any other for *pot-au-feu,* the times must be approximate—the cut of the meat, the kind of chicken, the tenderness of the vegetables—all these vary and the time needed to cook them will vary accordingly. A long fork for testing will be your handiest aid. Vegetables can be removed and set aside if they cook too quickly.

This recipe is a generous dinner for six, but with the addition of a few more vegetables, potatoes or one other kind of meat, it could easily serve eight or ten. It is quite common to include pork. Vegetables vary with the season. Cabbage, turnips, parsnips can be used, but have a dangerously pervasive flavor. You may prefer potatoes or noodles instead of bread. They must be cooked separately to keep the broth from becoming cloudy. Don't

have both the bread and the potatoes—in fact, do not serve oversize helpings. The bouillon looks innocent, but is surprisingly rich. It is so good that people will accept seconds if you offer them. Don't. And remember too that each helping of the main course will contain three kinds of meat, so it too is heartier than it seems.

4 pounds boneless beef	6 parsley sprigs
1 4- to 5-pound stewing chicken	4 cloves garlic, split
	1 large bay leaf
2 pounds beef bones, cracked	10 peppercorns, cracked
	6 cups beef broth or stock
2 tablespoons vegetable oil	6 cups water
4 large onions, each studded with a whole clove	Salt
	1 pound Polish sausage ring
3 carrots, cut up	12 whole carrots
2 celery stalks with leaves, cut up	18 whole white onions
	6 small whole leeks

Heat the oil in a large pot. Add the whole chicken and

brown it all over, turning frequently. Remove chicken. Discard any oil that remains. Put chunk of beef, bones, onions, cut-up carrots and celery, parsley, garlic, bay leaf and peppercorns into the pot. Pour in beef broth and water. Add one tablespoon of salt now—after dish is cooked taste and add more if needed. Bring to a boil, skimming broth until no more scum surfaces. Reduce heat, cover and simmer for one hour. Add browned chicken, bring back to a simmer. Skim thoroughly, cover and simmer for two hours. Add sausage, whole carrots, white onions and leeks and simmer one hour longer or until vegetables are tender. After testing to be sure they are done, carefully remove cooked meats, whole carrots, white onions and leeks and arrange in a large deep serving platter. Strain the broth left in the pot through a sieve lined with cheesecloth. Check seasoning and add salt and pepper if needed. Discard leftover vegetables, herbs and bones. Ladle a cup or two of the bouillon over the meat and vegetables on the platter and keep warm by covering with foil. Serve the bouillon at the table in a tureen. After the soup course bring on the platter. Serve Dijon mustard and an assortment of sour pickles, freshly grated horseradish, if you can get it—commercially prepared if not.

HOMEMADE BREAD

Think twice before deciding to bake the bread. It takes work and if you are content to serve store-bought bread, do so. However, making bread at home is an interesting and productive way to kill some of the *pot-au-feu* cooking time. If you can get small loaf tins, cook individual loaves. They're distinctive and no more work.

1 cup milk	2 envelopes dry yeast
4 tablespoons butter	1 cup lukewarm water
2 tablespoons sugar	6 1/2 cups sifted flour
1 tablespoon salt	

Scald the milk. Remove from heat and stir in butter, sugar and salt. Cool to lukewarm. Meanwhile, stir yeast into the lukewarm water in a large bowl. When yeast is completely dissolved, stir in the milk mixture. Then gradually stir in about three cups of flour. Mix well and then beat with a spoon for one minute. Add all but one-half cup of remaining flour and mix well, using your hands if necessary. Sprinkle remaining one-half cup of flour on a pastry board. Turn dough out onto this and knead it for about 10 minutes or until dough becomes smooth, elastic and satiny. It's apt to be hard work. Grease a large bowl generously. Place the dough in the bowl, then turn it over so the entire surface is lightly greased. Cover the bowl with a damp cloth and put it in a warm draft-free place (an unlighted oven serves well). Let dough rise until it has doubled in bulk—about 45 minutes. Press it firmly with a finger. If fingermark remains, it has risen enough. Now ball your fist up and punch the dough down.

Divide dough into the number of pieces desired and grease bread tins generously. This recipe makes 12 small (4x2x1-inch) loaves or six medium (5x3x2-inch) or two large (9x5x3-inch) loaves. Shape each piece into a ball, then flatten balls into oblongs. The width of each oblong should be about the length of the loaf tin and it should be twice as long as it is wide. Roll up lengthwise like a jelly roll. If the roll is longer than the tin push it gently together to shorten to the size of tin. If it's too short, gently stretch it—it is important that the ends touch ends of pan. The sides may or may not touch the sides of the pan —it doesn't matter. Place the rolls into the greased tins. Cover them with a damp cloth and let them rise until about double in bulk (another 45 minutes) or until the dough will pass the fingermark test. They will now fill the pans. Meanwhile preheat the oven to 400°. Bake the loaves on the lowest rack of the oven for 40 to 45 minutes or until rich brown. The loaves should sound hollow when turned out and thumped. Cool bread on wire racks.

GINGERBREAD WITH HOT LEMON SAUCE

This is not the usual gingerbread made with molasses, but a lighter, spicier version made with maple syrup. Heat it in a moderate oven for 10 minutes before serving. Heat sauce in a double boiler.

1 1/2 cups sifted flour	1/4 teaspoon allspice
1/2 cup sugar	1/4 teaspoon nutmeg
1/2 teaspoon baking soda	1/4 cup melted shortening
1/2 teaspoon baking powder	1/4 cup maple syrup
1/2 teaspoon salt	1/2 cup sour milk
1 teaspoon ground ginger	1 egg, well beaten
1 teaspoon cinnamon	

Preheat oven to 350°. Grease and flour the bottom of an 8x8x2-inch cake pan. In a mixing bowl, sift together the flour, sugar, baking soda and powder, and the spices. In a smaller bowl, stir shortening with the maple syrup, sour milk and egg, until well blended. To make sour milk, pour one tablespoon of lemon juice in a measuring cup, fill with regular milk. Stir well and let stand for 10 minutes. Add liquid ingredients to the flour and spice and beat until batter is smooth and creamy, about two minutes. Spoon batter into prepared baking pan. Bake until cake springs back when lightly touched, about 30 to 35 minutes. Serve warm with hot lemon sauce.

LEMON SAUCE

3/4 cup sugar	1 teaspoon grated lemon
1 tablespoon plus 2	rind
teaspoons cornstarch	3 tablespoons lemon juice
Pinch of salt	3 tablespoons butter
1 1/2 cups boiling water	

In a saucepan, mix the sugar, cornstarch and salt together. Gradually stir in the water. Bring to a boil, and cook for 10 minutes, stirring occasionally. Add the lemon rind, lemon juice and butter. Cook for another minute or two, until butter is melted and sauce is hot.

Lamb Curry with Condiments

Suddenly, with autumn here, you realize you owe dinner to six couples, haven't seen some old friends since they got back from vacation and ought to do something for the family whose pool your kids used all summer. That means a crowd—half a dozen people on the floor, half a dozen more at tippy little tables and, inevitably, a number balancing dinners on their knees. For this party you need lap food.

Curry is an exotic but at the same time sensible solution. The pieces of meat are small, the rice sops up the sauce. And, as arranged here, it will dazzle the guests. At right are condiments that can accompany a lamb curry. From left to right, row by row from top are: scallions, watermelon pickle, coconut, sambal, sweet relish, Bombay duck, chutney, green pepper, crystallized ginger, mandarin oranges, pimiento, peanuts, chives, sour cream, bacon and egg yolks. Guests move down the buffet table, choosing from these sweet and sour, hot and bland garnishes—which spice up both the meal and the talk. After all, you can't have a dull party with built-in conversation openers such as "Have you tried Bombay duck?"

A successful dinner party for 24 is as much a triumph of planning as of cooking. Preparing food in vast quantity is a production in itself, and in addition there are things to be rented, others to be borrowed, massive marketing to do. But this menu, for which everything can be made ahead of time, is designed to keep the work to a minimum and make things flow smoothly.

Decide early how much help, if any, you can afford to have and engage it well ahead of time. A maid who will help serve and clean up will make you feel like giving another party sooner than you might otherwise. And unless your husband's pride will be hurt hire a professional bartender. You will probably need four huge pots—two for the rice, two for the curry. Borrow what you need from friends. One bottle of liquor for every six people will insure against running out—and offer a reasonable range of drinks—gin, Vodka, Scotch, bourbon and a blended whiskey. Lay down the law that you're not serving any finicky mixed drinks tonight. Serve a light white California wine with dinner—and buy it by the gallon.

A few days before the party, start feeding the family ev-

HORS D'OEUVRES
Cheese cookies
Chicken liver pâté
Salami wedges
Onion sandwiches

LAMB CURRY
Boiled rice
Garnishes
White wine

SACHER TORTE

Fresh fruit

erything that's left in the refrigerator. You will be filling it up with dishes for the dinner. Two days beforehand bake the pâté and store it in the refrigerator; also order the lamb so the butcher has time to bone it. Make the cheese cookies and store at room temperature. One day before the party make the two chief dishes: the curry and the Sacher torte. Plan what serving bowls, glasses, linens you'll need. (Be sure you have enough little dishes to arrange the curry condiments attractively.) On the big morning set up the bar and buffet table. Chill the wine. Prepare any homemade garnishes for the curry. Make salami wedges and onion sandwiches, arrange trays, cover and refrigerate. Late in the day set out the condiments. Take out the pots for the rice, measure rice and water. Put the curry into a large pot on top of the stove. Measure water and coffee into the coffee pot. Spread pâté on squares of pumpernickel. Put the cheese cookies on a serving plate. During cocktails start the rice water, as it may take half an hour to come to a boil. About half an hour before serving put the rice in. Bring the curry to a simmer to warm through. Whip the cream at the last minute.

RECIPES

HORS D'OEUVRES

Hors d'oeuvres take the place of a first course. They are all made ready to eat in the kitchen—and, because people arrive slowly and many will spend the inevitably long cocktail hour standing up at a party this size, they are designed not to drip on the rug or crumble.

CHEESE COOKIES

2 cups grated Cheddar cheese
1 cup soft butter
2 cups sifted flour
1 teaspoon salt

Cream the cheese and butter together. Add flour and salt and mix until dough is smooth and well blended. Shape dough into rolls, about one inch in diameter. Chill two hours, until dough is firm. Preheat oven to 350°. Slice the dough into thin rounds. Place on ungreased baking sheets at least one inch apart. Bake for 12 to 15 minutes. Makes about eight dozen.

CHICKEN LIVER PÂTÉ

1 medium onion, cut up
1 clove garlic, cut up
2 eggs
1 pound chicken livers
¼ cup flour
½ teaspoon ginger
½ teaspoon allspice
1 teaspoon salt
1 teaspoon white pepper
¼ cup butter
1 cup heavy cream
Pumpernickel bread

This recipe is made for a blender. If you haven't one, don't try it. Content yourself with serving three hors d'oeuvres. Preheat oven to 325°. Combine onion, garlic and eggs in blender at high speed for one minute. Add livers and blend two minutes longer. Add flour, spices, salt, pepper, butter and cream. Blend at high speed two minutes more, until smooth. Pour into well-greased one-quart baking dish and cover with foil. Set in pan of hot water and bake for three hours. Remove foil and cool. Re-cover and chill at least four hours, or overnight. To serve, spread pâté on squares of pumpernickel.

SALAMI WEDGES

36 thin slices of hard salami
8 ounces cream cheese, softened
2 tablespoons prepared horseradish
Dash of Tabasco

Combine cream cheese with horseradish and Tabasco. Make three-decker sandwiches by spreading one slice of salami with two teaspoons of the cheese mixture, topping with another slice of salami, spreading that with cheese and putting a final slice of salami on top. Chill for at least one hour. Cut into quarters and spear with toothpicks.

ONION SANDWICHES

48 thin bread slices	1 cup mayonnaise
3-4 red onions	2 cups minced fresh parsley
½ cup soft butter	Salt

With a cookie cutter cut two two-inch rounds from each bread slice. Using a very sharp knife, slice onions into paper-thin rounds. Peel off outer rings to make onions the same size as bread. Salt them slightly. Lightly butter bread rounds. Make a sandwich of two rounds of bread with an onion slice between. Spread edges with mayonnaise and roll in chopped parsley. Chill at least one hour.

LAMB CURRY

The only trick to this dish is arriving at the right amount of spice—and you can only determine that by tasting. There are some 200 curry powders available in the U.S., each one different in intensity. No matter how hot you like your own food, a large party is not the time to concoct a curry hot enough to make your eyes water. Those who like it searing can use the hot garnishes.

Because of the quantity of food you will probably have to make the curry in two pans. Divide the ingredients more or less in half, putting half in one pan, half in another. If one pan turns out to be spicier or more liquid or in any way different from the other, mix the two batches so that when finished they are alike.

12 pounds boned lamb	16 apples, peeled and
2 cups butter or oil	chopped
16 large onions, chopped	6 cups chicken broth
24 cloves garlic, crushed	2 tablespoons salt
8 tablespoons curry powder	1 teaspoon coarsely ground
8 lemons, sliced	black pepper

Have the butcher bone the lamb and cut it in bite-size pieces. Brown the lamb in butter or oil; remove from pans and set aside. Add onions and garlic to fat remaining in pans and sauté, stirring constantly, until onions are soft but not brown. Add curry powder and cook, still stirring, for five minutes. Put the meat back into the pans. Stir in lemon slices, apples, chicken broth, salt and pepper. Bring to a boil, reduce heat, cover and simmer one and a half to two hours or until meat is tender and the apples and onions have cooked down into the sauce. Stir the curry from time to time. After an hour or so of cooking, check seasoning and add more if needed. If the sauce seems thin, continue the cooking uncovered. When you make curry ahead of time and refrigerate it overnight, stir a cup of chicken broth into it before reheating. Serve with rice, allowing 8 cups of uncooked rice for 24 people.

GARNISHES

There is virtually no limit to the condiments to serve with curry. The garnishes can be salty, sweet, hot or sour. There are dozens of others besides those shown on pages 196-197. There is, for instance, a larder full of different chutneys. Any kind of pickle goes, especially if it's homemade. Olives, capers, cocktail onions are all admissible. For sweetness a plum jam, apple butter or even marmalade is good, and best if homemade. Choose a variety of tastes, textures and colors. You can have as few as half a dozen, but the fun of this meal really comes from a splendid array of garnishes.

SACHER TORTE

This is probably the most high-toned chocolate cake in the world. It has a lively history, a distinguished pedigree and even a lawsuit in its past. The cake was invented by Franz Sacher, chef to Metternich, who one day in Vienna in the year 1832 asked for a dry, masculine chocolate cake. He got Sacher torte. It has character: a strong bitter chocolate flavor and slightly dry texture—softened by a dollop of whipped cream with which it is served.

¾ cup butter	1 cup sifted flour
¾ cup sugar	¼ cup apricot jam
6 eggs, separated	Chocolate icing
6 ounces unsweetened	1 pint heavy cream,
baking chocolate, melted	whipped

Preheat oven to 325°. Cream butter with one quarter cup of the sugar and beat until fluffy. Add egg yolks, one at a time, beating well after each addition. Stir in chocolate. Beat egg whites until foamy. Gradually add the remaining one half cup of sugar and continue beating until a stiff meringue is formed. Fold the meringue gently into the chocolate batter until no white shows. Then fold in the flour. Pour into a greased and floured eight-inch spring form pan. Bake for one hour. Let stand 10 minutes then remove rim. Cool on base. Cut torte in half crosswise to make two layers. Spread apricot jam between the layers. If the jam doesn't spread easily, thin it with a little water. Replace top layer of torte and frost with the chocolate icing. To serve, slice the torte into thin wedges and top each slice with a spoonful of whipped cream. For 24 people, you will need two tortes. Make each torte separately—don't try to double the batter.

CHOCOLATE ICING

9 ounces milk chocolate	¼ teaspoon vanilla
3 tablespoons milk	flavoring

Break chocolate into pieces and put in the top part of a double boiler. Place over simmering water, and cook, covered, until chocolate is melted, about 10 minutes. Stir in the milk and the vanilla, keeping the pan over the simmering water. The mixture will lump somewhat and harden, but it will melt again and become smooth with heat and stirring. When it is smooth and shiny, remove from the heat and spoon it, all at once, on the top of the torte. Working with a small spatula, smooth the icing evenly over the top and sides of the cake.

Beef Stew from Provence

Beef stew, which can be as straightforward as a Boy Scout, can also put on fancy airs. Boeuf bourguignon, cooked in red wine, has been turning up like a too-familiar friend at dinner parties. *Daube de boeuf à la Provençale,* shown at left, is less well known and its embellishments are far more unexpected. As its name suggests, it is cooked in the style of southern France, and its ingredients clearly show its heritage. The daube in its name comes from daubière, a French cooking pot designed for lengthy braising. Here the braising is done in white wine—not usually associated with beef—which gives this stew a delicate background flavor for the triumvirate that is the key to Provençal cooking: garlic, so much admired locally that it is known as the "truffle of Provence," olives that provide a salty zip and ripe tomatoes, juicy and fresh.

This dinner is Mediterranean from start to finish. The first course, like the main-course stew, is Provençal; in fact its very name comes from the Provençal word *tapéna,* meaning capers. The dessert, a silken caramel custard, is a favorite in all the Latin countries.

If you are the least bit nervous about cooking while guests are in the house, this is the ideal dinner for you. There is virtually nothing to do once the guests have arrived. In fact, aside from the stew, there is only about an hour's work involved, and the whole meal is done ahead of time.

This is not a spur-of-the-moment party, for to be at its best, the stew should be started two days beforehand. At that time make the marinade for the stew and let the meat sit in it overnight. Next day cook the stew up to the point of adding the tomato and olive garnish. The stew should then mellow in the refrigerator for another

MENU FOR SIX

MUSHROOMS TAPÉNADE

DAUBE DE BOEUF À LA PROVENÇALE
Boiled potatoes
Spinach salad
Red wine

CARAMEL CUSTARD

day before serving—it will be a richer-tasting dish for having waited.

On the morning of the day of the dinner, make the custard. It will take you half to three quarters of an hour to get it into the oven, where it will bake for an hour. Chill it until shortly before the guests arrive. During the afternoon prepare the mushroom caps and make the *tapénade,* which won't take you more than 15 minutes. Peel the tomatoes for the stew and refrigerate them; peel the potatoes and put them in cold salted water. Take the stew out of the refrigerator, remove the fat and let the stew come to room temperature. Unmold the custard, put it back in the refrigerator. Half an hour before sitting down to dinner, start the potatoes cooking and start warming the stew. Just before serving the *tapénade,* stir it vigorously and spoon it over the mushrooms. As you start clearing the dishes of the first course, add the olives and tomatoes to the stew.

RECIPES

MUSHROOMS *TAPÉNADE*

Tapénade is a strongly flavored sauce that in the south of France is served with cooked eggs, cold fish or beef. Its main ingredients are specialties of the region: capers, which grow on prickly shrubs throughout the area, anchovies and olive oil. The mixture is rather like a psychedelic French dressing.

It is served here on raw mushrooms. If you are able to get small, perfect ones (about 30 to the pound), leave the caps whole. If they are too big or blemished, cut the caps into thin slices.

4 tablespoons capers	1/4 cup lemon juice
6 anchovy fillets, drained	Freshly ground black pepper
1 cup olive oil	1 pound small mushrooms

Take two tablespoons of capers, rinse off the vinegar in which they were bottled and dry them with a paper towel. Pound them and the anchovies in a mortar or press them in a sieve with a spoon. When the mixture has been reduced to a paste, transfer it to a mixing bowl. Add the oil little by little, stirring as you do it. Add the lemon juice and pepper to taste. Let the sauce stand in a covered container at least four hours before serving. Remove the stems from mushrooms and clean the mushroom caps with damp paper towel. If you have small mushrooms, leave the caps whole. Place five on each plate and spoon three tablespoons of the *tapénade* over them. The *tapénade* separates very quickly when it stands, and all the oil comes to the top so be sure to stir thoroughly before pouring. Garnish the plates with the other two tablespoons of rinsed whole capers sprinkled over all.

DAUBE DE BOEUF À LA PROVENÇALE

For all its French airs, this is basically a hearty beef stew. The pitted black olives should be widely available, but don't leave getting them to the last minute. To peel the tomatoes, drop them into boiling water for about 10 seconds. Don't leave the tomatoes in the water any longer than that or they will start to cook. Then pour them into a colander, rinse with cold water and peel. The skins should slip off easily.

MARINADE

1/4 cup olive oil	1 teaspoon salt
2 yellow onions, sliced	1/2 teaspoon rosemary
1 stalk celery, cut up	1/2 teaspoon thyme
1 carrot, cut up	12 peppercorns
3 cloves garlic, minced	1 1/2 cups white wine

Heat olive oil in saucepan. Add onions, celery, carrot and garlic. Sauté until onion is translucent, stirring several times. Add remaining ingredients and simmer 15 minutes, stirring occasionally. Transfer to bowl and let marinade cool.

DAUBE

3 pounds boneless beef, cut in 1 1/2-inch cubes	1/2 teaspoon salt
	1/4 teaspoon rosemary
1/4 pound salt pork	1/4 teaspoon thyme
12 small white onions, peeled	2 cloves garlic, crushed
	12 small carrots, peeled
1/2 cup white wine	3/4 cup pitted green olives, drained
2 cups beef broth	

| ³/₄ cup pitted black olives, drained | 24 cherry tomatoes, peeled |
| | Freshly ground black pepper |

When marinade has cooled, add the cubed beef to it. Cover and refrigerate overnight, stirring once or twice. Next day—this is still the day before the party—remove beef from marinade. Pat each piece dry with paper towels. Strain the marinade and set aside the liquid, which will be about one cup. Discard the vegetables. Blanch the salt pork in boiling water for 10 minutes. Remove and cut salt pork into one-half-inch cubes and brown them in a large skillet. Brown the beef in the fat rendered from salt pork. As they brown, transfer the cubes of beef and salt pork to a large casserole. Then brown the onions quickly in the fat and set them aside. Preheat the oven to 350°. Pour the drained marinade into the casserole, add the wine and enough beef broth to barely cover the meat—about two cups. Refresh the seasoning by adding one-half teaspoon salt and one-quarter teaspoon each of rosemary and thyme; add the two cloves of crushed garlic. Cover tightly. Bring the stew to a simmer on top of the stove, then transfer it to the oven and cook one and a half hours. Add the browned onions and the carrots and cook one hour longer, until tender. Remove from oven. Let cool slightly, then refrigerate, covered, overnight. Remove from refrigerator about one hour before serving. Take fat from surface, then slowly bring the stew to a simmer. Rinse and drain the olives and add them, along with the peeled tomatoes, to the stew. Stir in a generous grinding of black pepper. The olives and tomatoes should be warmed through, not cooked. Serve the hot stew with boiled potatoes, which should be passed separately.

SPINACH SALAD

1 10-ounce package fresh spinach	2 drops Tabasco sauce
¹/₂ teaspoon coarse salt	3 tablespoons lemon juice
¹/₂ clove garlic	7 tablespoons olive oil
¹/₂ teaspoon dry mustard	Freshly ground black pepper

Wash the spinach carefully to remove all traces of sand. Drain well and tear into small pieces. Set aside while making the dressing. Sprinkle the salt over the bottom of the salad bowl and rub the garlic clove into the salt, then discard the garlic. Add the dry mustard, Tabasco sauce, lemon juice, olive oil and black pepper. Mix all together thoroughly with a fork. Add the spinach and toss lightly.

CARAMEL CUSTARD

The second time you make this dessert, it will be the easiest thing in the world. So if you haven't made it before, you might try it once on the family. The area of trouble lies in lining the mold with caramel, which is simply cooked sugar. Boiling sugar is hotter than boiling almost anything else, so you must be very careful in handling it: you must preheat the mold, even if it is ovenproof china, or you may crack it. If you use a metal charlotte mold, the mold itself becomes too hot to handle easily and the caramel will harden fast. It is easy to overcook the caramel—it goes from the desired golden brown to burned very fast and then it acquires some of the characteristics of cement.

The unmolding is easy—just be sure to turn the custard into a serving dish with sides, since a fair amount of caramel sauce will come with it.

1 cup sugar	2 egg yolks
1 quart milk	²/₃ cup sugar
6 eggs	1¹/₂ teaspoons vanilla

Preheat oven to 325°. Warm one-and-one-half-quart soufflé dish or mold in pan of hot water so that it will not crack when you add the caramel syrup. To make the syrup, pour one cup of sugar into a heavy skillet. Cook over medium heat until the sugar begins to melt, about five minutes. Stir with a wooden spoon until sugar is completely melted and a golden color, which will take five to 10 minutes more. Remove soufflé dish from the water and immediately pour in the caramel syrup. Hold the dish with pot holders and rotate it until the bottom and sides are thoroughly coated with syrup. Let it sit.

Heat the milk to just below scalding. Beat the six eggs and the two extra egg yolks together. Add two-thirds cup sugar and beat until well combined, but do not overbeat or you will have air bubbles in the custard. Add vanilla. Slowly add the hot milk to the egg and sugar mixture. If there is any sign of scum, strain the milk mixture, then pour into caramel-lined soufflé dish, stirring lightly. Place the soufflé dish in a shallow pan and pour boiling water into the pan until it reaches halfway up the side of the soufflé dish. Bake one hour or until a knife inserted in center of custard comes out clean. Cool, then chill until ready to serve. To unmold, run a small knife around edge of dish to loosen the custard. Place a serving dish upside down over the custard, then invert it quickly, shaking gently if necessary.

A Romanian Casserole

Autumn is an ideal season for *ghivetch*. Now that roadside stands are spilling over like cornucopias with fresh vegetables, this Romanian stew provides a fine excuse to stop the car and browse among the peppers and zucchini. *Ghivetch* (pronounced ghee-vetch) can contain as many different vegetables as happen to catch your eye. What saves it from blandness is the pungent addition of three cloves of garlic and a spray of herbs. If you want to add meat or fish, you will have a main course.

There are isolationist cooks who claim that in making *ghivetch*, you must cook each of the dozen or so vegetables separately. Unless you're secretly fond of scouring pots, it's best not to listen to them—you will have enough to do just chopping everything up. The recipe here has every ingredient going in the same kettle on the principle that each one works to enhance the good of all.

Be sure to have eight to this dinner —unless you want leftover *ghivetch*. That dish requires such an assortment of vegetables that eight people are needed to eat up the results. You may also feel that eight enthusiastic appreciators are necessary to make the trouble worthwhile. For this dinner requires a fair amount of dull work.

Cut up the vegetables for *ghivetch* the night before the dinner. Allow an hour for the job. Assemble the vegetables, a cutting board, a good sharp knife and a large bowl for the chopped vegetables—and set to. Listen to the radio or talk to a friend but resign yourself to an hour of chopping, slicing, dicing and mincing. But leave potatoes for the next afternoon —cut and prepare them not more than a couple of hours ahead, or they will darken.

In the morning make the apple pie. Prepare the chicken up to the point of putting it in the oven—place the prepared pieces on a baking tray, seal the tray tightly in foil or plastic wrap and refrigerate it. Make the soup—it will take only 15 or 20 minutes—and chill it until serving time. You are now finished with all preparation until two hours before dinner. At that time take the chicken out of the refrigerator and let it come to room temperature. Chill the wine. Transfer the vegetables for the *ghivetch* to the dish you will cook them in, add the potatoes, and prepare the bouillon in which you will cook the *ghivetch*. An hour before the dinner put the *ghivetch* and the chicken in the oven. When you serve the bisque, check on the vegetables and the chicken. They will probably both need 15 minutes more cooking—the time it will take to eat the bisque. But if the *ghivetch* looks done, take it from the oven and let it stand, covered, in a warm place. It will keep hot—and the only sin you can commit with this dish is to overcook it. Put the rolls in a low oven to warm. When you serve the main course put the pie in the oven to warm slightly too.

MENU FOR EIGHT

AVOCADO BISQUE

BAKED CHICKEN PARMESAN
GHIVETCH
Rolls and butter
Dry white wine

STREUSEL-TOPPED
APPLE PIE

RECIPES

AVOCADO BISQUE

Though this soup has a delicate color and an equally delicate taste it is quite rich, so don't offer your guests too much of it. You can serve it either hot or cold. It has more flavor cold, but if the night turns out to be unexpectedly bitter the bisque is easily transformed into a steaming first course.

2 tablespoons butter	1 tablespoon prepared
1/4 cup minced onion	horseradish, drained
2 tablespoons flour	1 teaspoon salt
3 cups chicken broth	1/4 teaspoon curry powder
1 tablespoon fresh lemon	1/4 teaspoon tarragon
juice	Freshly ground black pepper
1 tablespoon tarragon	1 large ripe avocado
vinegar	1 cup milk
1 clove garlic, crushed	1 cup light cream

Melt the butter in heavy three-quart saucepan. Add the onion and sauté until it is just tender but not browned. Blend in the flour. Stir in the chicken broth and heat, stirring, until it boils and thickens. Add the lemon juice, vinegar, garlic, horseradish and seasonings. Cover and simmer for 10 minutes. Peel the avocado, remove the pit and cut the avocado into chunks. Purée these pieces in the blender, adding one cup of the broth to make the procedure easier. If you do not have a blender, cut the avocado into cubes, dip them in a little lemon juice and put them through a food mill. Work quickly because avocado discolors rapidly. Stir the purée into the soup, mixing well. Add the milk and the cream. Bring to a boil, then simmer for five minutes. Transfer to a bowl, cover, then refrigerate until thoroughly chilled.

BAKED CHICKEN PARMESAN

This dish is full of different flavors—cheese, mustard, garlic—that blend beautifully. There is garlic in the *ghivetch* too (turn on the kitchen fan, or open the window when you're cooking), but then there's hardly any point to eating just a *little* garlic.

3 chickens (2 1/2 to 3	1/3 cup chopped fresh
pounds each) cut up for	parsley
frying	1 1/2 cups butter
4 1/2 cups fresh bread	1 clove garlic, crushed
crumbs	1 tablespoon Dijon mustard
1 1/4 cups grated Parmesan	1 1/2 teaspoons
cheese	Worcestershire sauce
1 tablespoon salt	

Wash the chickens and pat them dry. Prepare the bread crumbs in a blender, using day-old, firm-type white bread with the crusts removed. If you do not have a blender use the fine side of a grater to make the crumbs. Add the cheese, salt and parsley to the crumbs and mix well. Spread the mixture in a shallow pan. Melt the butter in a medium-sized saucepan. Add the garlic, mustard and Worcestershire sauce. Stir well and let the butter mixture cool so that you can put your fingers in it but do not let it congeal. Preheat the oven to 350°. Dip the chicken pieces into the butter mixture, then roll them in the crumb-cheese mixture. Be sure each piece is well coated;

pat the coating on with your hands. Place the pieces of chicken on a large, shallow baking tray. You may have to use two. Pour remaining butter over the chicken. Bake until golden and tender, about one hour to an hour and a quarter. Baste once or twice with the pan drippings.

GHIVETCH

Don't stint on the seasonings and don't cook it too long —those are the only rules for success with *ghivetch*. When you serve them, the vegetables should still be crisp and have a lot of their original color. It will help to preserve their brightness if you don't lift the lid to look in at them any more often than necessary. You can substitute other vegetables if you like—turnip for carrots, eggplant for zucchini, cabbage for celery.

1 cup thinly sliced carrots
  (2 medium)
1 cup fresh green beans,
  sliced into 1/2-inch
  diagonals
1 cup diced potato (2 small)
1/2 cup celery, sliced about
  1/4 inch thick on the
  diagonal (1 stalk)
2 medium tomatoes, cored
  and cut into quarters
1 small yellow squash,
  thinly sliced
1 small zucchini, thinly
  sliced
1/2 Bermuda onion, thinly
  sliced

1/2 head small cauliflower,
  broken into small
  flowerets
1/4 cup julienne strips sweet
  red pepper
1/4 cup julienne strips green
  pepper
1/2 cup frozen green peas,
  thawed
1 cup beef bouillon
1/3 cup olive oil
3 cloves garlic, crushed
2 teaspoons salt
1/2 bay leaf, crumbled
1/2 teaspoon savory
1/4 teaspoon tarragon

Wash and prepare all the vegetables, cutting them into the sizes and shapes given above. Preheat the oven to 350°. Put vegetables in ungreased shallow baking dish (13x9x2-inch). They should be mixed, not arranged in layers. Put the bouillon in a small saucepan, add the oil, garlic, salt, bay leaf, savory and tarragon, and heat to boiling. Pour the bouillon mixture over the vegetables. If the casserole does not have a tight lid, cover it with heavy aluminum foil. Bake until the vegetables are tender, about one hour to one hour and a quarter. Stir the vegetables once or twice so they cook evenly.

STREUSEL-TOPPED APPLE PIE

1 9-inch unbaked pie shell
2/3 cup flour
1/3 cup light brown sugar
1/3 cup butter
2 1/4 pounds tart
  cooking apples (about

7 cups sliced)
2/3 to 3/4 cup sugar
2 tablespoons flour
3/4 teaspoon cinnamon
1/2 teaspoon nutmeg

Preheat the oven to 400°. Prepare the pie shell using your favorite recipe or a mix, building up and crimping the edges. Refrigerate until ready to use. For the topping, mix the flour with the brown sugar in a medium-sized bowl. Cut in the butter until it resembles coarse meal, using a pastry blender or two knives. Set aside. For the filling, peel, core and cut the apples into thin slices. As they are sliced, put them into a bowl of cold water with a little lemon juice added to prevent them from darkening. When all the apples are sliced, drain them well. Taste one and if it is very tart, use the full amount of sugar; if a little on the sweet side, use only two thirds of a cup. Mix the sugar, flour, cinnamon and nutmeg together. Toss this mixture lightly with the apples. Turn them into the chilled pie shell, spreading them as evenly as possible. Sprinkle the topping mixture over the apples, patting it down evenly. Place the pie on the middle rack of the oven. Bake until apples are tender and juices bubble around the edges, from 45 to 60 minutes, depending on the apples. Place some foil on the rack below the pie to catch any juices that might bubble over. Serve the pie either warm or at room temperature.

Choucroute Garnie

The French region of Alsace, perched on the German border, has had plenty of reason throughout history to regret its geography. But food lovers have been de-

lighted, for Alsace puts a French touch on German cooking. Sauerkraut, an Alsatian specialty, reaches a pinnacle in *choucroute garnie*. The *choucroute*, or sauerkraut, is garnished with a combination of meats such as kielbasa, veal sausage, knockwurst, pork butt and bratwurst. The *choucroute* itself is simmered for hours in wine and seasonings. Every element in this peasant dish has an identifiable taste, but they all blend into one pungent, smoky flavor.

This is a substantial dinner which will taste its best on a cold winter night after a day of outdoor exercise. Since its preparation demands your attention over a period of several hours, plan to serve it on a day when the family is doing something —like shoveling snow—that you would just as soon skip.

This dinner is hearty, but not overwhelming. The first course is as light as any bouillon. The dessert is far less weighty than it sounds.

Although you must spend most of the day at home when you make this dinner, not all your time will be spent working. A lot of the cooking needs only an occasional kitchen check.

Shop for the meat ahead. This *choucroute* calls for a pork butt plus four varieties of sausage, each of which contributes a different flavor. If you can't get all the ones specified here, ask your butcher to suggest a com-

bination, but remember that some should be spicy, others should be more delicate.

If you are adept at doing several things at once you can make the soup and dessert while the *choucroute* is cooking. But if you feel more comfortable with the first and last courses out of the way, start them early on the day of the dinner. Once they are done, let the *choucroute* cook slowly and start the sausages at the appropriate times. Whenever convenient, prepare the watercress and the dressing. Five hours before you plan to serve dinner start the *choucroute*. This allows an hour to get it ready since it takes four hours of cooking time. Two and a half hours before serving start the pork butt, putting the sausages on to cook as necessary. Before the guests arrive, take the pudding out of the refrigerator (if you have made it ahead) and heat it up slowly.

RECIPES

MUSHROOM SOUP

This is a very unusual soup. Before tasting it your guests may assume, from the looks, that it is a rich beef broth. They will be startled by its intense mushroom flavor.

If you have a food grinder it is worth getting it out to make this dish, for you can put the mushrooms through it, stems and all, in very short order. The next simplest procedure is to put them in a blender, and use a slow speed to chop them. But you will have to do them a handful at a time. Lacking any machinery, the mushrooms can always be finely chopped by hand.

2 tablespoons butter	6 cups chicken broth
2-3 minced shallots	½ teaspoon salt
1½ pounds mushrooms, ground or chopped fine	1 teaspoon lemon juice
	1 lemon, thinly sliced

Heat the butter in a large saucepan. Add the shallots and cook until they are translucent, about three minutes. Add the mushrooms and cook five minutes longer, stirring occasionally. Add the chicken broth and bring to a boil. Reduce heat and simmer, uncovered, for 30 minutes. Cool. Strain the soup through a coarse sieve, pressing the mushrooms firmly to extract all the liquid. The strainer must be coarse enough so that some specks of mushroom will go through. Season with the salt and lemon juice. Garnish with lemon slices.

CHOUCROUTE GARNIE

Making the *choucroute* and making the *garnie* are two separate operations. They can be cooked together but the end result will be less greasy if the meats are cooked in a different pot from the sauerkraut.

In some traditional recipes a layer of salt pork is used to line the casserole. This version uses bits of bacon instead. They are first blanched to remove some of the salt, then mixed through the sauerkraut along with the carrots and onions. These improve the texture and visual appeal of the dish—large quantities of uninterrupted sauerkraut do not look particularly attractive.

The traditional accompaniment to this dish is boiled potatoes, which you may serve if you want to stretch things. If you do, dust the potatoes with caraway seeds.

You may use either canned sauerkraut or the kind that comes in plastic bags. It's not the kind of sauerkraut you buy but what you do to it that makes the difference. If you can't get juniper berries, substitute one quarter of a cup of gin—the flavor will be the same and perhaps you'll be able to detect just the faintest extra kick.

As to the meats, get the smallest pork butt that you can find—it will easily yield six slices. The *kielbasa* has an edge of garlic, the knockwurst tastes a bit like frankfurters, bratwurst is a spicy pork sausage and the unsmoked veal sausage, also called Swiss bratwurst, has a delicate taste. Since there are 200 kinds of sausages available, if you can't get these particular ones you can find others that will do. Kosher frankfurters, beef highly flavored with garlic, would substitute for the *kielbasa*. Bockwurst, an unsmoked veal sausage, could take the place of the Swiss bratwurst. Thuringer *cervelat* would do instead of smoked bratwurst. Serve the *choucroute* on the biggest platter you have. Heap the sauerkraut in the center and place the pork and sausages around it. Serve each person a heaping spoonful of sauerkraut and a slice of each of the meats. Don't hesitate to slice into the sausages—no one could possibly eat one of each kind and the important thing is to have a taste of everything.

3 pounds sauerkraut	bouillon
½-pound chunk of bacon	¾ cup water
2 tablespoons butter	1 cup dry white wine
½ cup carrots, thinly sliced	Salt
1 cup onions, thinly sliced	1 2- to 3-pound smoked
Parsley sprigs	pork butt
1 bay leaf	1 *kielbasa*
6 peppercorns	4 knockwurst
10 juniper berries	3 smoked bratwurst
1 10½-ounce can beef	3 unsmoked veal sausages

Drain the sauerkraut. Place in a large bowl and cover with cold water. Soak it for 20 minutes, changing the water twice. Drain again. Then take up large handfuls and squeeze out as much water as possible. Set aside. Remove the rind from the bacon and cut into strips about two inches long and one half inch wide. Blanch bacon by placing in a saucepan and covering with two quarts of cold water. Bring to a boil, then simmer 10 minutes. Drain. Melt the butter in a two-and-one-half- or three-quart casserole. Add the blanched bacon, carrots and onion and cook slowly, covered, for 10 minutes. Do not let the vegetables brown. Stir in the sauerkraut, breaking up any clumps in it to be sure that each strand gets coated. Cover and cook on top of the range slowly for 10 minutes. Preheat the oven to 325°. Tie the parsley, bay leaf, peppercorns and juniper berries in cheesecloth and bury them in the sauerkraut. Pour in the bouillon, water, wine and gin if you are using it. Add salt to taste. Continue cooking on top of the stove until it comes to a boil, then place in the oven and cook, covered, for four hours. Check now and then to be sure the sauerkraut is not too dry. If all the liquid has cooked away, add a little more bouillon or wine. The sauerkraut should just bubble.

Start the meat two and one-half hours before serving. Place the pork butt in a pot, cover with cold water, and bring to a boil. Then reduce the heat and simmer, covered, two hours. Start the sausages one hour before serving time. Place the *kielbasa* in a large pot with cold water to cover. Bring to a boil, then simmer, covered, 20 minutes. Add the knockwurst and smoked bratwurst to the *kielbasa* pot. Bring to a boil again, then simmer 10 minutes. Add the veal sausages and simmer five minutes longer. Turn off the heat and let stand five minutes more. Remove the herb bouquet before transferring the *choucroute* to a platter.

WATERCRESS SALAD
WITH MUSTARD VINAIGRETTE DRESSING

2 bunches watercress	6 tablespoons olive oil
1½ teaspoons Dijon	Salt
mustard	Freshly ground black pepper
2 tablespoons lemon juice	

Cut off and discard the tough lower stems of the watercress, then wash and shake it dry. For the dressing, combine the Dijon mustard, lemon juice, olive oil, salt and pepper and whisk them in a salad bowl. Taste for seasoning, add more salt (and pepper) if necessary. Just before serving, add the watercress and toss lightly.

INDIAN PUDDING

This is one of the oldest New England dishes. It was certainly not an Indian invention—they did not have the spices it requires—but it was a staple with the colonists. Their version baked for 10 hours, usually on Saturday, side by side with baked beans, and was served with thick sweet cream, as it is here. It tastes somewhat like pumpkin pie without the pastry, although there isn't a bit of pumpkin in it.

½ cup corn meal	½ teaspoon cinnamon
4 cups milk	1 teaspoon salt
1 cup brown sugar	½ cup dark molasses
1 teaspoon ginger	2 cups light cream
½ teaspoon nutmeg	2 cups heavy cream

Preheat oven to 275°—very low. Combine the corn meal with one cup of milk. Scald the remaining three cups of milk in a saucepan over medium heat. Stir in the corn meal mixture a little at a time and cook, stirring constantly, for 15 minutes or until the mixture is about as thick as a breakfast cereal. It is important to keep stirring to prevent lumps. Remove from heat. Combine sugar, spices and salt, stir them into the corn meal mixture. Add the molasses and light cream. Pour into a greased two-quart baking dish and bake for two hours. Set aside at least an hour. Serve pudding warm with a pitcher of heavy cream to pour over each portion at the table.

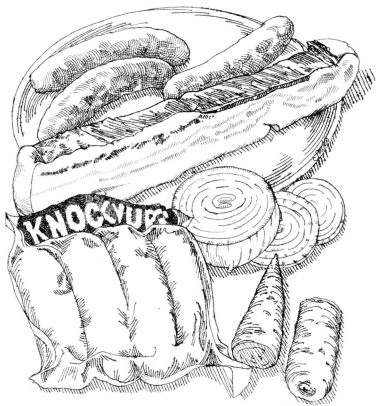

Pears Made Perfect

Say this about pears: they are sensitive, easily damaged, generally expensive, hard to appraise from the outside and their ripeness is so absolutely critical that it is said one may have to sit up all night—just waiting—to eat a perfect one. Say all that and then try to remember the last time you heard a gourmet exclaim: "What a marvelous banana!" Lesser fruits may be more rugged, but when pears are perfect—buttery, succulent and subtle—they soar.

The dessert at left, poached pears served with a *crème anglaise*, does not depend on finding the ultimate pear. Any reasonably healthy Bosc or Anjou will be superb gently simmered in syrup and spices and then coated with a smooth custard. The results of this classic French combination literally melt in the mouth.

Give some extra thought to your guest list when you serve this dinner. It will be a bit like eating at a sophisticated French restaurant, and a sense of adventure will stand your guests in good stead. Sweetbreads have an unusual soft texture. And to people used to eating their pears raw, poaching them and coating them with a custard sauce may seem like an odd trick indeed.

Despite the fact that this is quite a dressy dinner, it is very little work —and that's an unusual combination. Order the sweetbreads ahead of time. Fresh or frozen crabmeat is widely available. Your butcher may need a day or two advance warning to get sweetbreads.

Make the dessert ahead, either the night before or on the morning of the dinner. Refrigerate the pears and the custard separately until ready to serve. Sometime during the day soak, blanch and trim the sweetbreads. Prepare the crab and the sauce. Refrigerate them separately un-

---

MENU FOR SIX

CRAB LOUIS

SAUTÉED
SWEETBREADS WITH HAM
Artichoke hearts
Rice
Dry white wine

POACHED PEARS
WITH CRÈME ANGLAISE

---

til ready to serve. From this point on everything is last-minute cooking. But the procedures are simple and will not keep you from your guests for long provided that you assemble all the ingredients and pots, pans and serving dishes ahead of time. Be sure that the parsley is chopped, the lemon juice squeezed, the rice and flour measured. Just before your guests are due set out the ingredients that have been kept in the refrigerator. Twenty minutes before dinner sauté the sweetbreads and the ham, transfer them to a serving platter. Then turn on the artichokes and rice. When you serve the crab turn the oven down as low as possible and put the sweetbread platter in. After you finish eating the crab make the mustard-butter sauce for the sweetbreads—it takes only a moment. By then the artichokes and rice should be ready. Serve the pears in a serving dish and pass the custard sauce in a separate bowl at the table.

RECIPES

CRAB LOUIS
The story goes that Enrico Caruso, whose appetite was as grand as his voice and who is given credit for dozens of rich dishes, is supposed to have put this one on the map. He discovered it in a Seattle club and was so taken by it that he kept the creator of the dish, a chef named Louis, busy making it over and over again until he finally ran out of ingredients.

Many recipes for it exist, some quite sweet with whipped cream. This version is tangier. If you can get fresh local crabmeat, use it. Otherwise use frozen Alaska king crabmeat. It is served on a mound of crisp shredded lettuce. Iceberg is excellent for adding texture here.

1/2 cup mayonnaise	parsley
1/2 cup sour cream	2 teaspoons grated onion
2 tablespoons chili sauce	1/2 teaspoon salt
2 tablespoons salad oil	4 drops Tabasco
1 tablespoon vinegar	1 pound frozen crabmeat
1 tablespoon prepared horseradish	1 medium head iceberg lettuce
1 tablespoon fresh lemon juice	Watercress sprigs
	Lemon wedges
1 tablespoon chopped fresh	

In a small bowl, mix together all the ingredients listed above down through the Tabasco. Cover and refrigerate. Thaw the crabmeat and pat it dry with a paper towel. Break the lumps into bite-size pieces. Keep refrigerated until ready to use. Shred the lettuce by cutting the head in half, then slicing it thinly. Arrange a portion of the shredded lettuce on individual salad plates. Mound crabmeat over it, then top with sauce. Garnish with watercress and lemon wedges.

SAUTÉED SWEETBREADS WITH HAM
Sweetbreads, the thymus glands of the calf, come in pairs, are expensive, perishable and very messy-looking when bought. They should be soaked in cold water and then blanched. This process firms them up and also makes it easier to trim them, cutting away any tubes or veins that may have escaped the butcher.

3 pairs sweetbreads (about 3 pounds)	1 shallot, minced, or 2 teaspoons minced onion
2 tablespoons lemon juice	1 teaspoon prepared Dijon mustard
1/2 cup flour	2 tablespoons fresh lemon juice
1 teaspoon salt	
1/4 teaspoon freshly ground black pepper	2 tablespoons chopped fresh parsley
8 tablespoons butter	
6 thin slices boiled ham	

Soak the sweetbreads in cold water for two hours, changing the water once. To blanch them, place in a large saucepan, cover with water and add two tablespoons lemon juice. Bring to a boil slowly. Simmer for 20 minutes. Drain and plunge them into very cold water. When cool, slip off covering membrane with fingers. Trim, if necessary. Pat dry with paper towels.

Mix the flour with the salt and pepper. Dust the sweetbreads very lightly with the flour mixture. Be certain there is only the thinnest possible veil or the sweetbreads will absorb the flour and become soggy. In a skillet, melt four tablespoons of the butter. When it is bubbly and lightly browned, add the sweetbreads and sauté them over medium-high heat until they become a rich brown color on both sides. This will take eight to 10 minutes. Transfer them to a serving platter and cover it lightly with foil to keep warm. In the same skillet, sauté the ham slices a minute or two until lightly browned. Slip a slice of ham under each sweetbread.

Add the remaining four tablespoons of butter to the skillet with the shallot or chopped onion, and sauté for just a minute or two. Stir in the mustard and lemon juice. Bring to a boil, stir until frothy with a wire whisk or a fork and pour this sauce over the sweetbreads. Sprinkle with the chopped parsley.

Serve with the artichoke hearts *(below)* and white rice, cooked according to the directions on the box. Make the rice portions smaller than the amount suggested for six on the box as the sweetbreads are quite rich and filling.

ARTICHOKE HEARTS WITH LEMON

2 15-ounce cans artichoke hearts, or 3 10-ounce packages frozen	1 tablespoon butter
	1 cup chicken broth
	3 tablespoons fresh lemon juice
1/2 cup minced onion	1 teaspoon salt
1 small clove garlic, crushed	1 teaspoon oregano

Sauté onion and garlic in the butter until the onion is tender, but not browned. Add the drained artichoke hearts, the broth, lemon juice, salt and oregano. Simmer gently until heated through, about 10 minutes. If you use the frozen artichoke hearts, cook them a little longer, according to the time given on the package.

POACHED PEARS WITH CRÈME ANGLAISE

Use winter pears—Bosc or Anjou. They should be slightly underripe. If you use pears that are ready for eating they will fall apart in the poaching. It is not hard to find underripe pears because this fruit is always picked before it is tree-ripened. Watch the sauce attentively as it cooks. If you let it boil, it will curdle. To prevent this, stir steadily and keep the pot at a very low temperature. Use a vanilla bean if you can get it; if not, one teaspoon of vanilla extract, added when the sauce has cooled, will do. If you use the bean, fish it out of the sauce after it has finished cooking, wash it, dry it, and save it to use once again.

6 pears, slightly underripe	1 teaspoon grated lemon rind
4 cups water	
2 cups sugar	1 cinnamon stick
1 tablespoon fresh lemon juice	3 whole cloves

Peel the pears, leaving the stems on if desired. Drop them immediately into cold water containing a little lemon juice to prevent them from darkening. In a large pot or Dutch oven, bring the four cups water, sugar, lemon juice and lemon rind to a boil. Add the cinnamon stick, cloves and the pears. Cover and keep the syrup at a rolling boil —which keeps the pears moving and cooking evenly —until the pears are tender. This should take about 30 minutes, depending on the ripeness and the size of the pears. When finished cooking they should be slightly translucent, and easily pierced with a kitchen fork. With a slotted spoon, carefully transfer pears to a shallow, flat-bottomed dish. Stand them up if possible so that they keep their shape—they are very pliable and apt to flatten out slightly if they lie on their sides. If necessary, trim the bottoms when pears are cooler to help them stand up. Pour a little of the syrup over the pears, cover and chill for several hours.

CRÈME ANGLAISE

1 cup milk	6 tablespoons sugar
1/2 cup heavy cream	4 large egg yolks
1-inch piece vanilla bean	2 teaspoons cornstarch

Combine the milk, cream and vanilla bean in a saucepan. Bring just to a boil; let stand 10 minutes to absorb the flavor of the vanilla bean. Gradually beat the sugar into the egg yolks, and continue beating for about three minutes until the mixture is pale yellow and creamy. Beat in the cornstarch. Stir the milk-and-cream mixture into the yolks, beating vigorously with a wire whisk. Return this mixture to the saucepan and cook it over very low heat, stirring with a wooden spoon, until the mixture is quite thick and coats the back of a silver spoon. This will take about 15 minutes. Do not let it boil. Remove from heat and cool, stirring frequently. Remove vanilla bean, cover the custard sauce and chill thoroughly.

Equipping the Kitchen

On the following pages is an array of things useful for—but not essential in—making the recipes in this book. There are gleaming copper pots, colorful casseroles, gadgets galore, and an assortment of seasonings and food to encourage you to start cooking right away. You can cook all the LIFE dinners with the equipment of any average kitchen and the staples on most pantry shelves. But many of the utensils will make your cooking more efficient and more enjoyable, while the handsome casseroles will make your dinners more attractive. A well-stocked larder will certainly aid in the preparation of any meal. What equipment you furnish your kitchen with will depend on what kind of cooking you are going to do, how much storage space you have and how much money you want to spend. The pots and pans and gadgetry that follow show the range of the best kitchenware available. It is meant neither to be a complete catalogue nor to entice you into buying more than you can use. There is no point in having a large, heavy casserole if you have to store it on a high, inaccessible shelf. Nor is there much point to a lot of baking equipment if you never make desserts. Don't buy copper pans if you cannot face cleaning them regularly. As you add to your existing equipment, buy the best—it outlasts and outcooks the bargains. Don't try to buy matching sets of everything—different materials have their special advantages and disadvantages, and it is more efficient to buy a little of this and a little of that and so end up with cooking utensils that are adaptable and versatile.

As a minimum your kitchen should have a set consisting of two-, three- and four-quart saucepans with lids, and you will probably want more than just those three. Buy ones that nest to save space. A couple of very small saucepans are useful for heating up soups or gravy and for melting butter. Heavy aluminum or aluminum lined with stainless steel is the most practical. When you cook with wine, lemon juice or eggs, use any cookware except aluminum (lined aluminum is satisfactory, however), because the food will discolor. Be sure the lids are tight-fitting and have secure handles that are going to stay on. You need a large soup or spaghetti pot, at least the six-quart size, also of aluminum. Have at least two casseroles —one small three-quart size and another that will hold six or seven quarts. You will want an open baking, or au gratin, dish. Buy enamel on iron in attractive colors and styles that can go directly to the table. You need a roasting pan and two skillets with covers. Get the frying pans with handles that can go into the oven, or with removable handles. If you want a nonstick finish, be sure to buy the most durable and the most expensive—anything else scratches easily. As for a double boiler—you are less likely to boil away the water if you get a glass one. You'll need some baking equipment: cake and pie tins, a spring-form pan, a soufflé dish. To this basic list, you can add a paella pan, a fish poacher and a chafing dish—but only if you feel extravagant.

Choose your knives as carefully as you do your pans. Carbon steel takes the best edge, but it will rust if not dried after each use. Stainless is easy to take care of and looks prettier. But except for a very few high-priced stainless knives, it does not keep as good an edge. All slicing and chopping jobs are infinitely easier if done with the sharpest possible knife. Get in the habit of sharpening your knives regularly with a steel or a stone. Get two paring knives (one is always mislaid), a large chef's knife for chopping, a narrow-blade boning knife and a serrated blade for bread. The safest, most accessible place to store them is on a magnetic knife rack. Always use a chopping board. It protects your kitchen counters, offers a good, flat, easily-wiped-clean surface, and there is something quite satisfying about chopping on a good board.

The whisk is another tool worth cultivating. Sauces and gravies somehow can be whisked to a smoothness they never seem to get any other way. However, while a balloon whip beats egg whites stiffer and higher than anything else, I must admit to using an electric hand beater for egg whites. Another electric gadget I would not be without is the blender. These machines do so much so quickly that one expects them to do everything. For some jobs you have to remind yourself that they don't chop as precisely as you can by hand. Keep the blender out on the counter in order to get the most use from it.

When setting up a larder, carefully consider how much space you have and what kind of food you like. Obviously, if you don't care for highly seasoned food, you will not need to give much space to condiments. If you do a lot of baking, you may want to keep more than one kind of flour on hand. If your family is strong for Italian food, you should store several varieties of pasta. The only other basic rule is that nothing lasts forever. Tea, coffee, spices, salad oils, even canned goods, all have only a certain life expectancy. Although life can be prolonged by proper storage, it is best to buy in quantity only those ingredients you have some hope of using up before they lose their flavor. This requirement is virtually impossible to fulfill with spices and herbs, even when they are stored in airtight containers with screw-on tops. It requires an act of will to go through the spice shelf once a year and throw away the faded, flavorless herbs that have outlived their usefulness. Other staples, such as sugar, flour, rice and wheat, should be kept in jars with tightly fitting lids. When you replenish the jars, check to see if the old flour has gotten buggy and if so do not add fresh supplies on top of old.

Don't start out buying every herb on your grocer's shelf. Unless you are already familiar with a wide range of them, it is best to begin with a few, learn their personalities and then gradually build up the collection. Don't use dried parsley: it has very little resemblance to the fresh product. Fresh mint has little resemblance to the kind that comes in jars. Use fresh chives if available,

freeze-dried if not. Keep a pepper mill at hand in the kitchen and always use freshly ground pepper in cooking—it has far more flavor.

Onions come in many varieties. Use shallots in sauces. Try leeks in stews, red onions in salads. Use small white onions as a garnish for roasts.

Potatoes will not keep indefinitely, particularly in summertime, so don't try to stock them too far ahead. Buy big oval ones for baking—their texture is fluffier. The round "old" potatoes are better suited to mashing, frying and, in fact, for use in most recipes that call for potatoes. But small "new" potatoes can enliven stews and casseroles. And yams, a brighter and deeper orange than sweet potatoes but interchangeable with them in virtually all recipes, are traditional with some meats and make good pies and soufflés.

Since all the starches *except* potatoes keep well, put in a supply of alternatives. You will find that they soon begin to make regular appearances at the dinner table. Kasha, or groats, is inexpensive, easy to prepare and combines well with onions, mushrooms, nuts or raisins for lots of variety. Bulgur wheat is similar. Beans, if not canned, take a bit longer to prepare, but red and white ones at the very least should be in your repertoire. My own favorite is black beans, excellent with sour cream, but sometimes hard to get. White rice is extraordinarily versatile: it can be cooked with saffron, with broth (as risotto), or mixed with herbs or cheese. Wild rice is a treat for a formal dinner but unbelievably costly.

Pasta means more than spaghetti. Broad noodles can be served *au beurre noir,* fettucine with a little cream and cheese, linguine with clam sauce.

For sugar, keep the regular granulated variety on hand; confectioners' sugar is needed for cakes and frostings. Regular brown sugar keeps poorly, so buy it only as you need it. Lump sugar is more attractive than granulated when served with tea and coffee. Your family's tastes will determine the selection of jams and jellies you keep on hand, but bear in mind that orange marmalade and currant jelly are useful in making sauces for poultry and meat as well as in glazes.

For salads you need to keep both salad oil and olive oil. To prepare a variety of dressings have a red wine and white wine vinegar as well as regular cider vinegar on hand. Condiments are largely a matter of preference, but you should store at least mustard, Tabasco and catsup —the last of which your children probably wouldn't let you be without anyway.

Food is good to look at even before it is cooked. If I had the space, I would store everything in glass jars on open shelves. Surely it would be an attractive way of keeping track of supplies at a glance as well as a source of inspiration to the cook.

A pantry-full of ideas to make your
cooking easier and more inventive; a spice
and herb shelf to give your dishes
a subtle range of flavor; an unexpected
array of sweeteners; condiments to make
them lively; and a bin
bursting with starches that will
give your dinner menus new variety.

larder

The Zests

220

are capers and mild, all-purpose mustard; chili peppers, to add heat; sweet Spanish onion, a rather pungent garnish; catsup, America's favorite condiment; chili sauce *(far right)*. In bottom row: vegetable oil; pure olive oil; earthy leeks, braised or used in stews; Dijon mustard, a French version; mustard relish; garlic, indispensable and indiscreet, to be used with caution; Tabasco, a fiery liquid seasoning; a prepared meat sauce; green pepper; chutney, essential with curry; olives; Worcestershire sauce; pimientos *(jar at bottom)*, a colorful, sweet-tasting garnish; white wine vinegar with tarragon; bottled horseradish, for meats and sauces; all-purpose yellow onions; red wine vinegar; dill pickles.

Spices and Herbs

Spices (roots, berries and seeds) and herbs (leaves) almost more than anything else determine how a dish will taste. Fresh herbs are infinitely more delicious —and more delicate—than dried herbs; use them if you can get them. Here is a basic, but far from skimpy, spice shelf. In the back row are marjoram, a member of the mint family, excellent with lamb; sage, often the dominant flavor of stuffing; ginger root, shaved, useful in curries and Chinese cookery; oregano, the "pizza taste"; mustard seed, for salad dressing; curry, a blend of many spices; fennel, a licorice-flavored seed, excellent with fish; caraway, the "rye bread seed"; basil, with an affinity for tomatoes; a container of salt, neither spice nor herb, but the cook's most essential seasoner, in regular or coarse grinds. At bottom are a tin of ground ginger; cinnamon sticks and cloves, both useful for pickling and marinating; tarragon leaves—a favorite with the French for chicken, demanded for Béarnaise sauce; nutmeg, classic on custards, excellent with some meats and vegetables; savory, a soup and salad herb; on the chopping block, parsley, perhaps the most useful of them all; thyme, for chowder and Creole cooking; bay leaves, for marinades and stews; rosemary; fresh dill, a Scandinavian standby; in the spoon, paprika, the Hungarian's delight; mace, nutmeg's outer husk and very like it in flavor; allspice, a single berry combining the flavors of cinnamon, clove, nutmeg and juniper; black peppercorns for grinding; hot chili flakes.

The Starches

Every starch pictured here has a singular advantage; it can be cooked and brought to the table to be eaten practically as is. Americans too seldom vary the old standbys, potatoes and rice, with starches equally as good, such as beans, pasta and the numerous grain products. From upper left: a bag of white rice; in the three-tiered jar are chick-peas, red kidney beans and lima beans, all excellent and nutritious additions to soup and casseroles. In the sack are potatoes of every kind: yams, darker in color than the sweet potato, and much more available; baking potatoes, fluffy when cooked; old, or all-purpose potatoes; and new ones, best for boiling. Christopher Morley once said, "No man is lonely while eating spaghetti—it requires too much attention." The apothecary jar bristles with a dozen ways to stave off loneliness, but there are at least 150 other shapes of pasta to choose from. Nutty-flavored wild rice *(at lower left)* is not a rice at all but a very expensive wild grain; curried rice is one of many seasoned rices recently available; lentils are in the small glass jar at right; barley, kasha and bulgur are in a ladle. Barley is most often used in soups. Kasha (buckwheat groats) and bulgur, a cracked wheat, are both popular in the Middle East and often served with lamb or chicken. Other cereal foods that can be used as part of the main course are cornmeal and hominy grits. Flour ranks as the principal starch for baking. Besides flour, arrowroot and cornstarch are used for thickening sauces, gravies and stews.

The Sweets

Most sweeteners fall into two categories: sugars, derived from sugar cane or sugar beets, and fruit-based jellies and preserves. Since one sweetener can often stand in for another, it is unnecessary to have them all. However, you should keep on hand a sprinkling of the principal varieties of sugar and a sampling of jams, whichever are your favorites. Left to right, top row: a jar of honey, with its own distinctive flavor; a bottle of corn syrup, less sweet than sugar, essential for many candies and icings; orange marmalade, sometimes used in cooking, more often served at breakfast; the common sugar cube; mint jelly, a favorite accompaniment for lamb; a red shaker containing powdered sugar, a superfine granulated type which is often confused with confectioners' sugar, which *is* a powder; sparkling white fast-dissolving granulated sugar for all-around use; light and dark brown sugars, tasting slightly like molasses. The light brown is milder and best for condiments and frosting; the dark is more for baked beans and glazed hams. Bottom row: a shaker of spicy cinnamon sugar for toast; red currant jelly, used in sauces, desserts, and often served with fowl; sugar lumps; maple syrup to drench pancakes; strawberry preserves; an apothecary jar of decoratively colored sugar crystals; a jar of comb honey with a chewy texture; a scoop full of confectioners' sugar for dusting cakes and doughnuts; a jug of molasses.

The tools you need to slice and
dice, grate and grind, to poach, roast,
simmer and stew—are all to be
found here. Pots and pans for
everyday, colorful casseroles to set off your
most ambitious creations,
and glowing copperware to
make even a neophyte feel like a chef.

utensils

Bowls, Boards and Knives

Wooden ware and cutlery are among the most satisfactory things in a kitchen. They have a good feel and rewarding heft. Wood improves with age, and it takes time to get to know any knife. Across the top are a slicing board to reduce the likes of potatoes to uniform

slivers; hanging from a chocolate-roll board are assorted spatulas, spoons and forks, and a pair of tongs; on chopping block are *(from top to bottom)* a pie slicer, poultry shears, a dough cutter, an oyster knife and a clam opener. Chopping bowls *(at right)* and double-edge chopper can be used on parsley and onions. Slicers and peelers *(at bottom left, counterclockwise)* are for apples, fruit, fish scales and vegetables. The melon scoop has two sizes. Pounders come in three shapes. Next to them are mortar and pestle, sieve, scoop, all-purpose rolling pin and thin rolling pin for pastry. Cutting tools include pizza slicer, cleaver, roast slicer, serrated carving knife, all-purpose paring knife, knife sharpener, chef's knife, long-handled fork and boning knife. Behind them are cheese slicer, pastry blender and egg slicer.

Colorful Cooking Ware

The days when pots and pans had to stay in the kitchen are long gone. A lot of today's cookware is good-looking enough to go straight to the dining room and to ornament the kitchen wall when not in use—a solution which helps considerably with the storage problem. Unless otherwise noted the colorful kitchenware at right is made either of cast iron or steel, coated with enamel. Cast iron heats particularly well, but is very heavy. Steel is easier to lift, but also easier to scorch. Both are expensive, but clean easily, wear well, are equally at home in the oven or on top of the stove, and enhance the appearance of anything you cook. Across the top row are a round open baking dish, a double rectangular baking dish, a pair of casseroles—one covered—a Swedish pancake maker, and a skillet. In the next row are two enamel colanders over a paella pan filled with paella, two casseroles, a butter melter, a bean pot, a fondue set and two covered skillets. In next row are a stack of oval au gratin dishes, an oval casserole of uncoated cast iron (inexpensive and durable but rusts easily), a Dutch oven, a fish poacher, a white glass ceramic casserole that can go directly from freezer to oven, an earthenware casserole—light, attractive, but easily broken. At bottom are a covered saucepan, a casserole, funnels and a chicken-size pot complete with chicken. Scattered in random fashion through the picture are enamel spoons, solid and slotted, and in the center there is a skimmer.

Stylish Pots and Pans

The most luxurious—and expensive —cookware of all is made of copper. It is handsome and it conducts heat quickly and evenly. But it must be polished often. For everyday use aluminum saucepans work out best. Some are lined with

stainless steel, which makes them easier to clean yet retains aluminum's virtues of durability and even heating—an ideal combination. Across the top are an oval skillet, good for fish; a crepes pan and warmer; a teapot; a turkey-sized roaster; a fondue set; and a covered saucepan of aluminum lined with stainless steel. In the next row are three heavy-weight aluminum skillets; a glass double boiler; a copper bowl with a handle, for making zabaglione; a nest of copper skillets; a stack of butter melters; and an espresso coffee pot. Across the bottom are lids and saucepans in copper; a cluster of aluminum-stainless saucepans; the ultimate luxury —a copper fish poacher; a copper stew pot; and a nest of baking dishes.

The Gadgets

Choose gadgets carefully. They can be time-savers—designed to do particular jobs with great efficiency—but if you rarely perform these chores the gadgets become clutter. Some specialized utensils are shown here. In top row is a basket

for cooking fish, handy since fish has a tendency to break apart; under it, a flour sifter; an omelet pan, low-sided to make it easy to slide the finished product out; a grater; a stainless double boiler, ideal for sauces like Hollandaise; a meat grinder; and a salad basket for drying greens (inside-out it serves as a steamer). In the next row is an egg beater; a bouquet of whisks, spoons and skimmers blooming out of a stainless stock pot; a melon mold; measuring spoons; a meat tenderizer, for flattening veal scallops; a deep fryer; under it, a charlotte mold (also for soufflés); and a garlic press. At bottom, a rotary grater; a nest of brioche pans; an aspic mold; a fluted mold for classic *pâté en croute;* a strainer; and a food mill.

Index

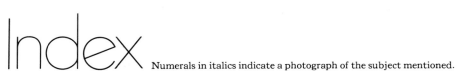

Numerals in italics indicate a photograph of the subject mentioned.

Designer: Eric Gluckman

Researchers: Mary Elizabeth Allison, Harriet Delihas,
Mary Jane Engel, Petty Nelson, Gerry Schremp

For their help in the production of this book
the editors wish to thank the following:
Azuma, Inc.; Bazar Français; The Bridge Company;
Copco, Inc.; Corning Glass Works; Dansk Designs Ltd.;
S.W. Farber; General Electric Co.; Hammacher Schlemmer;
Georg Jensen, Inc.; Revere Copper and Brass, Inc.;
H. Roth & Son Paprika Co.; Wear-Ever Aluminum, Inc.